THE LIFE OF
WILLIAM MAKEPEACE
THACKERAY

IN TWO VOLUMES

VOL. I

W. M. THACKERAY.

From a bust by Deville, in the National Portrait Gallery.   *Pellissier & Allen, Ph. Sc.*

THE LIFE OF
WILLIAM MAKEPEACE
THACKERAY

BY

LEWIS MELVILLE

WITH PORTRAITS AND ILLUSTRATIONS

IN TWO VOLUMES

VOL. I

HERBERT S. STONE AND COMPANY
CHICAGO AND NEW YORK
MDCCCXCIX

TABLE OF CONTENTS

VOLUME I

LIST OF ILLUSTRATIONS

VOLUME I

PREFACE

THOUGH it is more than five-and-thirty years since his death, until now there has never been published a Life of Thackeray which has had any pretensions to finality. Mr. Theodore Taylor's book, *Thackeray, the Humourist and the Man of Letters*, was admittedly only a stop-gap biography; the volume contributed eight years ago to the "Great Writers Series" by Mr. Herman Merivale and Mr. Frank Marzials can scarcely be regarded as much more than outlining the novelist's career; while Mrs. Ritchie's interesting Biographical Introductions are little more than material for a full Life.

No member of his family has come forward as a chronicler. There is a popular rumour to account for the unusual silence. Thackeray, so the story runs, some years before his death, was so disgusted with an unduly fulsome biography he was reading that he laid down the volume, saying to his daughters, "Let there be none of this when I go." They interpreted this remark literally, with the result that neither the members of his family nor his intimate friends have attempted to compile an "official" biography. Even assuming the story be true, I cannot think Thackeray wished the story of his life to remain unwritten. I think his only desire was that the truth should be told, that all the scars should be painted in the portrait; for he himself liked to read of the lives of literary men. "If the secret history of books could be written, and the author's private thoughts noted down

alongside of his story, how many insipid volumes would
become interesting, and dull tales excite the reader!'' he
wrote in one of his essays.

His stories are frequently autobiographical—there has
never lived an author whose writings have been more
personal. ''This is so like print that I think I shall
send it to *Punch*,'' he said of a letter he was writing to
Mrs. Brookfield; and this is true, in a larger degree, of
his life. He used his own experiences to a very great
extent, and the reader knowing the author's life must
certainly find an added pleasure in perusing the various
stories.

His departure from India, his arrival in England, his
early school-life, the Charterhouse days, Larkbeare,
Cambridge, the visit to Weimar, Paris, and elsewhere,
his misfortunes in London, his Deuceace, his life in the
Paris studios, the newspapers he was connected with,
the people he met, the places he visited, even his
illnesses, are all reproduced.

There is no lack of material for the biographer.
Nearly every one who knew Thackeray has recorded his
or her impression in a book or magazine-article. Sir
William Hunter has devoted his attention to the novelist's ancestors; Mr. C. P. Johnson has outlined the early
years of the literary career; *The History of Punch* contains
much information concerning his connection with that
journal; Mr. Eyre Crowe's book tells of his first American voyage, and Mr. Hodder has been the historian of
the return visit. Mrs. Brookfield published in 1887 a
most interesting and (to the biographer) instructive Collection of Thackeray's Letters, 1847—1855. Mrs.
Ritchie herself, besides the series of Introductions to
the *Biographical Edition of Thackeray's Works*, pub-

lished by Messrs. Harper & Brothers, has given us a
few chapters from "Some Unwritten Memoirs," also
issued by the same publishers. From both of these
works extracts have been made in this volume. These,
with the Lives and Letters of Edward Fitzgerald, Lord
Houghton, Alfred Tennyson, Professor Aytoun, Charlotte Brontë, Mr. Yates, and the Autobiographies of
Mr. Hollingshead and Mr. Vizetelly, together with information gleaned from little-known or less available
sources, have enabled me to expand the outline of his
life into the present work.

My own more personal acknowledgments are due to
Miss Saville, for very material assistance in the prepara-
tion of the work, and for her kindly encouragement;
to Mr. W. T. Stevens, who has allowed me the use of his
valuable collection of first editions of Thackeray's works;
and to Mr. Arthur Patchett Martin, who, giving me the
benefit of his extensive literary knowledge and long
experience, has read and revised these volumes in
manuscript.

Finally, I humbly claim for myself that, to the best
of my ability, I have endeavoured to fill a void in the
literary history of the century, and while therefore I
think no apology is needed for presenting these volumes
to the public, I would plead the great difficulty of the
task in palliation of those errors of omission and commission which the reader may discover.

LEWIS MELVILLE.

CHAPTER I

THACKERAY'S FAMILY HISTORY

CHAPTER I

THACKERAY'S FAMILY HISTORY

HISTORY has ignored the Thackerays until nearly the middle of the fourteenth century, when the family records mention John de Thakwa as holding at Hartwich, in 1336, a dwelling-house and thirty acres of land of the Abbot of St. Mary of Fountains, and in 1361 William de Thackwra, a tenant at will of a messuage and twenty-one acres at the same place. A century afterwards Robert Thackra kept the Grange of Brinham, and subsequently Edward Thacquarye held houses and lands from the Convent.

Early in the seventeenth century Walter Thackeray, first of the name as now spelt, established himself at Hampsthwaite, a little village close by the forest of Knaresborough, in the West Riding of Yorkshire. Here, through several generations, for two hundred years, the family lived, doing yeoman's duty, until 1804, when the last of the line, Thomas Thackeray, died childless, seven years before the novelist was born.

In 1682 Elias Thackeray had gone southwards to King's College, where he became M.A. in 1709, and two years later was given the rectorship of Hawkerswell, in the Archdeaconry of Richmond.

Probably at his suggestion, in January, 1706, Thomas Thackeray, then a boy of twelve, was sent from the ancestral home at Hampsthwaite to Eton, where he was

3

admitted on the foundation.   Here he remained until
1711, when he won a scholarship that took him to King's
College, Cambridge, where he qualified as B.A. in 1715,
four years later as M.A., and was eventually elected to
a fellowship.   He returned to Eton as assistant master,
and was an unsuccessful candidate for the provostship of
King's in 1744.   In 1746 he was appointed to the head-
mastership of Harrow School, which, although nearly
two hundred years old, had been almost ruined under a
"drunken, disorderly, idle" principal.   On his arrival,
there were but thirty-three boys, a number that under
his able rule was increased to a hundred and thirty.
He obtained several livings; was appointed a chaplain to
Frederick, Prince of Wales; and ultimately became
Archdeacon of Surrey.

In Richard's *History of Lynn*, published in 1812, a
letter dated 1756, from Dr. Edmund Pyle, is inserted,
having reference to Dr. Thackeray:

"Dr. Thackeray, who keeps a school at Harrow-on-
the-Hill, has one living and fourteen children; a man
bred at Eton, and a great scholar in the Eton way, and
a good one every way; a true Whig, and proud to be so
by some special marks of integrity.   He was a candidate
for the headship of King's, and would have beat all men
but George, and George, too, if Sir Robert Walpole had
not made George's promotion a point.   Since this disappointment he took the school at Harrow to educate his
own and other people's children, where he has performed
all along with great reputation.   The Bishop of Win-
chester [Hoadley?] never saw this man in his life, but
had heard so much good of him, that he resolved to
serve him some way or other if ever he could, but said
nothing to anybody.   On Friday last, he sent for this

Dr. Thackeray, and when he came into the room my Lord gave him a parchment, and told him he had long heard of his good character, and long been afraid he should never be able to give him any serviceable proof of the good opinion he had conceived of him; that what he had put into his hands was the Archdeaconry of Surrey, which he hoped would be acceptable to him, as he might perform the duty of it yearly at the time of his leisure in the Easter holidays.   Dr. Thackeray was so surprised and overcome with this extraordinary manner of doing him a favour, that he was very near fainting as he was giving him institution.''

The doctor died in 1760. He had married, in 1729, a daughter of John Woodward, of Butler's Marston, Warwickshire (another of whose girls was the wife of Dr. Nicholas Boscawen, Canon of Windsor), who bore him six sons and ten daughters during the first twenty years of their married life. The lady died in 1797, in her ninetieth year. Of these children Elias became Provost of Kings; another son chaplain at Saint Petersburg; another obtained an appointment in the Customs, and kept it for forty years; while two others studied medicine and practised, respectively, at Cambridge and Windsor.

For the youngest of this family a Writership in the East India Company's Service was obtained. This was William Makepeace (the curious name is said to be derived from a member of the family who suffered at the stake for his faith in the good old days), the grandfather of the author. After a preliminary training in book-keeping, in which it was necessary to be thoroughly grounded before entering the service, he sailed in February, 1746, in the Lord Camden for Calcutta. Placed in the Secretary's office, he at once attracted the notice of his superiors, and within twelve months of his arrival was promoted to be assistant-treasurer or cash-keeper under the new governor, Verelst, at a salary of one thousand one hundred and fifty-eight rupees, or one hundred and forty-five pounds, while most of the other Writers only received eighty pounds. In 1771 he was appointed Factor and Fourth in Council at Dacca, where he proceeded to take up his residence with the two sisters who had come to him from home. Both these ladies married during their stay in India—the elder, Jane, to Major James Rennel, a celebrated geographer; the younger, Henrietta, to James Harris, the Chief of Dacca, and the head of the Company's Service in Eastern Bengal.*

Under Warren Hastings William Makepeace was made a Chief of the frontier province of Sylhet, and in 1774 returned as Third in Council to Dacca, where his sister Jane and her husband were still living. A year later he fell in love with a very charming girl, Amelia, the daughter of Lieutenant-Colonel Richmond Webb, a descendant of the famous victor of Weynendal, who is so well portrayed in *Esmond*. The young couple (William Makepeace was six-and-twenty, and Miss Webb eighteen) were married at St. John's Cathedral, Calcutta, on January 31, 1776, and sailed for England immediately. The young civil servant had been absent for nine and a half years, during which time he had amassed a fortune sufficient to enable him to purchase a small estate at Hadley, near Chippine Barnet, where for the rest of his days he led a simple, hospitable country life. His wife

*When James Harris died, it was found that his extravagance had made deep inroads into his fortune; but enough was left for his widow to live comfortably, and in 1790 she settled down at Hadley, near her brother. Of her sons, two distinguished themselves at Balliol College, several entered the Army and Navy, and at least one went to India.

bore him twelve children, of whom eleven lived. She died in 1810, at the age of fifty-three, and was followed to the grave three years later by her husband (who was then in his sixty-fifth year), that is, more than three years before the boy Thackeray was sent to England.

Of the eleven children of this marriage, no less than nine went to the East. Three sons entered the Madras Civil Service, a fourth the Bengal Civil Service, and a fifth the Bengal Army. The sixth, who died in 1846, became a barrister at Calcutta, but, obtaining little practice, wrote leading articles for the *Englishman*, and probably also for other newspapers. Five of the brothers died in India, the sixth on a voyage to the Cape for the recovery of his health. Two of the daughters married Bengal civilians, and a third the Attorney-General of Ceylon. The fourth daughter remained in England. Francis, another son, entered the Church, and lived among his books in a Hertfordshire parish, where he wrote on the *State of Ancient Britons under the Roman Emperors*, and produced a *History of the Earl of Chatham*, that was quoted by Carlyle in *Frederick the Great* and reviewed by Lord Macaulay.

The eldest son, William Makepeace, was born in 1778, and in his twentieth year went to Madras as a Writer. He was the first Madras civilian who earned a reward under the rules of 1797 which encouraged the study of Oriental languages. For proficiency in Telugu he received a government grant equivalent to about £400, and a good appointment. His rise was rapid. He was appointed by Clive, Translator to the Government, then assistant to Sir Thomas Munro, and was the first judge of the Court established at Masulipatam. In 1806 he became a member of the Board of Revenue, and four years later Chief Secretary to the Madras Government. In 1813 he returned to England for the recovery of his health, and the Court of Directors mentioned his services in a despatch. He came back to India in 1816; was appointed a provisional member of Council; took his seat on June 10, 1820; and three days after became also President of the Board of Revenue. But the climate had undermined his health, and in November, 1822, a sea-voyage to the Cape was ordered. He died upon the voyage on January 11, 1823, in his forty-sixth year.

Webb Thackeray, who went out to Madras as a Writer in 1806, at the age of eighteen, died within a year.

St. John Thackeray, born in 1791, was one of the first civilians sent out by the East India College that eventually grew into Haileybury. He spent three years in the Board of Revenue, five years in the diplomatic department, and was killed in 1824 at Kittúr Fort, where, hoping to bring the insurgents to terms, he advanced, without a flag of truce, and was fired upon.

Lieutenant Thomas Thackeray, of the Bengal army, was killed in an action in the Nepal War during 1814. He was a brave man, and his death called forth enthusiastic mention in despatches from the Commander-in-Chief and the Governor-General.

Richmond Thackeray, the second son, and father of the novelist, was born either on September 1, 1781, or October 21, 1782.* He was sent to Eton at the age of ten, and remained there until 1796, when he underwent

---

*Sir William Hunter has pointed out that the tombstone says Richmond Thackeray died on September 13, 1815, aged thirty-two years, ten months, and twenty-three days, which would make the birthday October 21, 1782, instead of September 1, 1781, as stated in the Family Book of the Thackerays.

the usual training before proceeding to Bengal, where he had been nominated to a Writership in the Civil Service. He arrived at Calcutta on October 27, 1798—the year in which Lord Wellesley undertook the government—but was almost immediately prostrated by fever, and was sent on a voyage to Madras for the recovery of his health. On his return he studied in the College of Fort William, and, as a reward for his proficiency in Arabic and Persian, was appointed Collector of Midnapir.

In 1802 he was joined by his two sisters, Emily and Augusta, both of whom married very shortly after their arrival. Augusta was won by a great friend of her brother, Mr. Elliot, and Emily (who died in India) by John Talbot Shakespear. Of the latter alliance came nine children, the eldest of whom, Colonel John Dowdeswell Shakespear, seems to have some claim to be regarded as one of the men who sat for Colonel Newcome. A daughter Augusta married General Sir John Low. A younger son was Colonel Sir Richmond Shakespear, who became Agent to the Governor-General for Central India, and was appointed by Lord Canning to the Chief Commissionership of Mysore, which post he had just accepted when death terminated his career. The novelist made appreciative reference to him in a *Roundabout Paper*:

" 'Can I do anything for you?' I remember the kind fellow asking. He was always asking that question: of all kinsmen; of all widows and orphans; of all the poor; of young men who might need his purse or his service. I saw a young officer yesterday to whom the first words Sir Richmond Shakespear wrote on his arrival in India were, 'Can I do anything for you?' His purse was at the command of all. His kind hand was always open.

It was a gracious fate which sent him to rescue widows and captives. Where could they have had a champion more chivalrous, a protector more loving and tender?''

To return to Richmond Thackeray. He became Collector of Birbhum in 1803, and three years later was appointed Judge of Ramgarh. In 1807 he was promoted to the Secretaryship of the Bengal Board of Revenue, and from this time, with the exception of some months during which he acted as Judge of Midnapir, he remained in the capital, where, apart from his official position, he became a noted personage in the little social world. Here he met and married Anne Becher, a beautiful young girl, and a connexion of an old Bengal civilian family, of whom perhaps the most distinguished member was Richard Becher, who held high office during the administration of Lord Clive. Her father, John Harman Becher, whose arrival in Calcutta as a Writer is dated 1779, after a long illness, or series of illnesses, had died in 1800 while she was a child of seven.

CHAPTER II

BIRTH AND CHILDHOOD

CHAPTER II

BIRTH AND CHILDHOOD

WILLIAM MAKEPEACE THACKERAY was born at Calcutta, July 18, 1811. In the following December Richmond Thackeray was promoted to the Collectorship of the Calcutta districts, the most important appointment in the Governor's gift. The young couple resided at the official Collector's house at Alipur (which enabled them to continue their intercourse with the society of the capital) until the husband's death. Then the widow, only three-and-twenty, and her four-year-old son, stayed with relatives in India until, in 1817, the boy was sent to England to be educated.

Thackeray never forgot this parting, and referred to it five-and-forty years after in a *Roundabout Paper:*

"In one of the stories by the present writer, a man is described tottering 'up the steps of the ghaut,' having just parted with his child, whom he is despatching to England from India. I wrote this, remembering in long, long distant days, such a ghaut, or river-stair, at Calcutta; and a day when, down those steps, to a boat which was in waiting, came two children, whose mothers remained on the shore." The other child was Richmond Shakespear.

"When I first saw England she was in mourning for the young Princess Charlotte [died November 6, 1817], the hope of the Empire," Thackeray himself has written. "I came from India as a child, and our ship touched at an island on the way home, where my black servant took me a long walk over rocks and hills until we reached a garden, where we saw a man walking. 'That is he,' said the black man; 'that is Bonaparte! He eats three sheep every day, and all the little children he can lay hands on!' There were people in the British dominions besides that poor Calcutta serving-man, of an equal horror of the Corsican ogre.

"With the same childish attendant I remember peeping through the colonnade at Carlton House, and seeing the abode of the great Prince Regent. I can yet see the guards pacing before the gates of the Palace. The palace! What palace? The palace exists no more than the palace of Nebuchadnezzar. It is but a name now."

In England, he stayed partly with his grand-uncle Moore at the Manor House at Hadley, near Chipping Barnet, and partly at Chiswick with an aunt, Mrs. Ritchie, from whose house and probably under whose dictation on February 12, 1818, he wrote his first recorded letter to his "Mama": "I hope you are quite well. I have given my dear Grandmamma a kiss. My Aunt Ritchie is very good to me. I like Chiswick, there are so many good boys to play with. St. James's Park is a very fine place. St. Paul's Church, too, I like very much. It is a finer place than I expected. I hope Captain Smyth is well; give my love to him and tell him he must bring you home to your affectionate little son, William Thackeray." Captain Carmichael Smyth was the second husband of his mother.

One amusing anecdote of this time has been preserved. His aunt one day found that her husband's hat fitted the little boy, and she was so astonished, and perhaps alarmed, that she at once took him to Sir Charles Clark, the eminent physician, who, smiling, told her not to be afraid: "He has a large head, but there's a good deal in it." No doubt in after years the doctor was much surprised to find how much was in that head. At his death his brain weighed nearly fifty-eight and a half ounces.

At a very early age he was sent to a school in Chiswick Mall, of which, it is suggested, he wrote in the opening chapters of *Vanity Fair* when he described Miss Pinkerton's establishment. The school was kept by Dr. Turner, a distant relative of the Thackerays, and Mrs. Ritchie remembers it was said in the family that when the headmaster used to read the Ten Commandments of a Sunday to his boys, his wife and several members of the congregation had been heard to declare that to hear his resounding tones reminded them of Mount Sinai itself. The little boy was not happy there. Indeed, soon after he came he made an attempt to run away, and, in later years, when driving to Richmond or elsewhere, would show the corner of the lane by Hammersmith Road where, frightened, he turned back and arrived safely at the school, no one being any the wiser.

As years went by, however, the unpleasant recollections faded, and while at Charterhouse he would go on half-holidays to his old school, and play chess with Mrs. Turner and whist with the young ladies, until, wishing to enact a part in private theatricals, he borrowed a barrister's wig from the Doctor (who had been at the bar before he went into the Church), and, losing it, did not venture to call at Chiswick for some time. He was still at the Chiswick school when his mother and his stepfather came home in 1822. "He had a perfect memory of me," Mrs. Smyth has since said; "he could not speak, but kissed me, and looked at me again and again."

Thackeray and his step-father became excellent friends; and so admirable a man was the Major that those who knew him insist that the finest of all English gentlemen—that *preux chevalier* Colonel Newcome—was drawn from him. Thackeray loved his mother deeply, and was as proud of her as she, in the time to come, was of him. In his letters are frequent affectionate references to her, and his only amusing complaint was that "in her imperial manner" she would always endeavour to make his friends understand that her son was "the divinest creature in the world."

Mrs. Smyth had a *salon* in Paris some thirty years later.

She was a very beautiful woman, "a daughter of the gods, divinely tall," and, as became an Englishwoman of social position in Paris, with an inborn taste in dress of an unconventional kind; for we are told she "used to walk out in a red merino cloak, trimmed with ermine, which gave her the air of a retired empress wearing out her robes." Furthermore, "she was a woman of strong feeling, somewhat imperious, with a passionate love for little children, and with extraordinary sympathy and enthusiasm for any one in trouble. How benevolently she used to look round the room at her many *protégés* with her beautiful grey eyes!"*

Anthony Trollope, in his more matter-of-fact, prosaic fashion, also described this lady. "All who knew William Makepeace, remember his mother well, a handsome, spare, grey-headed lady, whom Thackeray treated with a courtly deference as well as constant affection."

Chapters from some unwritten memoirs.

"There was, however, something of discrepancy between them as to matters of religion," he continued. "Mrs. Carmichael Smyth was disposed to the somewhat austere observance of the evangelical section of the Church. Such, certainly, never became the case with her son. There was disagreement on the subject and probably unhappiness at intervals, but never, I think, quarrelling. Thackeray's house was his mother's home whenever she pleased, and the home also of his step-father."

CHAPTER III

AT THE CHARTERHOUSE

CHAPTER III

AT THE CHARTERHOUSE

IN August, 1822, Major Smyth, with his wife, took up
his residence at Addiscombe, where he had been
appointed Governor, and the boy, William Makepeace,
was sent to the Charterhouse School, where at least two
of the *English Humorists*, Addison and Steele, were
educated.

It was a bad time for a little boy to enter the school,
for just then Dr. Russell was trying his great experiment
of offering education in a famous school at a very cheap
rate. This was effected by what was called the
"Madras" or "Bell" system, in which, to a great extent,
the school teaches itself. Russell never had more than
seven assistant masters, and the lower forms were taught
by "præpositi"—boys of a form just below the Sixth
(or, as Russell called it, the first) which bore the name
of the "Emeriti." The reduction of fees was followed
by a great increase in the number of boys. Far more
pupils were accepted than could be comfortably accom-
modated, and the natural result was overcrowded class-
rooms and packed boarding-houses. I have read of his
first interview with the headmaster: "Take that boy and
his box," were the imperious directions thundered by Dr.
Crushall in his big, brassy voice to the school janitor, as
though sentencing a culprit for execution, "to Mrs.
Jones" [the matron of the boarding-house], "and make

my compliments to Mr. Smiler" [then junior master] "and tell him the boy knows nothing and will just do for the lowest form." Not a pleasant introduction to public-school life for a timid and sensitive boy, certainly. And Thackeray cordially detested Doctor Russell, and took him off in *Pendennis*.

"Pendennis, sir," he makes the Doctor say, "your idleness is incorrigible, and your stupidity beyond example. You are a disgrace to your school, and to your family, and I have no doubt will prove so in after-life to your country. If that vice, sir, which is described to us as the root of all evil, be really what moralists have represented (and I have no doubt of the correctness of their opinion), for what a prodigious quantity of future crime and wickedness are you, unhappy boy, laying the seed! Miserable trifler! A boy who construes *d e and*, instead of *d e but*, at sixteen years of age is guilty not merely of folly and ignorance, and dullness inconceivable, but of crime, of deadly crime, of filial ingratitude, which I tremble to contemplate. A boy, sir, who does not learn his Greek play cheats the parent who spends money for his education. A boy who cheats his parents is not very far from robbing or forging upon his neighbour. A man who forges on his neighbour pays the penalty of his crime at the gallows. And it is not such a one that I pity (for he will be deservedly cut off); but his maddened and heart-broken parents, who are driven to a premature grave by his crimes, or if they live, drag on a wretched and dishonoured old age. Go on, sir, and I warn you that the very next mistake that you make shall subject you to the punishment of the rod!"

But he lets the Doctor explain himself to Major Pendennis: "He is a very good boy, rather idle and unenergetic, but he is a very honest gentlemanlike little fellow, though I can't get him to construe as I wish."

Thackeray was at first a boarder in Mr. Penny's house in Wilderness Row, Clerkenwell Road, until the middle of 1825, when he became a day boy and stayed with Mrs. Boyes, a lady who took in boys belonging both to the Charterhouse and the Merchant Taylor's Schools.

Among his schoolfellows of 1825 were Edmund Lushington, the captain of the school; Francis Edgworth and Charles Freshwater, monitors; George and Richard Venables, John Murray, and Martin Tupper, in the First Form; Ralfe Bernal (afterwards Bernal Osborne), Pakenham Edgworth, Francis Beaumont, and John Stewart Horner in the Second; in the Third, besides Thackeray himself, James Reynolds Young; and in the Fourth, Henry George Liddell. Henry Ray Freshwater was in the Seventh; Richmond Shakspear and Alfred Gatty in the Eighth; and in the Twelfth, just entering the school, John Leech and Alfred Montgomery. Other contemporaries, whose forms I cannot ascertain, were George Shakespear, George Lock, Robert Curzon, J. F. Boyes, Eubank, Carne, Stoddart, Garden, and Poynter.

Mrs. Ritchie, Mr. Merivale, and many others have declared that Thackeray hated the school as long he was there, and in support of their statement they quote a part of one of his letters. "I really think I am becoming terribly industrious, though I can't get Dr. Russell to think so. It is so hard, when you endeavour to work hard, to find your attempts nipped in the bud. . . . There are but 370 in the school. I wish there were only 369." But I am inclined to think, with Mr. Davies, that more pathos has been extracted from that passage

than perhaps it really bears. It was written in 1828,
when Thackeray was second monitor [James Young was
the first] in Day-boys. He was a big fellow, just going
to Cambridge, and was probably anxious to have done
with his school-days. No doubt he disliked the headmaster, and no doubt also he was unhappy at first in the
great school—perhaps most of the time he was in Mr.
Penny's house; but I think he was more contented during his stay at Mrs. Boyes'. Certainly the numberless
parodies, poems, and caricatures he wrote and drew do
not suggest unhappiness in the schoolboy, and his letters
generally are not by any means dismal in tone. He
read everything he could lay his hands on; he acted
when he had the chance; he debated—"We are going to
have a debate to-morrow night on 'The Expediency of
a Standing Army.' We have not yet settled the sides
which we shall take in this important question"; he
drew—"His drawings are wonderful," said his mother;
and he felt the inclination to write—"I have not yet
drawn out a plan for my stories, but certain germs thereof
are yet budding in my mind, which I hope by assiduous
application will flourish yet and bring forth fruit." "I
always feel as if I were at home when I am writing," he
said in a letter, in which he apologizes for writing so
much every day.

At least three of his schoolfellows have recorded their
recollections. Here is Dr. Liddell's letter, inserted by
Mr. Davies in his interesting article on Thackeray in the
Greyfriars.

"The Doctor inserted a Form between the VI. and V.
(or, as he would say, First and Second), which he called
the Emeriti, consisting of those boys *who had served
their time* in the lower Forms and were entitled to be

placed in the VI. as vacancies occurred. But before
joining the Emeriti we were obliged to learn all the odes
and epodes of Horace by heart, and to translate them
without book, and to answer all questions, grammatical,
geographical, and historical, that arose out of the book.
Having achieved this task, we passed into the Emeriti,
and were supposed to learn the same lessons as the VI.
We sat by and were expected to drink in the wisdom of
the Head Form, but seldom were called on to have our
diligence or attention tested. I need hardly say we did
not trouble ourselves to prepare the lessons; and when,
on rare occasions, it occurred to the Doctor to 'put us
on,' great was our consternation, grievous the ignorance
displayed, and vehement the wrath of the master. I
cannot remember whether it was in this curious Form
(between VI. and V., or in the Form below) that I constantly sat next to Thackeray in school. It must, I
think, have been the Form below (the V.): for he was
very lazy in school-work, and I cannot think he ever
exerted himself sufficiently to grapple with the Horace
so as to rise into the Emeriti. In whichever Form it
was, I recollect that we spent much—most—of our time
in drawing. His handiwork was very superior to mine,
and his humour exhibited itself at that time in burlesque
representations and scenes from Shakespeare. I remember one—Macbeth as a butcher—brandishing two blood-
reeking knives, and Lady Macbeth as the butcher's wife
clapping him on the shoulder to encourage him in his
bloody work.''

In after life, Thackeray accused the Dean of ruining
his chance of scholarship by doing his verses for him;
but, as Mr. Davies remarks, there is little trace of Liddell's hand in the Latin *Sapphics*, a fac-simile of the MS.

of which is given in the *Greyfriars*, nor is there any evidence of divided authorship in the *Holyday Song*, August 1, 1826, some verses of which I reprint in this chapter.

In 1822 Thackeray was in the Tenth Form, in 1823 in the Seventh, in the next year in the Sixth, and the year after in the Third. The Blue Book of May, 1826, shows him in the Second (or Fifth) with Henry George Liddell next, and that of the following May in the First (or Sixth) Form. He seems to have jumped the "Emeriti."

"But, it so happens, that same year, 1826-7, was the beginning of the end, and the school ran down very fast in numbers," Mr. Davies (the Charterhouse Gold Medalist for 1864) has explained. "It was perhaps *force majeure* which pushed Thackeray up to that exalted position without the ordeal of the odes and epodes. Nay, more: Thackeray's copy of Horace (the writer's possession) lies on the table as he writes, and if it was the same copy which should have been the open sesame to the 'Emeriti,' then it may be safely said that no odes were ever learnt by heart out of it. It is clean, beautifully clean, unthumbed, unsoiled — what second-hand booksellers describe as 'in fine condition.'"

Read what some of his contemporaries have written of him.

"It was when he was between thirteen and fifteen and a half that I knew Thackeray best," Mr. J. F. Boyes has written in the very interesting article *Thackeray and His Schooldays*, printed in the *Cornhill Magazine* in 1865. "He was then eminently good-tempered to all, especially the younger boys, and nothing of a tyrant or bully. Instead of a blow or a threat, I can just hear him saying

to one of them: 'Hooky' (a soubriquet of a son of
the late Bishop Carr, of Bombay), 'go up and fetch me
a vol. of *Ivanhoe* out of my drawer, there's a good fellow; in the same drawer you will perhaps find a penny,
which you may take for yourself.' The penny was,
indeed, rather problematical, but still realized sufficiently
often to produce excitement in the mind of the youth
thus addressed, and would make the service a willing
one. When disappointed it was more than probable
that the victim would call Thackeray a 'great snob,' for
misleading him, a title for which the only vengeance
would be a humourous and benignant smile.

"In the two or three years I am recording I scarcely
ever saw Thackeray seriously angry, or even his brow
wrinkled with a frown. He has been called a cynic: it
is doubtful if a real cynic could ever be manufactured
out of a boy who had such powers as he had of sarcasm,
and who used them so little unkindly.

"Thackeray had nearly all the materials that usually
go to the making of a first-rate classical scholar. He
had wonderful memory, an absolute faculty of imitation;
. . . he had the power of acquiring language, and
an intense admiration of the beautiful. He got to love
his Horace, . . . but never was a highly classical
scholar.

"He had no school industry. No one in those early
days could have believed that there was much work in
him, or that he would ever rise to the top of any tree by
climbing. . . .

"His beau-ideal was the serious and sublime; he was
too familiar with, too much a master of, the humourous
to think as much of that mastery as his admirers did.
I have heard him speak in terms of homage to the genius

of Keats that he would not have vouchsafed to the whole tribe of humourists.

"A rosy-faced boy, with dark curling hair and a quick, intelligent eye, ever twinkling with humour and *good*-humour. He was stout and broad-set, and gave no promise of the stature which he afterwards reached. It was during a short but severe illness, just before he left school, that he grew rapidly, leaving his sick-bed certainly a good many inches taller than he was when he entered it, and heading at once nearly all his contemporaries. . . . For the usual schoolboy sports and games Thackeray had no taste or passion whatever, any more than in after-life for those field sports which seem to have been the delight of his fellow-humourist and school-fellow, Leech.

"Such amusement would have come probably next to Euclid and Algebra in his list of dislikes. But he was by no means what men of genius are said to have been in their youth—disposed to isolation or solitary musing. For a non-playing boy he was wonderfully social, full of vivacity and enjoyment of life; his happy insouciance was constant. Never was a lad at once so jovial, so healthy, and so sedentary. Good spirits and merriment seemed to enable him to dispense with the glow of cricket or football, and if in his still earlier days he ever 'fagged out' it must have been bitterly against his will. We were now and then, indeed, out together in small fishing parties, but it was for the talking, and the change, and the green fields, and the tea abroad instead of at home—cakes, etc., accompanying (for he was always gustative, never greedy)—that Thackeray liked these expeditions. I question whether he knew the difference between a roach and a gudgeon—

except when fried—whether he ever caught either the
one or the other I am much disposed to doubt; or
whether he cared about doing so. . . . Though
keenly ambitious and very sensitive of failure, Thackeray
was wonderfully free from anything like vanity or conceit.''

"My recollection of him," his friend George Stovin
Venables wrote to Anthony Trollope, "though fresh
enough, does not furnish much material for biography.
He came to school young—a pretty, gentle, and rather
timid boy. I think his experience there was not generally pleasant. Though he had afterwards a scholar-like
knowledge of Latin, he did not attain distinction in the
school, and I should think that the character of the
headmaster, Dr. Russell, which was vigorous, unsympa-
thetic, and stern, though not severe, was uncongenial to
his own. With the boys who knew him, Thackeray was
popular, but he had no skill in games, and I think no
taste for them.

"He was already known by his faculty for making
verses, chiefly parodies. I only remember one line of
one parody on a poem of L. E. L.'s about 'Violets,
dark blue violets'; Thackeray's version was 'Cabbages,
bright green cabbages,' and we thought it very witty.''

This parody, his first literary effort, has only once
been printed, and then in a magazine, so that it is practically unknown; and it shows so clearly the sense of
humour and the eye for the ridiculous which distinguished all Thackeray's later works, that I venture to
print it here, putting, for the sake of the reader's
convenience, the poem of which it is a parody by its
side.

VIOLETS (L. E. L.)

Violets! deep blue violets!
April's loveliest coronets:
There are no flowers grow in the
vale,
Kissed by the sun, woo'd by the
gale,
None with the dew of the twilight
wet,
So sweet as the deep blue vio-
let.

I do remember how sweet a
breath
Came with the azure light of a
wreath,
That hung round the wild harp's
golden chords
That rang to my dark-eyed lover's
words.
I have seen that dear harp
rolled
With gems of the East and bands
of gold,
But it never was sweeter than
when set
With leaves of the dark blue
violet.

And when the grave shall open
for me—
I care not how soon that time
may be—
Never a rose shall bloom on my
tomb,
It breathes too much of hope and
bloom;
But let me have there the meek
regret
Of the bending and deep blue
violet.

CABBAGES (W. M. T.)

Cabbages! bright green cabbages!
April's loveliest gifts, I guess.
There is not a plant in the gar-
den laid,
Raised by the dung, dug by the
spade,
None by the gardener watered,
I ween,
So sweet as the cabbage, the
cabbage green.

I do remember how sweet a
smell
Came with the cabbage I loved
so well,
Served up with the best that
beautiful looked
The beef that dark-eyed Ellen
cooked.
I have seen beef served with
raddish of horse,
I have seen beef served with
lettuce of cos,
But it is far nicer, far nicer, I
guess,
As bubble and squeak, beef and
cabbages.

And when the dinner-bell sounds
for me—
I care not how soon that time
may be—
Carrots shall never be served on
my cloth,
They are far too sweet for a boy
of my broth;
But let me have there a mighty
mess
Of smoking hot beef and cabbages.

To prophesy *after* the event is always an absurdity, but there is no doubt that *Cabbages* might easily have been worse. At least, *Cabbages* is a better parody than *Violets* is a poem—but it can, of course, be retorted that this is not necessarily imputing any great merit to the schoolboy parody. It is, moreover, worthy of note as an index to Thackeray's mind, and as showing that, while he always had a profound reverence for the beautiful in art, as his boyish appreciation of Keats and his later admiration for Tennyson demonstrate, he had a corresponding natural antipathy to the mawkish or feebly sentimental, which was the cause and mainspring of his genius for parody and burlesque.

Anthony Trollope has printed some lines of doggerel, attributed at Charterhouse to Thackeray, which show the marvellous tendency to almost impossible rhymes that was in itself a distinguishing merit of his humourous poetry. And now I must find space for a few of the eleven verses of the *Holyday Song*, to which I have already referred, and which is printed in fac-simile in the *Greyfriars* by Mr. Davies:

> Now let us dance and sing,
> While Carthusian bells do ring;
> Joy twangs the fiddle-string,
>   And Freedom blows the flute.

> Tiddle-dum and Tiddle-di—
> What a joke for you and I—
> Dulce domum, let us cry—
>   Charterhouse adieu.

> Purblind Cupid still drag on
> Some more days ere he can brag on
> Killing game to fill a waggon,
>   And thy shooting-jacket too!

Yet, oh stay! thou beauteous sister
Who has caused heartburn and blister
To that paragon young mister,
    Joseph Carne!

Queen of Beauty! Star of Harrow!
Thou has shot thro' heart and marrow
And stricken Makepeace with thy arrow
    In the head-brain.

"His change of retrospective feeling about his school-days was very characteristic," Mr. Venables continued. "In his earlier books he always spoke of the Charter-house as Slaughter House and Smithfield. As he became famous and prosperous, his memory softened, and Slaughter House was changed into Grey Friars where Colonel Newcome ended his life."

It was with Venables that Thackeray had the fight that he, at least, could never have entirely forgotten. "That unlucky fight!" Mr. Ronpell, the monitor at Penny's in 1822, has said. "It was on a wet half-holiday, I think, when a boy named Glossip came and asked leave for Thackeray and Venables to fight. We wanted some amusement, so I let them fight it out in our long room, with the important result to Thackeray's nasal organ." It says much for Thackeray's manliness and sweetness of disposition that he and his opponent became firm friends and remained so for the rest of their lives.

Yet it is from Thackeray's own pen that we have what is probably the best description of himself as a boy.

"Arthur Pendennis's school-fellows at the Greyfriars school state that, as a boy, he was in no ways remarkable either as a dunce or as a scholar," he wrote. "He did, in fact, just as much as was required of him, and no more. If he was distinguished for anything it was for

verse-writing; but was his enthusiasm ever so great, it
stopped when he had composed the number of lines
demanded by the regulations (unlike your Swettenham,
for instance, who, with no more of poetry in his composition than Mr. Wakley, yet would bring up a hundred
dreary hexameters to the master after a half-holiday; or
young Fluxmore, who not only did his own verses, but
all the fifth form's besides). He never read to improve
himself out of school-hours, but, on the contrary, devoured all the novels, plays, and poetry on which he
could lay his hands. He never was flogged, but it was a
wonder how he escaped the whipping-post. When he
had money he spent it royally in tarts for himself and
his friends; he has been known to disburse nine and sixpence out of ten shillings awarded to him in a single day.
When he had no funds he went on tick. When he could
get no credit he went without, and was almost as happy.
He has been known to take a thrashing for a crony without saying a word; but a blow, ever so slight, from a
friend, would make him roar. To fighting he was averse
from his earliest youth, as indeed to physic, the Greek
grammar, or any other exertion, and would engage in
none of them, except at the last extremity. He seldom
if ever told lies, and never bullied little boys. Those
masters or seniors who were kind to him, he loved with
boyish ardour. And though the Doctor, when he did
not know his Horace, or could not construe his Greek
play, said that that boy Pendennis was a disgrace to the
school, a candidate for ruin in this world, and perdition
in the next; a profligate, who would most likely bring
his venerable father to ruin and his mother to a dishonoured grave, and the like—yet as the Doctor made
use of these compliments to most of the boys in the

place (which has not turned out an unusual number of felons and pickpockets), little Pen, at first uneasy and terrified by the charges, became gradually accustomed to hear them; and he has not, in fact, either murdered his parents, or committed any act worthy of transportation or hanging up to the present day.''

Thackeray's sense of humour seems to have been very early developed, as the following practical joke shows. Dr. Senior, when a boy, sat next to Thackeray in the class-room, and he was dozing there on a sultry summer afternoon while Adam's *Roman Antiquities* was being read aloud. A sentence had just been concluded, when Senior was aroused by hearing his name called, and by being asked the question: "What was provided for the Senators when they met?" Not having the vaguest idea of what to answer, he was delighted to hear a neighbouring voice murmur, "Try 'Wine.'" Thereupon Senior answered boldly, "Wine"; and of course the boys were convulsed with laughter. "Try 'Bread and cheese,'" murmured the prompting voice. The other, however, would not try any more, and a severe imposition rewarded his first attempt.

The sentence on which the silly question had been founded was: "The Senators met periodically in the Temple of So-and-so, where seats or benches were provided for their accommodation"; and—it is almost needless to add—the voice of the tempter was the voice of Thackeray.

How clearly these days of boyhood were impressed upon the man's mind can be seen when, some forty years later, he wrote of these times in a *Roundabout Paper*— "Tunbridge Toys."

"At the beginning of August, 1823, Bartlemy-tide

holidays came, and I was to go to my parents, who were at Tunbridge Wells. My place in the coach was taken by my tutor's servant. 'Bolt-in-Tun,' Fleet Street, seven o'clock in the morning, was the word. My tutor, the Rev. Edward P——, had a parting interview with me; gave me my little account for the governor; the remaining part of the coach-hire; five shillings for my own expenses; and some five-and-twenty shillings of an old account which had been overpaid and was to be restored to my family. Away I ran and paid Hawker his three-and-six [for a pencil case purchased from him]. Ouf! what a weight it was off my mind! . . . The next morning, of course, we were an hour before the time. I and another boy shared a hackney-coach; two-and-six; porter for putting luggage on coach, three-pence. I had no more money of my own left. Rasherwell, my companion, went into the 'Bolt-in-Tun' coffee-room and had a good breakfast. I couldn't, because though I had five-and-twenty shillings of my parents' money, I had none of my own, you see. I certainly intended to go without breakfast, and still remember how strongly I had that resolution in my mind. But there was that hour to wait. A beautiful August morning—I am very hungry. There is Rasherwell 'tucking' away in the coffee-room. I pace the street, as sadly almost as if I had been coming to school, not going thence. I turn into a court by mere chance—I vow it was by mere chance—and there I see a coffee-shop with a placard in the window, *Coffee, Twopence, Round of Buttered Toast, Twopence.* And here I am, hungry, penniless, with five-and-twenty shilings of my parents' money in my pocket. What would you have done? You see I had had my money, and spent it in that pencil-case affair. The five-

and-twenty shillings were a trust—by me to be handed over.

"But then would my parents want their only child to be actually without breakfast? Having this money, and being so hungry, so *very* hungry, mightn't I take ever so little? Mightn't I at home eat as much as I chose?

"Well, I went into the coffee-shop, and spent four-pence. I remember the taste of the coffee and toast to this day—a peculiar muddy, not-sweet-enough coffee—a rich rancid, yet not-buttered-enough delicious toast. The waiter had nothing. At any rate, fourpence, I know, was the sum I spent. And my hunger appeased, I got on the coach a guilty being. At the last stage—what is its name? I have forgotten in seven-and-thirty years—there is an inn with a little green and trees before it: and by the trees is an open carriage. It is our carriage. Yes, there are Prince and Blucher, the horses; and my parents in the carriage. Oh, how I had been counting the days until this one came! Oh! how happy I had been to see them yesterday! But there was that fourpence. All the journey down the toast had choked me, and the coffee poisoned me.

"I was in such a state of remorse about the fourpence, that I forgot the maternal joy and caresses, the tender paternal voice. I pull out the twenty-four shillings and eightpence with a trembling hand.

" 'Here's your money,' I gasp out, 'which Mr. P—— owes you, all but fourpence. I owed three and six to Hawker out of my money for a pencil-case, and I had none left, and I took fourpence of yours and had some coffee at a shop.'

"I suppose I must have been choking whilst uttering this confession.

" 'My dear boy,' says the Governor, 'why didn't you go and breakfast at the hotel?'

" 'He must be starved,' says my mother.

"I had confessed; I had been a prodigal; I had been taken back to my parents' arms again. It was not a very great crime as yet, or a very long career of prodigality; but don't we know that a boy who takes a pin which is not his own will take a thousand pounds when occasion serves, bring his parents' gray heads with sorrow to the grave, and carry his own to the gallows. . . . Oh! Heaven be thanked, my parents' heads are still above the grass, and mine is still out of the noose."

The extract is long, but this picture of the *boy* is one to dwell upon, for it applies equally to the *man*. All his faults were of this fourpenny order, that is to say, of small importance—and he worried himself about them just as he did about the above trifle. How true this is may be gathered from the story Mr. Bayard Taylor has told of a visit that, in 1860, he paid with Thackeray to Baron Marochetti, the sculptor, who was then the novelist's next-door neighbour in Onslow Square. The Baron took down a small engraving of Albert Dürer's from the wall—the subject was St. George and the Dragon—and gave it to Thackeray, who inspected the gift with great delight for a few minutes; and then, suddenly becoming grave, turned to his companion and said, "I shall hang it near the head of my bed, where I can see it every morning. We have all our dragons to fight. Do you know yours? I know mine; I have not one, but two. Indolence and luxury. . . . I am serious. I never take up the pen without an effort. I work only from necessity. I never walk without seeing some pretty useless thing which I want to buy. Sometimes I pass the same shop window every day for months, and resist the temptation and think I am safe; then comes the day of weakness, and I yield. My physician tells me that I must live very simply, and not dine out so much; but I cannot break off the agreeable habit. I shall look at this picture, and think of my dragons, though I don't expect to overcome them.''

But I must return to the *Roundabout Paper*, from which I quote again. "As I look up from my desk, I see Tunbridge Wells and Common in the rocks, the strange familiar place which I remember forty years ago. Boys saunter over the green with stumps and cricket bats. Other boys gallop by on the riding-master's hacks. I protest it is 'Cramp, Riding Master,' as it used to be in the reign of George IV., and that Centaur Cramp must be at least a hundred years old. Yonder comes a foot-man with a bundle of novels from the library. Are they as good as *our* novels? Oh! how delightful they were! Shades of Valancour, awful ghost of Manfroni, how I shudder at your appearance! Sweet image of Thaddeus of Warsaw, how often has this almost infantile hand tried to depict you in a Polish cap and richly embroi-dered tights! And as for Corinthian Tom in light blue pantaloons and hessians, can all the splendour of real life which their eyes have subsequently beheld, and all the will I have heard or read in later times, compare with your fashion, with your brilliancy, with your delightful grace and sparkling vivacious rattle? . . . [My eyes] are looking backwards, back into forty years off, into a dark room, into a little house hard by on the Common here, in the Bartlemy-tide holidays. The parents have gone to town for two days: the house is all his own, his own and a grim old maid-servant's, and a little boy is seated at night in the lonely drawing-room, poring over *Manfroni, or the One-Handed Monk*, so frightened that he scarce dared to turn round."

Thackeray left Charterhouse in May, 1828, but he revisited it many times. In 1859 we hear of his dining with Mr. John Irvine in the Masters' Common Room at Charterhouse, when after dinner and chapel they went to the headmaster's house, where the headmaster (Canon Elwyn) produced the "Green Book," so that Thackeray might con over the names of his school contemporaries. When he came to his own name, Thackeray found recorded, after Trin. Coll. Camb., in the space devoted to "subsequent career": "Michel (?) Angelo Titmarsh, sub-editor of *The Globe*; and he exclaimed with much (probably feigned) indignation, "I never was sub-editor of *The Globe*. I worked for *The Globe*, but I never was sub-editor." This statement was erased, and the new entry is: "Author of *Vanity Fair*, *The Newcomes*, etc., died Christmas, 1863."*

His last visit was on Founder's Day (December 12th), 1863, and the scene has been described by eye-witnesses.

"He was there in his usual back seat in the quaint old chapel. He went thence to the oration in the Governor's room; and as he walked up to the orator with

---

*The bed upon which Thackeray died was given by his daughters to Charterhouse, and to the Head Gownboy and his successors has been accorded the privilege of lying upon it; and Archdeacon Hale, then Master of the Charterhouse, wrote the following inscription, which was engraved at its head:—

HOC LECTO RECUMBENS
OBDORMIVIT IN CHRISTO
GULIELMUS MAKEPEACE THACKERAY
IX KAL. JANVAR: AN. MDCCCLXIV
SCHOLÆ CARTHUSIANÆ QUONDAM DISCIPULUS
MATURA ÆTATE HUJUSCE LOCI AMANTISSIMUS
UTI TESTANTUR EJUS SCRIPTA
PER ORBEM TERRARUM DIVULGATA
VIXIT ANNOS LII.

his contribution, was received with such hearty applause as only Carthusians can give to one who has immortalised their school. At the banquet afterwards he sat at the side of his old friend and artist-associate in *Punch*, John Leech; and in a humorous speech proposed, as a toast, the noble foundation which he had adorned by his literary fame, and made popular in his works. . . . Divine Service took place at four o'clock in the quaint old chapel; and the appearance of the brethren in their black gowns, of the old stained glass and carving in the chapel, of the tomb of Sutton, could hardly fail to give a peculiar and interesting character to the service. Prayers were said by the Rev. J. J. Halcombe, the reader of the House. There was only the usual parochial chanting of the *Nunc Dimittis;* the familiar Commemoration Day psalms, 122 and 100, were sung after the third collect and before the sermon; and before the general thanksgiving the old prayer was offered up expressive of thankfulness to God for the bounty of Thomas Sutton, and of hope that all who enjoy it might make a right use of it. The sermon was preached by the Rev. Henry Earle Tweed, late Fellow of Oriel College, Oxford, who prefaced it with the 'Bidding Prayer,' in which he desired the congregation to pray generally for all the public schools and colleges, and particularly for the welfare of the house founded by Thomas Sutton for the support of age and the education of youth.''

In many of his books Thackeray has mentioned the school, and young Rawdon Crawley, Pendennis, Colonel Newcome and his son, Philip Firmin, and many other "living" characters spent their boyhood there; but *The Newcomes* immortalised the establishment, and well earned for him the title of "Carthusianus Carthusian-

orum.'' It was while at the School on Founder's Day,
1854, that Thackeray suddenly exclaimed, "I shall put
all this in my book"; and in the following April he asked
John Irvine, then a boy at Charterhouse, to introduce
him to a "Codd" (a colloquial term for the Poor Brothers of the Charterhouse), adding, "Colonel Newcome is
going to be a Codd." Young Irvine, whose acquaintance with the "Codds" was very limited, took him to
see Captain Light, an old army man whom blindness and
reduced circumstances had compelled to seek the privileged shelters of Thomas Sutton's Hospital, where he
was tended during the day by his daughter. Many
times Thackeray went to see the veteran, who, it is
related, used to gleefully declare, "I'm going to sit for
Colonel Newcome"; and he wound up his series of visits
by giving a lecture to the boys. I have only found this
lecture mentioned in an article by "D. D." in the
National Review for 1889.

" 'You little fellows perhaps won't understand a word
of what I'm going to say,' he addressed the juniors;
'but you don't care; you're so full of delight at the
thoughts of going home to-morrow that no words of mine
could make any difference, or make you feel a bit jollier.'
Then, turning to the elder boys, 'The predecessor of
your friend, Dr. Senior, whom I well remember in that
chair, and who gave me the soundest reasons for well
remembering him, was the author of two highly popular
treatises, one the *Grey Friars' Latin Grammar*, the other
its Greek ditto, to which amusing works we all subscribed.
They ran through many editions, and, I believe, are not
yet quite obsolete.' Then came some facetiously pen-
sive recollections of his days as a fag, making So-and-
so's toast and blacking So-and-so's boots for a leave-day

outing. Then, looking round at the 'Uppers,' 'Is there still in the Purlieus of this venerable foundation a Red Cow? I'm not referring to Smithfield, or rather, to speak quite classically, "Smiffel." There was in my time. She lived up a lane, and to the milk of that animal many of us were strongly addicted.' Some notice of the story-books he loved as a boy, and a handsome compliment to 'Boz' for having provided the youngster with Pickwick and Nickleby, concluded the lecture."

Well may the Captain have been proud, for he had inspired some of the grandest pages of English literature, with the quotation of one of which I shall conclude my account of Thackeray's connection with the Charterhouse School.

"Mention has been made once or twice in the course of the history of the Grey Friars school—where the Colonel and Clive and I had been brought up—an ancient foundation of the time of James I., still subsisting in the heart of London city. The death day of the founder of the place is still kept solemnly by Cistercians. In their chapel, where assemble the boys of the school, and the fourscore old men of the Hospital, the founder's tomb stands, a huge edifice, emblazoned with heraldic decorations and clumsy carved allegories. There is an old Hall, a beautiful specimen of the architecture of James's time; an old Hall? many old halls; old staircases, old passages, old chambers decorated with old portraits, walking in the midst of which we walk as it were in the early seventeenth century. To others than Cistercians, Grey Friars is a dreary place possibly. Nevertheless, the pupils educated there love to revisit it; and the oldest of us grow young again for an hour or two as we come back into those scenes of childhood.

"The custom of the School is, that on the 12th December, the Founder's Day, the head gown-boy shall make a Latin oration in praise Fundatoris Nostri and upon other subjects; and a goodly company of old Cistercians is generally brought together to attend this oration; after which we go to Chapel and tea and sermon; after which we adjourn to a great dinner, where old condisciples meet, old toasts are given and speeches are made. Before marching from the Oration Hall to chapel, the stewards of the day's dinner, according to old-fashioned rite, have wands put into their hands, walk to church at the head of the procession, and sit there in places of honour. The boys are already in their seats, with shining fresh faces and shining white collars; the old black-gowned pensioners are on their benches; the chapel is lighted, and Founder's Tomb, with its grotesque carvings, monsters, heraldries, darkles and shines with the most wonderful shadows and lights. There he lies, Fundator Noster, in his muff and gown, awaiting the great examination day. We oldsters, be we ever so old, become boys again as we look at that familiar old tomb, and think how the seats are altered since we were here, and how the doctor—not the present doctor, the doctor of our time—used to sit yonder, and his awful eye used to frighten us shuddering boys on whom it lighted; and how the boy next us would kick our shins during service time, and how the monitor would cane us afterwards because our shins were kicked. Yonder sit forty cherry-cheeked boys thinking about home and holidays to-morrow.* Yonder sit some three score old

*"Little Rawdon was there sitting, one of fifty gown-boys in the Chapel of Whitefriars School, thinking, not about the sermon, but about going home next Saturday, when his father would certainly tip him, and perhaps would take him to the play."—*Vanity Fair.*

gentlemen, pensioners of the hospital, listening to the
prayers and psalms.   You hear them coughing feebly in
the twilight—the old reverend black-gowns.   Is Codd
Ajax alive you wonder?—the Cistercian lads called the old
gentlemen 'Codds,' I know not wherefore—I know not
wherefore—but is old Codd Ajax alive, I wonder? or
Codd Soldier? or kind old Codd Gentleman? or has the
grave closed over them?   A plenty of candles light up
this chapel, and this scene of age and youth and early
memories, and pompous death.   How solemn the well-
remembered prayers are, here uttered again in the place
where in childhood we used to hear them!   How beautiful and decorous the rite; how noble the ancient words
of the supplications which the priest utters, and to which
generations of fresh children and troops of bygone seniors
have cried Amen! under those arches.''

Thackeray spent his holidays at Addiscombe until
Major Smyth, retiring in 1825, settled down as a gentleman farmer at Larkbeare, on the confines of the parish
of Ottery St. Mary.   Here Thackeray also stayed for
some months in the interval between leaving school and
going up to Cambridge, while his stepfather coached him
for his university career; and Mrs. Ritchie remembers
being told that while Euclid was child's play to her
father, he disliked algebra, and to the end of his days
declared he could never understand the difference between latitude and longitude.

Doctor Cornish, who was the Vicar at this time, has
inserted in his *Short Notes on the Church and Parish of
Ottery St. Mary, Devon*, an interesting page, headed
Clavering St. Mary and Pendennis.   ''No person of these
parts,'' he wrote, ''can read Pendennis without being
struck with the impression which the scenery of this

neighbourhood must have made upon his mind, to be reproduced in that remarkable story after a lapse of more than twenty years. The local descriptions clearly identify Clavering St. Mary, Chatteris, and Baymouth, with Ottery St. Mary, Exeter, and Sidmouth; and in the first edition, which is ornamented with vignettes in the margin, an unmistakable representation of the 'cock-tower' of Ottery St. Mary is introduced. But though Clavering St. Mary and Chatteris are locally identified with Ottery and Exeter, the characteristics of the story found no counterpart in the inhabitants of either locality.

"In *Fraser's Magazine* for November, 1854, there is an article, entitled *Clavering St. Mary; a talk about Devonshire Worthies*, which confirms this identity, where it speaks of the birthplace of Pendennis, that 'little old town of Clavering St. Mary,' past which the rapid river Brawl holds on its shining course, and which boasts a fine old church with great grey towers, of which the sun illuminates the delicate carving, deepening the shadows of the deep buttresses, and gilding the glittering windows and flaming vane. Things have, however, changed at Clavering since Mr. Thackeray spent many a pleasant summer holiday there in his boyhood. The old Collegiate church has been swept and garnished, bedizened with finery until it scarcely knows itself; and the Wapshot boys no longer make a good cheerful noise, scuffling with their feet as they march into church and up the organ-loft stairs, but walk demurely to their open seats in the side aisle." Thus we see that even Dr. Portman existed, in a modified form, as Dr. Cornish; and it was this gentleman who sent some of Thackeray's verses to *The County Chronicle and Chatteris Champion*, which, however, was known at Exeter as *The Western Luminary*.

And Miss Fotheringay? Did young Thackeray find an angel disguised as an actress in the Exeter Theater? If we think so we shall be in good company, for Mr. Herman Merivale entertains a secret belief that there was some one somewhere that the youngster wooed and loved and (fortunately) lost. But it is only supposition. Even the poem in the *Western Luminary* is not a love-verse, but only a parody of an intended speech of Lalor Sheil's upon Penenden Heath, which he was not allowed to deliver, but of which, before he left town, he had taken the precaution to send copies to some of the leading journals for insertion. This *jeu d'esprit* was the first appearance in print of the future author of *Esmond*, and as such, rather than on account of its merits, obtains quotation here.

IRISH MELODY

(Air: *The Minstrel Boy*.)

Mister Sheil into Kent has gone
  On Penenden Heath you'll find him;
Nor think you that he came alone,
  There's Doctor Doyle behind him.

"Men of Kent," said the little man,
  "If you hate Emancipation,
You're a set of fools." He then began
  A cut and dry oration.

He strove to speak, but the men of Kent
  Began a grievous shouting,
When out of the waggon the little man went,
  And put a stop to his spouting.

"What though these heretics heard me not!"
  Quoth he to his friend Canonical,
"My speech is safe in the *Times*, I wot,
  And eke in the *Morning Chronicle*."

We gather from these stray recollections of Thackeray's school-life at the Charterhouse, and the glimpses we get of his holiday pursuits at Ottery St. Mary, that, like most men of genius, his distinct bias was already apparent, both in his studies and his amusements. It is evident, as in the case of many another sensitive boy with a predestined leaning toward literature and art, that William Makepeace Thackeray was neither a model student, nor had he any keen enjoyment in the rude sports and pastimes of English boyhood. But he was a clever, manly, and affectionate lad, with a fine sense of fun and an innate gift of literary expression. Moreover, his early bent was distinctly in the direction of humourous parody, in which he displayed a keen eye for the foibles and futilities of his fellows, and but little of that love of mere sentiment which distinguishes the juvenile efforts of even so masculine a mind as Byron's. In Thackeray's case, as in most others, the Child was father to the Man.

CHAPTER IV

AT CAMBRIDGE

CHAPTER IV

AT CAMBRIDGE

WHEN he was barely nineteen, in February, 1829, exactly one year after Charles and Alfred Tennyson, Thackeray went up to Trinity College, Cambridge. Major Smyth accompanied him (even as Major Pendennis went with his nephew), and they stayed for a few days at Slaughter's Coffee House, in London, from whence Thackeray wrote to his mother, telling her of a visit to Charterhouse, where he had seen Dr. Russell and some old school-fellows, of calls paid upon members of the family, of one especially to his aunt, Mrs. Ritchie, who had recommended him to her cousin, the Provost of King's. He stayed at Cambridge for two years, and then came down without taking his degree. This, however, was not because, like Pendennis, he was "plucked," but because, going up in February instead of October, he had either to meet men who had three months' advantage of him at the May examination, or to wait for a whole year until the next examinations. It was decided that he should adopt the only other possibility, and he left the University "unplucked" and degreeless. As with the three famous Cambridge poets, Byron, Wordsworth, and Tennyson, *Alma Mater* was able to confer no scholastic title or distinction on the future novelist.

There is not a great deal to record of these years. His letters tell of his work, his books, and his friends,

and form a journal of his daily doings that differed to no
particular extent from those of far less intellectual young
men.   The tutors at this time included Whewell, Julius
Hare, and Cannop Thirlwall; and among the undergrad-
uates were the Tennysons (Frederick, Charles, and
Alfred), G. S. Venables, E. Blakesley, James Spedding,
Arthur Hallam, Robert Monteith, Ralph Bernal (since
known   as   Bernal - Osborne),   Hailstone,   Heyworth,
Badger, Mazzingli, the Lushingtons (E. L., and Henry),
W. H. Thompson (subsequently Master of Trinity),
Charles Kennedy, Edward Horsman, Thomas Sunder-
land, John (now Archdeacon) Allen (the prototype of
Dobbin), Henry (afterwards Dean) Alford, Richard
Trench (afterwards Archbishop of Dublin), and Richard
Monckton Milnes, the first Lord Houghton.   In other
colleges were his Charterhouse comrades: Carne, Young
(Caius), Moody (St. John's), and Fawcett (Corpus
Christi); and his friends Wells, Hine (Corpus Christi),
and Baker (Caius).

He was dull at first, and suffered from headache.
Dr. Thackeray attended him, and ordered diet and
leeches, and refused to take a fee.   "What!" he de
manded, "do you take me for a cannibal?"   He read
classics and mathematics, alternatively, with Whewell;
attended lectures on political economy; and indulged in
an immense amount of desultory reading, principally
fiction, poetry, and history.   Indeed, Thackeray always
advocated the study of this last branch of learning.
"Read a tremendous lot of history," he one day advised
a young cousin, Mr. Bedingfield, as they were leaving
the Reading Room in the British Museum; though,
speaking of this same subject to Mr. Jeaffreson, he
declared, "There's nothing new, and there's nothing

true, and it don't much signify." It was probably at this time that he laid the foundation of his love for the writers of the eighteenth century in general, and, in particular, for Fielding's works. "My English would have been much better if I had read Fielding before I was ten," he said years after.

According to a letter written in March, 1830, he went to Fawcett,* his coach, three times a week, from eight to nine; to Fisher, the mathematical lecturer, from nine to ten; and to Stan, the classical lecturer, from ten to eleven. He read Greek plays with Badger—Badger was a freshman—from eleven to twelve, devoted the next hour to Euclid and Algebra, and worked in the evening at some one or other of these subjects, or at some collateral reading connected with Thucydides or Æschylus. "This is my plan, which I trust to be able to keep," he concluded. His good intentions paved the way to Fame. Indeed, his craving for work was apparently insatiable, and, if he could find time, he determined to write for a college prize competition an English essay on "The Influence of the Homeric Poems on the Religion, the Politics, the Literature and Society of Greece." However—he could not find the time.

He was fortunately not too much occupied to go to supper-parties, where, "though not talkative,—rather observant,—he enjoyed the humour of the hours, and sang one or two old songs ["Old King Cole" was a favourite with him] with great applause, nor to practise fencing, nor to play chess, nor (as he took care to record) to fall asleep over a *Life of Cardinal Wolsey*.

*In another letter he wrote of Fawcett as a "most desperate, good-hearted bore," and mentioned how the coach, while endeavouring to make him *au fait* in trigonometry, made obscure even what he thought he already understood.

In the *Transactions of the Union Society*, printed in 1834, Thackeray is mentioned as a speaker in a list that includes Charles Buller, Kemble, Sterling, Blakesley, Milnes, Trench, Praed, Hallam, Venables, Alford, King-lake, and, above all, Sunderland, who was *the* orator, and, in the belief of the undergraduates, destined to be the greatest of them all,—his promising career, it is well known, was unhappily cut short by insanity. Thackeray spoke at the Union upon the character of Napoleon, and with so little success that he wrote home of his intention never to speak again. However, he subsequently determined to venture, when Shelley was the subject of debate; but the meeting was adjourned for a few days, and I do not think it is known if he ultimately delivered his speech.

Shelley was the rage at Cambridge then, while Byron was the ideal of the undergraduates of Oxford. Sir Francis Doyle and Mr. Gladstone at Oxford invited a deputation from Cambridge to discuss the supremacy of these poets, and Hallam, Milnes, and Sunderland were deputed to maintain the fame of Shelley. Thackeray wrote that he would bring with him, when he came home, Shelley's *Revolt of Islam*, which he thought "a most beautiful poem—though the story is absurd, and the republican sentiments conveyed in it, if possible, more absurd." But soon after he altered his mind; he would not take the poem with him to Larkbeare, for "it is an odd kind of book, containing poetry that would induce me to read it through, and sentiments which might strongly incline one to throw it in the fire."

Shelley had, nevertheless, a certain interest for him, since, when the scheme of a magazine to be called the *Chimera* was mooted at Cambridge, he volunteered—and actually wrote at Paris during the Long Vacation in 1829—*An Essay on Shelley*. But there seems to be no trace of publication of either essay or magazine.

At Cambridge Thackeray contributed to a little weekly paper called *The Snob, a literary and scientific journal not conducted by members of the University*.

In 1829 the subject of the English poem for the Chancellor's medal was the singularly unpromising one of *Timbuctoo*—the medal was awarded to an undergraduate of Trinity College, by name Alfred Tennyson—and Thackeray sent to the *Snob* a poem which (so runs his letter to the Editor) "was unluckily not finished on the day appointed for delivery of the several copies of verses on "Timbuctoo." The poem opens as follows:

> "In Africa (a quarter of the world)
> Men's skins are black, their hair is crisp and curled
> And somewhere there, unknown to public view,
> A mighty city lies, called Timbuctoo."

A description then follows of the fauna and flora of Timbuctoo, of a lion-hunt, of the home-life of the inhabitants and the misery caused by the introduction of slavery; and the whole winds up with a prophecy of dire disaster to Europe.

> "The day shall come when Albion's self shall feel
> Stern Afric's wrath and writhe 'neath Afric's steel.
> I see her tribes the hill of glory mount,
> And sell their sugars on their own account,
> While round her throne the prostrate nations come
> Sue for her rice and barter for her rum."

The skit, read with the notes and elucidations provided by the author, is amusing enough, though it would be difficult to discover in it any promise of his future greatness. But whatever may be thought now among his companions at Cambridge, "*Timbuctoo* received much laud," as Thackeray wrote to his mother, adding naïvely: "I could not help finding out that I was very fond of this same praise. The men knew not the author, but praised the poem; how eagerly I sucked it in. All is vanity!"

Thus even at eighteen he piped the tune that he was to sing in such magnificent tones in after-life. Note, too, the name of the paper—*The Snob!*

In his correspondence from Cambridge there are many references to the little weekly. On the 23rd of May, 1829, he wrote: "On Monday night myself and the Editor of the *Snob* sat down to write the *Snob* for next Thursday. We began at nine and finished at two; but I was so afflicted with laughter that I came away quite ill."

A few days later he tells his parents that "the *Snob* goeth on and prospereth. Here is a specimen of my wit in the shape of an advertisement therein inserted:— Sidney Sussex College. Wanted, a few freshmen. Apply at the Butteries, where the smallest contribution will be gratefully received." From yet another letter it appears that *Guinivere* verses, written over the signature of "A Literary Snob," are his; and several critics have ascribed to him the *Ramsbottom Papers*, and the *Extract from a Letter from one in Cambridge to one in Town.* It is possible, too, that he may have written a rhyming letter published in No. 3 over the signature of "T. T."*

The first number of the *Snob* appeared on April 9, and the eleventh and last bore the date of June 18. It had been intended by Thackeray and others after the long vacation to set up a periodical of a higher class, but

*The letters in the *Constitutional* and the *Corsair* were also signed "T. T."

the intention fell through, and the *Snob* was revived in
November under the new name of the *Gownsman*. To
this he contributed *I'd be a Tadpole* (air: *I'd be a But-
terfly*)." Probably *From Anacreon*, and the continued
Ramsbottom Papers were from his pen; and Anthony
Trollope has suggested also the dedication:

> "To all Proctors, past, present, and future—
> Whose taste it is our privilege to follow,
> Whose virtue it is our duty to imitate,
> Whose presence it is our interest to avoid."

I venture to say, in spite of Anthony Trollope's contrary belief, that Thackeray's university career did him
an immense amount of good. Enough has been said of
the course of his studies to show that, without being
carried to any great depths, he obtained a good general
knowledge of many things which proved to be of great
use to him in after life. Indeed, Thackeray himself
never underrated the value of a classical education; and
once when "Eöthen" Kinglake was laughing at the five
or six years' enforced composition in Latin to which he
had been subjected at Eton, he said to him, "It has
made you what you are."

But another great benefit was derived from Thackeray's stay at Cambridge, for (as Mr. Richmond Ritchie
has pointed out) "Cambridge fixed his social status.
Though afterwards he was to consort with Bohemians
and other strange acquaintances into which a man is
forced by adversity, he was never a Bohemian and
always faithful to the traditions of the class in which he
was born and bred." There can be no question as to
the truth of this; it is beyond all cavil or argument.
The university life gave the lad the ballast necessary to
carry him safely through his troubles by imbuing him

with a liking for the society of his equals, and a great dislike to everything that smacked of vulgarity.

Sir Walter Besant and many others, who are unable to understand how Thackeray could have known enough of the manner of the Upper Ten to be able to depict Society (the Society with the capital S) in *Vanity Fair*, since, they insist, it was only on the success of that book that he obtained the *entrée* into those exclusive circles, forget that Thackeray was the son of well-to-do parents of the upper stratum of the middle classes, that he had a public-school and university education, and that, at Cambridge, he met and made lasting friendships with Edward Fitzgerald, Monckton Milnes, W. H. Thompson, R. C. Trench, John Sterling, Alfred Tennyson, James Spedding, John Allen, William Brookfield, and many others whose names are now well known—several of whom were among the choice and master spirits of the time, and all gentlemen of good social standing. We should ever bear in mind the dictum of Walter Bagehot, that the value of an English University training consists more in the youthful friendships there formed with fellow-students and contemporaries than in the actual studies and examinations.

CHAPTER V

IN GERMANY

CHAPTER V

IN GERMANY

I T was arranged that, after coming down from Trinity, Thackeray should travel for a couple of years, and with this end in view he took a course of German lessons from a Herr Troppeneger, in London. During this continental tour he visited many places of interest, and spent several months at Dresden and Rome and Paris and Weimar. Commencing at Godesberg, as, for some unknown reason, everybody did in those days, he stayed there with a friend for a month, improving his knowledge of the language and reading—or at least buying—Schiller's works. He spent some time, too, in the studios at Paris, and these experiences and those of later years have been reproduced in *The Newcomes* and *Philip*, just as the German travels have borne fruit in *Vanity Fair* and other stories.

Weimar, however, is the place around which is centered most of the interest of these early travels. Dr. Norman McLeod was there, and also his friend and fellow-student at Trinity, W. C. Lettson, since Her Majesty's *chargé d'affaires* at Uruguay, but then attached to the suite of the English Minister at Weimar; and the three young men learnt German together from Dr. Weissenborne.

He must have arrived there not later than the end of August or the beginning of September. In the last week of the latter month he was presented at Court, where the etiquette, in his opinion, was absurdly ceremonious. The lack of a uniform in which to appear seems to have worried him; and he wrote home asking for a cornetcy in Sir John Kennaway's yeomanry, as he objected to the makeshift dress of black coat, waistcoat, and (trousers cut down into) breeches, in which he declared he looked half footman, half Methodist parson.

He liked Weimar so well that in December he said that he would much appreciate an *attaché*-ship which would enable him to settle down there, where I think he must have spent some of the happiest months of his life. He wrote during his stay there, and read too. He translated Körner, and promised to send his mother two pieces—though whether they were prose or verse I do not know. He read *Faust*, but without much enthusiasm. "Of course I am delighted," he said, "but not to that degree I expected." For Schiller, on the other hand, he had unbounded admiration. "I have been reading Shakespeare in German," he wrote; "if I could ever do the same for Schiller in English, I should be proud of having conferred a benefit on my country. . . . I do believe him to be, after Shakspere, 'the poet';" and it was, I think, Thackeray who, on being told that some one had translated *Wilhelm Tell* into English, and had bettered the drama in the translation, replied that he held the latter process to be quite superfluous.

As, on the ground of *merit*, nothing that Schiller ever wrote—not *Wilhelm Tell*, or *Maria Stuart*, not even the magnificent *Wallenstein*—can bear comparison with Goethe's masterpiece—*the* masterpiece of German literature—it is necessary to seek some other reason for the

SIMPLE MELODIES

with illustrations

CHOISY LE ROI.

PRINTED FOR EDWARD TORRE.

1832

young Englishman's preference for the lesser genius.   I
believe the solution of the problem is to be found in the
fact that *Faust* is, in its very essence, metaphysical, while
the predominant feature of *Tell* is love of home, which
latter quality appealed to Thackeray, while the former
made little impression on him.   This will be found to be
only one of many instances in which his judgment came
from his heart, and not from his intellect; and remembering this, it is all the more remarkable to note how the
majority of his criticisms in art and literature have been
accepted by the critics of our generation.

He had his flirtations; he laughingly wrote to his
mother about a certain mademoiselle whom he adored,
and whom a gentleman of the Guards, with his magnificent waistcoats and his ten thousand a year, took away
from him.   He bemoaned his fate by merrily translating
Schiller:—

> "The world is empty,
> This heart is dead,
> Its hopes and its ashes
> Forever are fled."

Here, too, he may have met a Miss Löwe, who, with
the aid of her father and *fiancé*, swindled him; and a
Dorothea, for whom he learnt to dance, and did dance
with her on the slippery floor—aye, and fell too.   "O
Dorothea! you can't forgive me—you oughtn't to forgive me; but I loved you madly still.   My next flame
was Ottilia."   Five-and-twenty years after, when he
revisited the town, he pointed out the house where Frau
von X. (presumably Dorothea's mother) used to live.
"At Venice, a year or two after our visit to Weimar,"
Mrs. Ritchie has recorded, in the charming *Chapters
from Some Unwritten Memoirs*, "we were breakfasting at

a long table, where a fat lady also sat a little way off,
with a pale, fat little boy beside her.   She was stout,
she was dressed in light green, she was silent, she was
eating an egg.   The *sala* of the great marble hotel was
shaded from the blaze of sunshine, but streaky gleams
shot across the dim hall, falling in on the palms and the
orange-trees beyond the lady, who gravely shifted her
place as the sunlight dazzled her.   Our own meal was
also spread, and my sister and I were only waiting for
my father to begin.   He came in presently, saying he
had been looking at the guest-book in the outer hall, and
he had seen a name which interested him very much.
'Frau von Z., geboren von X.   It must be Amalia!
She must be *here*—in the hotel,' he said; and as he
spoke he asked a waiter whether Madame von Z. was
still in the hotel.   'I believe that is Madame von Z.,'
said the waiter, pointing to the fat lady.   The lady
looked up, and then went on with her egg, and my poor
father turned away, saying in a low, overwhelmed voice,
'*That* Amalia!   That cannot be Amalia!'   I could not
understand his silence, his discomposure.   'Aren't you
going to speak to her?   Oh, please do go and speak to
her,' we both cried.   'Do make sure if it is Amalia.'
But he shook his head.   'I can't,' he said; 'I had rather
not.'   Amalia, meanwhile, having finished her egg, rose
deliberately, laid down her napkin, and walked away,
followed by her little boy.   Does not this description
seem to recall Thackeray's version of the *Sorrows of
Werther,*—

"Charlotte, having seen his body
    Borne before her on a shutter,
Like a well-conducted person
    Went on cutting bread and butter."

The most memorable day in Thackeray's earlier
years, and one which he never forgot, was Wednesday,
October 20, 1830. On that day he wrote to his
mother:—

"I saw for the first time old Goethe to-day; he was
very kind, and received me in rather a more *distingué*
manner than he has used the other Englishmen here;
the old man [Goethe was eighty-one] gives occasion-
ally a tea-party to which the English and some special
favourites in the town are invited; he sent me a sum-
mons at twelve. I sat with him for half an hour."

Many years later Thackeray wrote again of Goethe
and the happy Weimar-Pumpernickel days in a letter to
George Henry Lewes, published in the *Life of Goethe*,
which, though written forty-four years ago, is of lasting
interest, and calls for reproduction here:—

"LONDON, *April* 28, 1855.

"DEAR LEWES,—I wish I had more to tell you
regarding Weimar and Goethe. Five-and-twenty years
ago, at least a score of young English lads used to live
at Weimar for study, for sport, or society. The Grand
Duke and Duchess received us with the kindliest hospitality. The Court was splendid, but yet most pleasant and homely. We were invited in our turns to dinners, balls, and assemblies there. Such young men as
had a right appeared in uniforms, diplomatic and military. Some, I remember, invented gorgeous clothing:
the kind old Hof Marschall of those days, M. de Spiegel
(who had two of the most lovely daughters eyes ever
looked on), being in no wise difficult as to the admission
of these young Englanders. Of the winter nights we
used to charter sedan chairs, in which we were carried
through the snow to those pleasant Court entertain-

ments. I, for my part, had the good luck to purchase
Schiller's sword, which formed a part of my Court costume, and still hangs in my study, and puts me in mind
of days of youth, the most kindly and delightful.*

"We knew the whole society of the little city, and
but that the young ladies, one and all, spoke admirable
English, we surely might have learned the very best
German. The society met constantly. The ladies of
the Court had their evenings.

"The theatre was open twice or thrice in the week,
where we assembled a 'large family party.' Goethe had
retired from the direction, but the great traditions
remained still. The theatre was admirably conducted,
and besides the excellent Weimar company, famous
actors and singers from various parts of Germany performed Gastrolle through the winter. In that winter I
remember we had Ludwig Devrient in Shylock, Hamlet,
Falstaff, and the Robbers; and the beautiful Schröder
in Fidelio.

"After three-and-twenty years' absence, I passed a
couple of summer days in the well-remembered place,
and was fortunate enough to find some of the friends of
my youth. Madame de Goethe was there, and received
me and my daughters with the kindness of old days.
We drank tea in the open air, at the famous cottage in
the park, which still belongs to the family, and had been
so often inhabited by her illustrious father.

"In 1831, though he had retired from the world,
Goethe would nevertheless very kindly receive strangers.
His daughter-in-law's tea-table was always spread for us.

*Thackeray gave the sword to his friend Bayard Taylor in 1857
or 1858, and he, in his turn, bequeathed it to the Schiller House in
Germany.

We passed hours after hours there, and night after night, with the pleasantest talk and music. We read over endless novels and poems in French, English, and German. My delight in those days was to make caricatures for children. I was touched to find that they were remembered, and some even kept until the present time; and very proud to be told, as a lad, that the great Goethe had looked at some of them.

"He remained in his private apartments, where only a very few privileged persons were admitted; but he liked to know all that was happening, and interested himself about all strangers. Whenever a countenance struck his fancy, there was an artist settled in Weimar who made a portrait of it. Goethe had quite a gallery of heads, in black and white, taken by this painter. His house was all over pictures, drawings, casts, statues and medals.

"Of course I remember very well the perturbation of spirit with which, as a lad of nineteen, I received the long-expected intimation that the Herr Geheimerath would see me on such a morning. This notable audience took place in a little ante-chamber of his private apartments, covered all round with antique casts and bas-reliefs. He was habited in a long grey or drab redingot, with a white neckcloth, and a red ribbon in his button-hole. He kept his hands behind his back, just as in Rauch's statuette. His complexion was very bright, clear and rosy. His eyes extraordinarily dark, piercing and brilliant.* I felt quite afraid before them, and recollect comparing them to the eyes of the hero of a

*This must have been the effect of the position in which he sat with regard to the light. Goethe's eyes were dark brown, but not very dark.—G. H. L.

certain romance called *Melnoth the Wanderer*, which used to alarm us boys thirty years ago; eyes of an individual who had made a bargain with a Certain Person, and at an extreme old age retained these eyes in all their awful splendour. I fancied Goethe must have been still more handsome as an old man than even in the days of his youth. His voice was very rich and sweet. He asked me questions about myself, which I answered as best I could. I recollect I was at first astonished, and then somewhat relieved, when I found he spoke French with not a good accent.

"Vidi tantum. I saw him but three times. Once walking in the garden of his house in the Frauenplatz; once going to step into his chariot on a sunshiny day, wearing a cap and a cloak with a red collar. He was caressing at the time a beautiful little golden-haired granddaughter, over whose sweet face the earth has long since closed too.

Any of us who had books or magazines from England sent them to him, and he examined them eagerly. *Frazer's Magazine* had lately come out, and I remember he was interested in those admirable outline portraits which appeared for a while in its pages. But there was one, a very ghastly caricature of Mr. Rogers, which, as Madame de Goethe told me, he shut up and put away from him angrily. 'They would make me look like that,' he said, though in truth I could fancy nothing more serene, majestic, and healthy looking than the grand old Goethe.

"Though his sun was setting, the sky roundabout was calm and bright, and that little Weimar illumined by it. In every one of those kind salons the talk was still of art and letters. The theatre, though possessing no very extraordinary actors, was still conducted with a noble intelligence and order. The actors read books, and were men of letters and gentlemen, holding a not unkindly relationship with the Adel. At Court the conversation was exceedingly friendly, simple and polished. The Grand Duchess (the present Grand Duchess Dowager), a lady of very remarkable endowments, would kindly borrow our books from us, lend us her own, and graciously talk to us young men about our literary tastes and pursuits. In the respect paid by this Court to the Patriarch of letters, there was something ennobling, I think, alike to the subject and sovereign. With a five-and-twenty years' experience since those happy days of which I write, and an acquaintance with an immense variety of humankind, I think I have never seen a society more simple, charitable, courteous, gentlemanlike, than that of the dear little Saxon city where the good Schiller and the great Goethe lived and lie buried.

"Very sincerely yours,
"W. M. THACKERAY."

It is interesting to think of the meeting of these two men. The one in his old age, the other in his youth. The one famous beyond all living men, as poet, dramatist, romancist, and philosopher; the other only as yet dreaming of becoming a famous artist, and, perhaps, flushing with pleasure to think that his host had approved of some of his early drawings and youthful caricatures.

One cannot help wondering whether the aged and illustrious author of *Faust* discerned in the English youth of twenty the germs of a greatness almost rivalling his own. Probably not. We know how slightingly

Coleridge, as an old man, regarded the more than promising juvenile verse of Tennyson.   Rarely indeed does the old world-worn man who has achieved fame and universal recognition look upon the most promising of the aspirants of the new generation with any sense of their coming greatness or recognition of their personal genius.

CHAPTER VI

THE MIDDLE TEMPLE, GRUB STREET, AND PARIS

CHAPTER VI

THE MIDDLE TEMPLE, GRUB STREET, AND PARIS

IN the autumn of 1831 Thackeray entered himself as a student at the Middle Temple. He had abandoned all thought of the Diplomatic service, and though he did not look forward with much pleasure to practising at the Bar, yet he regarded his profession (he wrote to his mother) as "a noble and tangible object, an honourable calling, and, I trust in God, a certain fame."

He became the pupil of the special pleader and conveyancer, Taprell, and took chambers at No. 1, Hare Court, and, no doubt (as did Pendennis and Warrington), he and his friends, "after reading pretty hard of a morning, and, I fear, not law merely, but politics and general history and literature, which were as necessary for the advancement and instruction of a young man as mere dry law, after applying with tolerable assiduity to letters, to reviews, to elemental books of law, and, above all, to the newspapers, until the hour of dinner was drawing nigh . . . would sally out upon the town with great spirits and appetite, and bent upon enjoying a merry night as they had passed a pleasant forenoon." Indeed, he confirmed this theory in a letter to his mother: "I go regularly to my pleader's and sit with him until half-past five and sometimes six; then I come home and read and dine till about nine or past, when I am glad enough to go out for an hour and look at the

73

world." His only grievance at this time seems to have been that his uncle Frank, who was very kind, *would* ask him to dinner too often—three times a week.

Thackeray does not appear to have overworked himself. His diary and letters show that, far rather than study mere dry law, he preferred to spend a day with Charles Buller, discussing poetry (they could not agree upon the merits of the poets), or to stroll with a friend in Kensington Gardens and lunch at Bayswater. With Maginn, too, he spent much time. It seems, from Mr. Blanchard Jerrold's account, that Father Prout in Paris introduced Dr. Maginn to Thackeray as a possible editor of a magazine which the ambitious young man wished to bring out. Maginn, who was a big man in those days, would not go into the matter until he had five hundred pounds—which may explain the current tale that Thackeray lent him that sum. The magazine was never published, but the pair struck a lively friendship. The doctor took Thackeray to the *Standard* office in the spring of 1832, where he explained the mysteries of printing, and probably gave him an object-lesson in the art of leader-writing. On the next day he gave him dinner at the King's Head—Thackeray's comment on the other guests is not complimentary: "A dull party of low literary men." Maginn read Homer to him, and pointed out beauties that the listener had never perceived—bound him over, too, to read some Homer every day. Thackeray liked him for his wit and good feeling, and there is no doubt that, through Maginn, Thackeray obtained his introduction to *Fraser's Magazine*.

During June Charles Buller was summoned by his constituents at Liskeard, Cornwall, to come down immediately. Unfortunately, however, he was too ill to

Pen pursuing his law studies.

move, so he deputed his brother Arthur and Thackeray to attend. The young men worked hard; they canvassed farmers, dined with attorneys, wrote addresses, and attended meetings. One day, Thackeray told his mother, he was riding for twelve hours canvassing. He found time, however, in spite of the hard work, to amuse himself—to read Wallenstein, to draw caricatures, and to make a lifelong friend of Sir William Molesworth.

Thackeray was never a very keen politician, though he had decided views on some subjects, and was interested in and advocated certain Liberal measures of the day, particularly the passing of the Reform Bill, and the introduction of the Ballot, of Universal Suffrage, and some of those other changes that have come about in more recent years, but which at the time were thought so dangerous that when a very dignified old lady asked him to dinner Mrs. Ritchie is convinced it was with the intention of remonstrating with him on these socialistic opinions.

On the 18th of July he came of age. Almost the first step he took, when he was his own master, was to give up studying for the Bar. It was a cold-blooded profession at best, he said, and a good lawyer must think of nothing all his life long but law. Thackeray never altered his opinion—read an extract from *Pendennis:*

"On the other side of the third landing, where Pen and Warrington lived, till long after midnight sits Mr. Paley, who took the highest honours, and who is a fellow of his college, who will sit and read and note cases until two o'clock in the morning; who will rise at seven and be at the pleader's chambers as soon as they are open, where he will work until an hour before dinner time; who will come home from Hall and read and note

cases again until dawn next day, when perhaps Mr.
Arthur Pendennis and his friend Mr. Warrington are
returning from some of their wild expeditions. How
differently employed Mr. Paley has been! He has not
been throwing himself away: he has only been bringing
a great intellect down to the comprehension of a mean
subject, and in his fierce grasp of that, resolutely exclud-
ing from his mind all higher thoughts, all better things,
all the wisdom of philosophers and historians, all the
thoughts of the poets; all wit, fancy, reflection, art,
love, truth altogether—so that he may master that enormous legend of the law, which he proposes to gain his
livelihood by expounding. Warrington and Paley had
been competitors for University honours in former days,
and had run each other hard; and everybody said now
that the former was wasting his time and energies, whilst
all people praised Paley for his industry. There may be
doubts, however, as to which was using his time best.
The one could afford time to think, and the other never
could. The one could have sympathies and do kindnesses; and the other must needs be always selfish. He
could not cultivate a friendship or do a charity, or
admire a work of genius, or kindle at the sight of beauty
or the sound of a sweet song—he had no time, and no
eyes for anything but his law-books. All was dark outside his reading lamp. Love and Nature and Art,
(which is the expression of our praise and sense of the
beautiful world of God), were shut out from him. And
as he turned off his lonely lamp at night, he never
thought but that he had spent the day profitably, and
went to sleep alike thankless and remorseless. But he
shuddered when he met his old companion Warrington

on the stairs, and shunned him as one that was doomed to perdition.''

From Cornwall, it seems he went abroad—to Havre, first, on his way to Paris, where he arrived towards the end of August.   Here he stayed some months, learning the language, going into society, reading, and criticising what he read, drawing too, and frequenting the theatres as a matter of course.   It was probably the success of his contributions to the *Snob* and *Gownsman* that inclined Thackeray's thought towards a literary life.   Charles Buller wrote for the magazines, and Thackeray told his mother, even before he came of age, that he much desired to follow his example, only he was doubtful of his own powers.   How can a man know his own capabilities? he asked.   But on the other hand, he was always comparing himself with Bulwer, who was then at the zenith of his popularity.   When, however, in January, 1833, Major Carmichael Smyth, became associated with the production of *The National Standard and Journal of Literature, Science, Music, Theatricals, and the Fine Arts*, Thackeray, returning to London, formally entered Grub Street.

On January 5 the paper appeared, under the editorship of the then well-known ballad writer, F.W.N. Bayley.   Thackeray soon became a contributor, and with the nineteenth number took over the editorship, which change he himself announced in the columns of the paper:—

"Under the heading of the *National Standard* of ours, there originally appeared the following: 'Edited by F. W. N. Bayley, assisted by the most eminent men of the day.'   Now we have *changé tout cela*—no, not exactly *tout cela*, for we still retain the assistance of a host of literary talent; but Frederick William Naylor Bayley has gone. We have got free of the Old Bailey, and changed the governor."

Some weeks later he bought the paper.

His own early contributions included a *Sonnet* ascribed to W. Wordsworth; a review of Montgomery's *Angel of Life*, in which, by a supposed printer's error, ten or twelve lines are quoted in inverted order, but, as Thackeray explained, it is quite unnecessary to correct the mistake, as they have just as much sense one way as the other; a tale, *The Devil's Wager*,* which ends with the Thackerayesque touch, "The moral of this story will be given in several successive numbers," and some verses addressed to Louis Philippe, which are noticeable only because of the reference to 'a snob.'

> "He stands in Paris as you see him before ye,
> Little more than a snob—there's an end of the story."

The late Mr. Shepherd, in his bibliography, stated that Thackeray's contributions ceased on August 24. This is obviously inaccurate, for Thackeray himself, in a letter dated from the Garrick Club, September 6, mentioned that he was busily engaged in writing, puffing, and other delightul occupations for the *National Standard*, which, he added, was growing in repute. Another letter from Paris, October 23, referred to *A Tale of Wonder* (*National Standard*, September 13), translated from a clever French story, written in a sort of *patois*, which he had "sent to the printers as soon as it was finished, when one does not know good from bad," and he added

---

*When *The Devil's Wager* was reprinted in *The Paris Sketch Book*, this last sentence was changed to: "The moral of this story will be found in the second edition."

that he had done nothing but send a cheque to the paper, which, however, was rapidly improving, and which he hoped would form a property that would at once provide him with an occupation and an income! During the next three weeks the circulation only increased by twenty—at which rate he said the proprietor would assuredly be ruined before his venture succeeded. At Christmas he was very busy. "The only fault I find with the *National Standard* is that at the end of the day I am but ill disposed, after writing and reading so much, to read another syllable or write another line."

He was anxious that on the New Year the issue should be particularly good, as he was about to change the name to the *Literary Standard*, and to increase the price to threepence, hoping that with the alterations he would do better.

The last number for the old year announced the intended change of name—finally settled as *The National Standard and Literary Representative*—surely not much of an improvement—and contained an editorial note, in which the paper's future success was spoken of as certain. On January 18 he contributed *Father Gahagan's Exhortation*, and a long and interesting review of the *Étude sur Mirabeau, par Victor Hugo*, appeared in the paper, dated February 1; which issue, in spite of the confident tone of the New Year's address, was the last appearance of the *National Standard, etc.*

It is generally, and I think correctly, believed that Thackeray related the tale of this newspaper venture in the pages of *Lovel, the Widower*, when he put the following words in the mouth of Mr. Batchelor:—

"They are welcome to make merry at my charges in

respect of a certain bargain which I made on coming to London, and in which, had I been Moses Primrose purchasing green spectacles, I could scarcely have been more taken in. My Jenkinson was an old College acquaintance, whom I was idiot enough to believe a respectable man. The fellow had a very smooth tongue and a sleek, sanctified exterior. He was rather a popular preacher, and used to cry a good deal in the pulpit. He and a queer wine merchant and bill discounter, Sherrick by name, had somehow got possession of that neat little literary paper, *The Museum*, which perhaps you remember, and this eligible literary property my friend Honeyman, with his wheedling tongue, induced me to purchase. . . . I daresay I gave myself airs as the editor of that confounded *Museum*, and proposed to educate the public taste, to diffuse morality and sound literature throughout the nation, and to pocket a liberal salary in return for my services. I daresay I printed my own sonnets, my own tragedy, my own verses. . . . I daresay I wrote satirical articles in which I piqued myself on the fineness of my wit, and criticisms, got up for the nonce out of encyclopædias and biographical dictionaries, so that I would be actually astonished at my own knowledge. . . . I daresay I made a gaby of myself to the world. Pray, my good friend, hast thou never done likewise? If thou hast never been a fool, be sure thou wilt never be a wise man.''

Thackeray lost the greater part of his fortune* very soon after he inherited it, and until recently there was much speculation, and many romantic stories circulated

---

*I have read many contradictory accounts, but I believe his patrimony could have been invested to produce an income of from four hundred to five hundred pounds. Sir William Hunter mentions twenty thousand pounds as the sum.

as to the manner in which it was dispersed. Now, however, the truth is more or less accurately known.

The *National Standard* cost a good round sum.
Social robbers eased him of much more, as he complains
in the *Roundabout Papers*, *On a Pear Tree*, and *Ogres:*

"When I first came to London, as innocent as Monsieur Gil Blas, I also fell in with some pretty acquaintances, found my way into several taverns, and delivered
my purse to more than one gallant gentleman of the
road. Ogres, nowadays, need not be giants at all. . . .
They go about in society, slim, small, quietly dressed,
and showing no especially great appetite. In my own
young day there used to be play ogres—men who would
devour a young fellow in one sitting, and leave him
without a bit of flesh on his bones. They were quiet,
gentlemanlike looking people. They got the young man
into their cave, champagne, *paté de foie gras*, and numberless good things, were handed about; and then, having eaten, the young man was devoured in his turn."
This question was finally laid at rest when Thackeray
pointed out to Sir Theodore Martin at Spa, a broken-
down but gentlemanly-looking man as "the original of
my Deuceace. I have not seen him since the day he
drove me down in his cabriolet to my broker's in the
city, where I sold out my patrimony and handed it over
to him." The method of procedure employed to ease
Thackeray of fifteen hundred pounds may be read in the
Yellowplush Papers. But Thackeray bore his Deuceace
no malice now, and only remarked to his companion,
with pity in his voice, "Poor devil! my money doesn't
seem to have thriven with him."

More money went in an Indian bank failure, to which
catastrophe we probably owe the Bundelkund Bank inci-

dent in *The Newcomes;* and much of his remaining capital was expended in "loans" to needy friends. All through his life Thackeray gave away in "loans" and gifts a far greater part of his monies than prudence advised; but then, Thackeray was extravagant and a cynic, and with him to see distress and to endeavour to alleviate it were two simultaneous impressions.

While acting as Paris correspondent of the *National Standard* in July, Thackeray had written home: "I have been thinking very seriously of turning artist. I can draw better than I can do anything else, and certainly I should like it better than any other occupation, as why shouldn't I?" When, therefore, in the winter, the paper came to an untimely end, he remained in Paris—his parents soon following—to devote himself in all seriousness to the study of art.

Here he stayed with his grandmother, Mrs. Butler, most of the time, and with other old ladies, friends and relations of hers, until at last he was able to settle down in rooms in the *Rue des Beaux Arts.*

He spent all his days in the studios, at one time with Brine, a well-known impressionist artist, and at another with Gros, a favourite pupil of David. He reported himself satisfied with his progress, and hoped in a year, if he worked hard, he might paint something worth looking at; but, he naïvely tells his mother, it would require at least that time to gain any readiness with his brush!

He spent much time at the picture-galleries, and now and then copied a picture—a Watteau or a Lucas von Leyden ("a better man, I think, than Albert Dürer, and mayhap as great a composer as Raphael himself"); and Hayward, the Edinburgh reviewer, in his article on *Vanity Fair*, published in January, 1848, says, "We well remember ten or twelve years ago finding him day after day engaged in copying pictures in the Louvre, in order to qualify himself for his intended profession." But I think instead of ten or twelve years ago, "thirteen or fourteen" should have been written.

In Paris he led the life of his companion students—a happy Bohemian existence, that he has graphically described in his article on *The French School of Painting:*—

"The life of the young artist is the easiest, merriest, dirtiest existence possible," he wrote. "He comes to Paris, probably at sixteen, from his province; his parents settle forty pounds a year on him, and pay his master; he establishes himself in the Pays Latin, or in the new quarter of Notre Dame de Lorette (which is quite peopled with painters); he arrives at his *atelier* at a tolerably early hour, and labours among a score of companions as merry and as poor as himself. Each gentleman has his favourite tobacco-pipe; and the pictures are painted in the midst of a cloud of smoke, and a din of puns and choice French slang, and a roar of choruses, of which no one can form an idea who has not been present at such an assembly. How he passes his evenings, at what theatres, at what guinguettes, in company with what seducing little milliner, there is no need to say. . . . These young men (together with the students of sciences) comport themselves towards the sober citizen pretty much as the German bursch towards the *philister*, or as the military man, during the Empire, did to the pekin: —from the height of their poverty they look down upon him with the greatest imaginable scorn—a scorn, I think, by which the citizen is dazzled, for his respect for the Arts is intense."

Thackeray waxed enthusiastic over the opportunities that Paris affords the art student.

"To account for a superiority over England,—which I think, as regards art, is incontestable—it must be remembered that the painter's trade in France is a very good one: better appreciated, better understood, and generally far better paid than with us. There are a dozen excellent schools in which a lad may enter here, and, under the eye of a practised master, learn the apprenticeship of his art at an expense of about ten pounds a year. In England there is no school except the Academy, unless the student can afford to pay a very large sum and place himself under the tuition of some particular artist. Here, a young man, for his ten pounds, has all sorts of accessory instructions, models, etc., and has farther, and for nothing, numberless incitements to study his profession which are not to be found in England!—the streets are filled with picture shops, the people themselves are pictures walking about; the churches, theatres, eating houses, concert rooms, are covered with pictures; Nature herself is inclined more kindly to him, for the sky is a thousand times more bright and beautiful, and the sun shines for the greater part of the year. Add to this incitements more selfish, but quite as powerful: a French artist is paid very handsomely; for five hundred a year is much where all are poor; and has a rank in society rather above his merits than below them, being caressed by host and hostesses in places where titles are laughed at, and a baron is thought of no more account than a banker's clerk."

And later in the same article, he declared:

"What a Paradise this gallery [of the Louvre] is for French students, or foreigners who sojourn in the

capital!   It is hardly necessary to say that the brethren
of the brush are not usually supplied by Fortune with
any extraordinary wealth or means of enjoying the
luxuries with which Paris, more than any other city,
abounds.   But here they have a luxury which surpasses
all others, and spend their days in a palace which all the
money of all the Rothschilds could not buy.   They
sleep, perhaps, in a garret, and dine in a cellar; but no
grandee in Europe has such a drawing-room.   King's
houses have at best but damask hangings and gilt
cornices.   What are these to a wall covered with canvas
by Paul Veronese, or a hundred yards of Rubens?
Artists in England who have a national gallery that
resembles a moderate-sized gin-shop, who may not copy
pictures, except under particular restrictions, and on rare
and particular days, may revel here to their hearts' content.   Here is a room half-a-mile long, with as many
windows as Aladdin's palace, open from sunrise till evening, and free to all manners and all varieties of study:
the only puzzle to the student is to select the one he
shall begin upon, and keep his eyes away from the rest."

Paris was Thackeray's favourite haunt all his life long.
He visited it for the first time in 1830—surreptitiously—
and recalls that visit more than thirty years later in a
Roundabout Paper.

"I remember as a boy," he wrote in *Desseius*, "at the
'Ship' at Dover, (imperante Carolo Decimo,) when, my
place to London being paid, I had but twelve shillings
left after a certain little Paris expedition (about which
my benighted parents never knew anything), ordering
for dinner a whiting, a beef-steak, and a glass of negus,
and the bill was, dinner seven shillings, a glass of negus
two shillings, waiter sixpence, and only half-a-crown left,

as I was a sinner, for the guard and coachman on the way to London! And I *was* a sinner. I had gone without leave. What a long dreary, guilty four hours' journey it was, from Paris to Calais, I remember. . . . I met my college tutor only yesterday. We were travelling, and stopped at the same hotel. He had the very next room to mine. After he had gone into his apartment, having shaken me quite kindly by the hand, I felt inclined to knock at his door and say 'Dr. Bentley, I beg your pardon, but do you remember when I was going down at the Easter vacation in 1830, you asked me where I was going to spend my vacation? And I said, with my friend Slingsby in Huntingdonshire. Well, sir, I grieve to have to confess that I told you a fib. I had got twenty pounds and was going for a lark to Paris, where my friend Edwards was staying.' . . . The doctor will read it, for I did not wake him up."

He spent a great deal of his leisure, and, indeed, did much of his writing there. He thoroughly enjoyed the social gaieties of Parisian life, and loved to mix with the gifted and artistic Bohemian lions.

Even in the early thirties he had a large acquaintance in all ranks of society, and was much sought after. He was especially a welcome guest at Mrs. Crowe's, and was a friend of all her children, Amy, Eyre, and Joseph. He is mentioned in the latter's *Reminiscences:* "Once a week, on Saturdays, my mother received guests in the evening. My mother at her evenings made every one bright by playing Irish jigs or Scotch reels, or accompanying on the piano Methfessel's students' songs and choruses, the supreme enjoyment being a song from Thackeray."

In 1835 he met with an accident that might have had very serious consequences, but any mention of which is only to be found in Mr. T. A. Trollope's *Reminiscences*. A picnic was organised for a visit to the woods of Mont-morenci, where the young people, including Thackeray, thought the day would not be passed properly without a ride on the famous donkeys. Half-a-dozen of the party started, and urged their animals into places and paces to which they were quite unused. Consequent struggles between men and beasts, and Thackeray's donkey tossed his rider over his head, depositing him upon a heap of newly-broken stones. The fall was so severe that it was thought the picnic would have a tragic ending. Soon, however, it was ascertained that no serious injury had been done—but Thackeray bore the mark of the accident to his dying day.

His natural powers of observation were not, however, dimmed by social pleasures. He studied the political, social, literary, and artistic manners and customs of the country, expressing his opinions in his private letters, and later in his writings for the *Constitutional*, and in the articles reprinted in the *Paris Sketch-Book*. He passed summary judgment upon matters that a great statesman or philosopher would only think of in fear and hesitation. The Thackeray of this time was the young Pendennis of whom it is written :—

"The courage of young critics is prodigious: they clamber up to the judgment seat, and, with scarce a hesitation, give their opinion upon works the most intri-cate or profound. Had Macaulay's history or Her-schel's astronomy been put before Pen at this period, he would have looked through the volumes, meditated his opinion over a cigar, and signified his august approval of either author, as if the critic had been their born superior, and indulgent master and patron. By the help of the *Biographie Universelle* or the British Museum, he would be able to take a rapid *résumé* of a historical period, and allude to names, dates, and facts, in such a masterly, easy way, as to astonish his mamma at home, who wondered where her boy could have acquired such a prodigious store of reading, and himself, too, when he came to read over his articles two or three months after they had been composed, and when he had forgotten the subject and the books which he had consulted.   At that period of his life Mr. Pen owns that he would not have hesitated, at twenty-four hours' notice, to pass an opinion upon the greatest scholars, or to give a judgment upon the encyclopædia.''

Yet many of the great novelist's decisions have coincided with those pronounced in later years by more qualified judges.

Thackeray was not destined to become a painter. Fortunately for the greater public, as well as for himself, he was driven by circumstances to the profession of letters.

CHAPTER VII

JOURNALISM AND MARRIAGE

CHAPTER VII

JOURNALISM AND MARRIAGE

IN 1836 Thackeray returned to London to settle the preliminaries of a scheme for establishing a daily newspaper projected by his stepfather. Major Smyth had chosen the moment when the old newspaper tax was about to be much reduced. It was proposed to form a small joint-stock company, with the Major as chairman, to be registered as the *Metropolitan Newspaper Company*, with a capital of £60,000 in six thousand shares of £10 each. To this end a respectable paper (with a small and ever-decreasing circulation) entitled *The Public Ledger* was bought. The first number, produced under the auspices of the company as the *Constitutional and Public Ledger*, and printed by Robert Dyer, of 162 Fleet Street, was issued on September 15, 1836, when the stamp duty on newspapers was reduced.

Laman Blanchard was appointed editor, and Thackeray Paris correspondent. Its politics were radical, or what was called radical in those days, and it advocated the ballot, triennial parliaments, complete freedom of the press, and religious liberty and equality. Joseph Hume, George Grote, George Evans, Charles Buller, William Ewart, Sir William Molesworth, John Arthur Roebuck, and other leaders of the advanced party, promised to support the new journal. Thackeray's Paris letters, signed T. T., began to appear on Septem-

ber 27.   They are very meagre and bare, and have absolutely no interest at all for us now; but they at least
show, as we expect them to do, a great dislike to the
government of July.   There are in all forty-four letters,
the last appearing on February 18 (1837), shortly after
which Thackeray came to town to assist at a meeting
called to discuss the paper's finances, which were in a
very precarious condition—when the paper, which, on
March 1, had been increased from six to seven columns
on each of its four pages, was now reduced to its former
dimensions, though the price still remained fivepence.
The *Constitutional* dragged on an almost saleless existence until July 1, when the last number (249) appeared,
with a black border for the death of the king, and an
announcement, probably written by Thackeray himself,
explaining the cause of the failure of the paper.

"The adverse circumstances have been various," he
wrote.   "In the philosophy of ill-luck it may be laid
down as a principle that every point of discouragement
tends to one common centre of defeat.

"When the fates do concur in one's discomfiture, their
unanimity is wonderful.   So has it happened in the case
of the *Constitutional*.

"In the first place a delay of some months, consequent upon the postponement of the newspaper stamp
reduction, operated on the minds of many who were
originally parties to the enterprise.   In the next the
majority of those who remained faithful were wholly
inexperienced in the art and practical workings of an
important daily journal.   In the third, and consequent
upon the other two, there was the want of those abundant means, and of that wise application of resources,
without which no efficient organ of the interests of any

class of men—to say nothing of the interests of the first and greatest class, whose welfare has been our dearest aim and most constant object—can be successfully established.

"Then came further misgivings on the part of friends, and the delusive undertakings of friends in disunion."

And so the *Constitutional* went down, and in the wreck was lost most of the fortune of Major Smyth, and all that was left of Thackeray's patrimony; for, though nominally a joint-stock company, the major and his stepson were such large shareholders that they practically owned the paper.*

Henry Reeve, the famous editor of the *Edinburgh Review*, wrote [*Diary*, January 16, 1836]:—

"That excellent and facetious being . . . has fallen in love and talks of being married in less than twenty years. What is there so affecting as matrimony! I dined yesterday with his object, who is a nice, simple, girlish girl; a niece of old Colonel Shawe, whom one always meets at the Sterling's." Early in the *Constitutional* days, on August 20, 1836, Thackeray married Isabella Gethen Creagh Shawe, *daughter* of Colonel Matthew Shawe; her mother was a Creagh.

[The following is an extract from the "Register Book of Marriages in the house of the British Ambassador in Paris":—

"William Makepeace Thackeray, of the Parish of St.

---

*Even the failure of both his newspaper ventures did not damp Thackeray's ardour. About two years later, writing from 13, Great Coram Street, he asks Jordan, "Is it fair to ask whether the *Literary Gazette* is for sale? I should like to treat, and thought it best to apply to the fountain head."

During 1840 he wrote to his mother that he was about to bring out, on his own account, a weekly paper called the *Foolscap Library*, which he laughingly adds will be so successful that he will not share the profits with any bookseller.

John Paddington, in the County of Middlesex Batchelor and Isabella Getkin Eneagh Shawe* of the Parish of Donerial in the County of Cork Spinster and a Minor was married in this House with the consent of her mother Isabella G. Shawe this twentieth day of August in the year one thousand eight hundred and thirty-six. By me M. H. Luscombe, Bishop and Chaplain. This marriage was solemnised between us W. M. Thackeray, I. G. E. Shawe, in the presence of V. Spencer, I. G. Shawe, senior, J. W. Lemaire."]

Thackeray had met Miss Shawe at his grandmother's, and (he told his eldest daughter) he lost his heart to her when he heard her sing. He was five-and-twenty now, but entirely dependent upon his salary as Paris correspondent of the *Constitutional*. He was not afraid of the future, and would never admit the imprudence of the step he had taken. In 1849 he told Mrs. Brookfield how much more he admired a friend of his after "he flung up his fellow and tutorship at Cambridge in order to marry on nothing a year;" and twenty years after his marriage he wrote to Mr. Synge, who was then about to commit matrimony: "I married at your age with £400 paid by a newspaper which failed six months afterwards, and always love to hear of a young fellow testing his fortune bravely in that way, . . . though my marriage was a wreck, as you know, I would do it again, for behold, Love is the crown and completion of all earthly good."

The young couple settled in Paris in the Rue St. Augustine, and it is especially interesting to those who have read the ballad of *Bouillabaisse* to know that the Rue Neuve des Petits Champs, with its restaurant, was

*This name should be Isabella Gethen Creagh Shawe.

quite close.   When they came to London in 1834 they
stayed with Major and Mrs. Smyth in Albion Street,
Hyde Park, where their eldest daughter, Anne Isabella—
now Mrs. Ritchie—was born in 1838.   Afterwards they
moved to Great Coram Street, where John Leech and
Charles Keene were living at the time.   Here they had
another child, who died in infancy.   How greatly he
regretted this loss readers of *The Great Hoggarty Diamond* will be able to estimate.

"The marriage was a very happy one," we are told,
"and in spite of the failure of the *Constitutional*, work
was abundant and the future promising."

It is into particulars of this work that we must now
enter.

His earliest writings—*Cabbages* and the other verses
composed at Charterhouse, the *Irish Melody*, and the
contributions to the *Snob* and *Gownsman*, were, of course,
purely boyish efforts; and even his writings in the ill-
fated *National Standard* may be counted as amateur
work.   It is now, arrived at the period when he first seriously adopted literature, that we are met by the question: When and for what papers did he first write
professionally?

Mr. James Payn has recorded that Thackeray told him
the first money he ever received in literature ("under
what circumstances he did not say, but I fancy they
must have been droll ones") was from Mr. G. W. M.
Reynolds.   Mr. Payn added he was so astounded that
he forgot to ask for what species of contribution Thackeray was paid.   This knowledge, therefore, advances us
very little and, after all, it is most probable that these
articles, criticisms, tales, verses, or what not, were of
very little importance, and may, with safety, be ignored.

Turning away from the writings of minor interest, we find ourselves face to face with another problem which has proved a stumbling-block to the bibliographers, which cannot be so lightly passed over: What were Thackeray's earliest contributions to the pages of *Fraser's Magazine?*

There are only two things to guide the perplexed searcher. The first is a letter from Thackeray at Weimar, in which he mentions that *Fraser* had just come out—this shows that he knew of the magazine from its first appearance in 1830. The second, however, is much more satisfactory, and proves beyond all doubt that he had written in *Fraser* before 1835—and this is to admit by inference that he had at that time obtained some standing in the world of letters, since the contributors to the magazine were not by any means a race of "leetle" men—for in the January (1835) number there appeared a picture by Maclure, showing the chief contributors to the periodical. Maginn (the editor), Barry Cornwall, Lockwood, John Gall, Ainsworth, Brydger Gleig, Edward Irving, Sir David Brewster, Count D'Orsay, Theodore Hook, Southey, Coleridge, Carlyle, etc., and our Mr. Titmarsh dining at the house of Mr. Fraser.

No article has yet been *positively* identified as Thackeray's before November, 1837, when a review appeared of a book that had just been published, called *My Book, or the Anatomy of Conduct*, by John Henry Skelton, a half-demented West-end linen draper, who had the immovable idea that his mission was to instruct the world in the true art of etiquette! The review was written in the form of a letter to 'Oliver Yorke,' and was headed *Fashnable Fax and Polite Annygoats. By Charles Yellowplush, Esquire*, and dated "No. —, Grosvenor Square, 18th

October (N. B.—Hairy Bell)." It winds up with a note, signed O. Y., though most certainly written by Thackeray, which concludes: "He who looketh from a tower sees more of the battle than the knights and captains engaged in it; and, in like manner, he who stands behind a fashionable table knows more of society than the guests who sit at the board. It is from this source that our great novel-writers have drawn their experience, retailing the truths which they learned. It is not impossible that Mr. Yellowplush may continue his communications, when we shall be able to present the reader with *the only authentic picture of fashionable life* which has been given to the world in our time."

There must, however, have been many articles from Thackeray's pen before this year. Mr. Swinburne, Dr. John Brown, and Mr. Shepherd, believe the gruesome *Elizabeth Brownrigge* (*Fraser*, August, September, 1832) to have been written by him; while, on the other hand, Mr. C. P. Johnson says that in his opinion "after most careful consideration of all they (Swinburne and Brown) have written on the subject and of the story itself, it seems to be impossible to concede to *Elizabeth Brownrigge* the honour of counting Thackeray as its author.* My belief is that Thackeray *did* write the story. The satirical dedication to the author of *Eugene Aram* and the *Advertisement* seem to me to be quite in Thackeray's early style. Indeed, to me the whole tale suggests an immature *Catherine*—the motive of the two tales is the same, and many of the passages are similar in intent, and not vastly different in text. And since Thackeray,

Elizabeth Brownrigge is naturally not to be found in Thackeray's collected works, but the curious will find it reprinted in the volume published by Redman in 1887, entitled *Sultan Stork*.

after publication, rewrote his imitation of Beranger's *Il était un Roi d'Yvetot*, why should he not have written two stories, endeavouring in each, but with stronger pen in the second, to aim a blow at what he regarded as a very pernicious literary tendency?

Elizabeth Brownrigge was the story of a wretched woman who murdered her two apprentices, while *Catherine*, supposed to be written by Ikey Solomons, Esq., junior, himself a convict, tells of a woman, named Catherine Hayes, who was burned at Tyburn for the deliberate murder of her husband under very revolting circumstances.* The object of each book is avowedly "to counteract the injurious influence of some popular fictions of that day, which made heroes of highwaymen and burglars, and created a false sympathy for the vicious and criminal."

In each story it is endeavoured, by ridiculing such books as *Eugene Aram*, *Jack Sheppard*, and similar productions, to bring about a healthier taste.

Read the advertisement to *Elizabeth Brownrigge:*—

"The author of the foregoing tale begs leave to state that he is prepared to treat with any liberal and enterprising publisher, who may be inclined to embark in the speculation, for a series of novels, each in three volumes,

---

*In 1850 Mr. Briggs, an Irishman, suddenly declared that *Catherine* had reference to a Miss Catherine Hayes, an Irish singer of some repute. The angry Irishman wrote to Thackeray that he would thrash him, and took lodgings opposite to the house in Young Street. After a time, finding the situation ludicrous and impossible, Thackeray called on Mr. Briggs and pointed out that when the story was written, in 1839, Miss Hayes was certainly unknown and probably in short frocks. There was no thrashing. Thackeray stood six feet three inches, or more. But the reported discovery had spread, and so many attacks were made upon him in the papers that at last the author settled the matter once for all in a letter, *Capers and Anchovies*, that on April 12, 1850, appeared in the columns of the *Morning Chronicle*. See appendix.

8vo, under the title of *Tales of the Old Bailey*, or *Romances of Tyburn Tree*, in which the whole Newgate Calendar shall be travestied after the manner of *Eugene Aram*."

And then the dedication of the same story:—

"From the perusal of older works of imagination I had learned so to weave the incidents of my story as to interest the feelings of the reader in favour of virtue, and to increase his detestation of vice. I have been taught by *Eugene Aram* to mix vice and virtue up together in such an inextricable confusion as to render it impossible that any preference should be given to either, or that the one indeed should be distinguishable from the other. . . . In taking my subject from the walk of life to which you had directed my attention, many motives conspired to fix my choice on the heroine of the ensuing tale; she is a classic personage,—her name has been already 'linked to immortal verse' by the muse of Canning. Besides, it is extraordinary that, as you had commenced a tragedy under the title of *Eugene Aram*, I had already written a burletta with the title of *Elizabeth Brownrigge*. I had indeed, in my dramatic piece, been guilty of an egregious and unpardonable error: I had attempted to excite the sympathy of the audience in favour of the murdered apprentices, but your novel has disabused me of so vulgar a prejudice, and, in my present version of her story, all the interest of the reader and all the pathetic powers of the author will be engaged on the side of the murderess."

And again:—

"I am inclined to regard you as an original discoverer in the world of literary enterprise, and to reverence you as the father of a new 'lusus naturæ' school. There is no other title by which your manner could be so aptly designated. I am told, for instance, that in a former work, having to paint an adulterer, you described him as belonging to the class of country curates, among whom, perhaps, such a curate is not met with in a hundred years; while, on the contrary, being in search of a tender hearted, generous, sentimental, high-minded hero of romance, you turned to the pages of the Newgate Calendar, and looked for him in the list of men who have cut throats for money, among whom a person in possession of such qualities could never have been met at all. Wanting a shrewd, selfish, worldly, calculating valet, you describe him as an old soldier, though he bears not a single trait of the character which might have been moulded by a long course of military service, but, on the contrary, is marked by all the distinguishing features of a bankrupt attorney, or a lame duck from the Stock Exchange. Having to paint a cat, you endow her with all the idiosyncrasies of a dog.''

The moral of *Elizabeth Brownrigge* and *Catherine* is identical. It is a purpose for which Thackeray was never tired of labouring in both these stories, and in his almost unknown article on Fielding.

''Vice is never to be mistaken for virtue in Fielding's honest, downright books; it goes by its name, but invariably gets its punishment. See the consequences of honesty. Many a squeamish lady of our time would throw down one of these romances with horror, but would go through every page of Mr. Ainsworth's *Jack Sheppard* with perfect comfort to herself. Ainsworth dared not paint his hero as the scoundrel he knew him to be. He must keep his brutalities in the background, else the public morals will be outraged, and so, he produces a book quite absurd and unreal, and infinitely

more immoral than anything Fielding ever wrote. *Jack
Sheppard* is immoral actually because it is decorous. The
Spartans who used to show drunken slaves to their children took care, no doubt, that the slave should be really
and truly drunk; sham drunkenness, which never passed
the limits of propriety, would be rather an object to
incite youth to intoxication than to deter him from it,
and the same late revels have always struck us in the
same light."

Still, the question of the authorship of *Elizabeth
Brownrigge* cannot be held as settled until fresh light
from some at present unknown source is thrown upon the
subject.

Mr. C. P. Johnson, with praiseworthy patience and
industry, has examined, article by article, the volumes
of *Fraser*, from its first appearance until *Fashnable Fax*,
but the result is not very satisfactory. "After all,"
Mr. Johnson says, "I have only been able conclusively
to identify one solitary ballad, though there are many
more pieces both in prose and verse that may have been
and probably were by Thackeray." The ballad to which
he refers is the well-known imitation of Beranger's *Il
était un Roi d'Yvetot*, which, however, was almost entirely
re-written before its re-publication in the *Ballads*.

The "doubtfuls" include:—

(i) *Hints for a History of Highwaymen* (March, 1834), a
review of *Lives and Exploits of English Highwaymen, Pirates,
and Robbers*, by C. Whitehead, Esq.

(ii) *A Dozen of Novels* (April, 1834) criticising stories
of which, with perhaps the exception of Miss Edge-
worth's *Helen*, the modern reader has never heard.

(iii) *Highways and Low-ways, or Ainsworth's Dictionary,
with notes by Turpin* (June, 1834), a review of *Rookwood*.

(iv) *Paris and the Parisians in* 1835 (February, 1836), an article on a book of the same name by Mr. Trollope.

(v) *Another Caw from the Rookwood: Turpin out again* (April, 1836), a further article on Ainsworth's novel, on the appearance of the third edition.

(vi) *The Jew of York* (September, 1836), a burlesque that certainly suggests the author of *Rebecca and Rowena*.

(vii) Mr. Grant's *Great Metropolis* (December, 1836). Thackeray reviewed the same author's *Paris and its People* in December, 1843.

(viii) *One or two Words about one or two Books* (April, 1837), dealing with Savage Landor's *Satire on Satirists*, and an anonymous tragedy entitled *The Student of Padua*.

But even if we accept all these articles as being from Thackeray's pen—and they most certainly bear traces of his workmanship — there must be a good many more papers still hidden, especially between 1830 and 1834; for Mr. Taylor says that it was early in 1834 that Thackeray was recognised as an established contributor, worthy to take a permanent place among the brilliant staff, and he hints at some papers chiefly referring to the Fine Arts (most of them having reference to Thackeray's French experiences) written while he was still studying painting in Paris, and before the pseudonyms of *Titmarsh, Fitzboodle, Yellowplush,* and *Mr. Wagstaff,* were thought of.

When the *Constitutional* failed, Thackeray, having a wife to provide for, and having no source of income, plunged into work with immense energy, and wrote for many magazines and papers, though, as most of the writings were published anonymously, it is possible to trace only a few of the articles. Most of the writing was hack-work, and with a fine indifference he supplied drawings, novelettes, stories, reviews, art criticisms, foreign correspondence, and poems, in great profusion to *Fraser's Magazine*, *Bentley's Miscellany*, *Colburn's New Monthly Magazine*, the *Westminster Review*, *Cruikshank's Omnibus and Comic Almanacs*, the *Times*, the *Morning Chronicle* (his favourite journal, with which, in spite of his frequent contributions, he never succeeded in establishing a permanent connection), the *Globe*, *Galignani's Messenger*,* etc.

In 1837, besides the already mentioned *Fashnable Fax* (*Fraser*, November) his other principal writings were:

(i) A review which appeared in the *Times* (August 3), on Carlyle's *French Revolution*, of which the sage of Chelsea did not entirely approve. "I understand there have been many reviews of a mixed character," the philosopher wrote to his brother; "I got one in the *Times* last week. The writer is one Thackeray, a half monstrous Cornish giant, kind of painter, Cambridge man, and Paris newspaper correspondent, who is now writing for his life in London. . . . His article is rather like him, and, I suppose, calculated to do the book good."

(ii) *The Professor, A Tale. By Goliah Gahagan* (*Bentley's Miscellany*, September); and

(iii) *A word on the Annuals* (*Fraser*, December), in which he makes a vigourous attack on the *Keepsake* sort of production which, after works of the class parodied in *Catherine*, were his pet aversion.

"It is hardly necessary to examine these books and designs one by one," he wrote; "they all bear the same

*Thackeray wrote to Mrs. Brookfield in October, 1848, saying: "We" [Longueville Jones and himself] "worked in Galignani's newspaper for ten francs a day very cheerfully ten years ago."

character and are exactly like *The Book of Beauty*, *Flowers of Loveliness*, and so on, which appeared last year. A large, weak plate, done in what we believe is called the stipple style of engraving, a woman badly drawn, with enormous eyes—a tear, perhaps, upon each cheek—and an exceedingly low cut dress—pats a greyhound or weeps into a flower pot, or delivers a letter to a bandy-legged, curly-headed page. An immense train of white satin fills up one corner of the plate; an urn, a stone railing, a fountain and a bunch of hollyhocks adorn the other; the picture is signed Sharpe, Parris, Corbould, Corbeaux, Jenkins, Brown, as the case may be, and is entitled *The Pearl*, *La Dolorosa*, *La Diondina*, *Le Gage d' Amour*, *The Forsaken One of Florence*, *The Water Lily*, or some such name. Miss Landon, Miss Mitford, or my Lady Blessington, writes a song upon the opposite page, about *Water Lily*, chilly, stilly, shivering beside a stream-let, plighted, blighted, love-benighted, falsehood sharper than a gimlet, lost affection, recollection, cut connexion, tears in torrents, true love-token, spoken, broken, sigh-ing, dying, girl of Florence; and so on. The poetry is quite worthy of the picture, and a little sham sentiment is employed to illustrate a little sham art. . . . It cannot be supposed that Miss Landon, a woman of genius—Miss Mitford, a lady of exquisite wit and taste—should, of their own accord, sit down to indite namby-pamby verses about silly, half-decent pictures; or that Jenkins, Parris, Meadows & Co., are not fatigued by this time with the paltry labour assigned to them. . . . Who sets them to this wretched work? To paint these eternal fancy portraits of ladies in voluptuous attitudes and various stages of *déshabille*, to awaken the dormant sensibilities of misses in their teens, or tickle the worn-

out palates of rakes and *roués?* What a noble occupation for a poet! what a delicate task for an artist! 'How
sweet!' says Miss, examining some voluptuous Inez, or
some loving Haidée, and sighing for an opportunity to
imitate her. 'How rich!' says the gloating old bachelor, who has his bedroom hung round with them, or
the dandy young shopman, who can only afford to purchase two or three of the most undressed; and the one
dreams of opera girls and French milliners, and the
other, of the 'splendid women' that he has seen in Mr.
Yates's last new piece at the Adelphi.

"The publishers of these prints allow that the taste
is execrable which renders such abominations popular,
but the public will buy nothing else, and the public must
be fed. The painter perhaps, admits that he abuses
his talent (that noble gift of God, which was given him
for a better purpose than to cater for the appetites of
faded débauchées); but he must live, and he has no
other resource. Exactly the same excuse might be made
by Mrs. Cole."

A little more is known of his articles in the following
year (1838), though there is nothing approaching a full
record yet compiled. To the *Times* he contributed
reviews on

(i) *The Duchess of Marlborough's Private Correspondence*
(January 6), which review is chiefly interesting for the
following passages:—

"The dignity of history sadly diminishes as we grow
better acquainted with the materials which compose it.
In our orthodox history books the characters move on as
in a gaudy play-house procession, a glittering pageant of
kings and warriors and stately ladies majestically appearing and passing away. Only he who sits very near the

stage can discover of what poor stuff the spectacle is
made. The kings are poor creatures, taken from the
dregs of the Company; the noble knights are dirty
dwarfs in tin foil; the fair ladies are painted hags with
cracked feathers and soiled trains. One wonders how
gas and distance could ever have rendered them so
bewitching. The perusal of letters like these produces
a very similar disenchantment, and the great historical
figures dwindle down into the common proportions as
we come to view them so closely. Kings, Ministers,
and Generals form the principal *dramatis personæ;* and if
we may pursue the stage parallel a little further, eye
never lighted upon a troupe more contemptible.
Weighty political changes had been worked in the country, others threatened equally great. Great questions
were agitated—whether the Protestant Religion should
be the dominant creed of the State, and the Elector of
Hanover a king, or whether Papacy should be restored
and James III. placed on the throne—whether the continental despotism aimed at by Louis should be established, or the war continued to maintain the balance of
power in Europe, or at least to assure the ascendency of
England—on these points our letter-writers hardly deign
to say a word. The political question is whether
Harley should be in or Godolphin, how Mrs. Masham,
the chambermaid, can be checked or won over, how the
Duchess of Marlborough can regain her lost influence
over the queen, or whether the duke is strong enough to
do without it, can force his Captain-Generalcy for life,
and compel the queen to ensure to his daughters the
pension and places of their mother.''

(ii) *Eros and Anteros, or Love*, by Lady Charlotte Bury
(January 11).

(iii) *A Diary relative to George IV. and Queen Caroline**
(January 11), which set Thackeray on the war-path
again, and rightly so, as may be seen from the opening
and closing passages of the article now quoted,—

"We never met with a book more pernicious or more
mean. It possesses that interest which the scandalous
chronicles of Brantome and Rabutin, and the ingenious
Mrs. Harriette Wilson, have excited before, and is pre-
cisely of a similar class. It does worse than chronicle
the small beer of a court—the materials of this book are
infinitely more base, the foul tittle-tattle of the sweepings
of the Princess of Wales's bed-chamber or dressing-room,
her table or ante-room, the reminiscences of industrious
eaves-dropping, the careful records of her unguarded
moments, and the publication of her confidential correspondence, are the chief foundations for this choice
work. Add to this scandal of the Princess of Wales,
sneering small talk about the Princess Charlotte, a few
old women's tales of familiar moving in what is called
high life, and paw-paw stories of their domestic infideli-
ties and peccadilloes, and we have an accurate catalogue
of the diary. . . . Was there, we ask, any need of
fresh information as to the Princess's life and follies?
Was it modest or decorous that a woman should record
them?—a woman, too, who has eaten at her table, and
dipped into her purse, shared in her wild revels, and
doubtless flattered her and cringed to her in her time.
. . We may read this diary, and say it is indeed a
ridicule to bear a towering name or to pretend to the old
virtue which characterised it, or the honour which for-
merly belonged to it. It is ridicule indeed to come of a

---

*This same book is the subject of a very similar attack by Yellow-
plush in a paper entitled *Skimmings from the Diary of George IV.*

noble race, and uphold the well-worn honour of an ancient line. What matters it if you can read in your family records the history of a thousand years of loyalty and courage, of all that is noble in sentiment, honest and brave in action?—the pride of ancestors is a faded super-stition—the emulation of them a needless folly. There is no need now to be loyal to your Prince, or tender of his memory. Take his bounty while living, share his purse and his table, gain his confidence and learn his secrets, flatter him, cringe to him, vow to him an unbounded fidelity,—and when he is dead, *write a diary and betray him.*"

(iv) *Memoirs of Holt, the Irish Rebel* (January 31); and

(v) *Poetical Works of Dr. Southey, collected by himself* (April 17).

Besides these articles, Thackeray, who was a regular contributor to the *Times*, must have written for it many articles that are as yet unknown—probably criticisms of books, plays, and pictures, chiefly.

It has been said—I do not know on what authority—that he wrote for the two short-lived periodicals, the *Torch* and the *Pantheon*.

The New Monthly Magazine published *The Story of Mary Ancel*, and *Some Passages in the Life of Major Gaha-gan;* but it was to *Fraser* that he contributed most of his best work.

(i) *On a Batch of Novels for Christmas* 1837 (January, 1838). Reviewing Mrs. Trollope's *Vicar of Wrexhill*, in which she writes with great bitterness against those who interpreted the Scriptures in other ways than she, while admitting the cleverness of her work, he said:—

"A woman's religion is chiefly that of the heart, and not of the head. She goes through, for the most part, no tedious processes of reasoning, no dreadful stages of doubt, no changes of faith: she loves God as she loves her husband—by a kind of instinctive devotion. Faith is a passion with her, and not a calculation; so that, in the faculty of believing, though they far exceed the other sex, in the power of convincing they fall far short of them. Oh! we repeat once more, that ladies would make puddings and mend stockings! that they would not meddle with religion (what is styled religion we mean) except to pray to God, to live quietly among their families, and more lovingly among their neighbours! Mrs. Trollope, for instance, who sees so keenly the follies of the other party—how much vanity there is in Bible meetings—how much sin even at Missionary Societies—how much cant and hypocrisy there is among those who desecrate the awful name of God, by mixing it up with their mean private interests and petty projects —Mrs. Trollope cannot see that there is any hypocrisy or bigotry on her part. She who designates the rival party as false and wicked and vain—tracing all their actions to the basest motives, declaring their worship of God to be only one general hypocrisy, their conduct at home one fearful scene of crime, is blind to the faults on her own side. Always bitter against the Pharisees, she does as the Pharisees do. It is vanity very likely which leads these people to use God's name so often, and to devote all to perdition who do not coincide in their peculiar notions. Is Mrs. Trollope less vain than they when she declares, and merely *declares*, her own to be the real creed, and stigmatises its rival so fiercely? Is Mrs. Trollope serving God, in making abusive and licentious pictures of those who serve Him in a different way? Once, as Mrs. Trollope has read—it was a long time ago!—there was a woman taken in sin: people brought her before a great Teacher of Truth, who lived in those days. 'Shall we not kill her?' said they; 'the law commands that all adulteresses should be killed.' We can fancy a Mrs. Trollope in the crowd shouting, 'Oh, the wretch! oh, the abominable harlot! kill her, by all means—stoning is really too good for her!' But what did the Divine Teacher say? He was quite as anxious to prevent the crime as any Mrs. Trollope of them all; but he did not make an allusion to it—He did not describe the manner in which the poor creature was caught—He made no speech to detail the indecencies which she had committed, or to raise the fury of the mob against her—He said, 'Let the man who is without sin himself throw the first stone!' Whereupon the Pharisees and Mrs. Trollopes slunk away, for they knew they were no better than she. There was as great a sin in His eyes as that of the poor erring woman—it was the sin of pride.''*

When *Ernest Maltravers* fell to him for criticism, the lash was applied with the utmost vigour. But in this article, in his zeal for the pure and healthy in literature, Thackeray went too far, and showed what might easily have been construed as personal animus, against the author, though it is certain none existed. He commenced with the following passage:—

"What a pity that Mr. Bulwer will not learn wisdom with age and confine his attention to subjects at once more grateful to the public and more suitable to his own powers. He excels in the *genre* of Paul de Koch, and is

---

*Mr. Bedingfield at this time asked Thackeray to a party, but he declined when he heard Mrs. Trollope would be among the guests. "O, by Jove! I can't come," he exclaimed. "I've just cut up her *Vicar of Wrexhill* in a review. I think she tells lies."

always striving after the style of Plato; he has a keen perception of the ridiculous, and, like Liston or Cruikshank, or other comic artists, persists that his real view is the sublime. What a number of sparkling magazine papers, what an outpouring of fun and satire, might we not have had from Neddy Bulwer, had he not thought fit to turn moralist, metaphysician, politician, poet, and be Edward Lytton heaven-knows-what Bulwer, Esq., and M. P., a dandy, a philosopher, a spouter at radical meetings. We speak feelingly, for we knew the youth at Trinity Hall, and have a tenderness even for his tomfooleries. He has thrown away the better part of himself—his great inclination for the LOW, namely: if he would but leave off scents for his handkerchief, and oil for his hair: if he would but confine himself to three clean shirts in a week, a couple of coats in a year, a beefsteak and onions for dinner, his beaker a pewter pot, his carpet a sanded floor, how much might be made of him even yet! An occasional pot of porter too much—a black eye in a tap-room fight with a carman—a night in a watch-house—or a surfeit produced by Welsh rabbit and gin and beer, might perhaps redden his fair face and swell his slim waist; but the *mental* improvement which he would acquire under such treatment—the intellectual pluck and vigour which he would attain by the stout diet—the manly sports and conversation in which he would join at the *Coal-Hole*, or the *Widow's*, are far better for him than the feeble fribble of the Reform Club (not unaptly called the *Hole in the Wall*); the windy French dinners, which, as we take it, are his usual fare; and above all the unwholesome radical garbage which forms the political food of himself and his clique in the House of Commons."

Miss Landon's *Ethel Churchill* pleased him with its wit and cleverness, but he found this book, too, unhealthy in tone. "Oh!" he cried out, "oh, for a little manly, honest, God-relying simplicity—cheerful, unaffected and humble."

(ii) *Half-a-Crown's Worth of Cheap Knowledge* (March), in which article he dealt with a round dozen of the penny and twopenny periodicals of the day. There is nothing particularly worth preserving here, except, perhaps, the following, as a literary curiosity:—

"We next come to *Oliver Twiss* by 'Bos'; a kind of silly copy of Boz's admirable tale. We have not, we confess, been able to read through *Oliver Twiss*. The only amusing part of it is an advertisement by the publisher, calling upon the public to buy Lloyd's edition of *Oliver Twiss* by 'Bos,' it *being the only genuine one*. By which we learn that there are thieves, and other thieves who steal from the first thieves; even as it is said about that exiguous beast the flea, there be other fleas, which annoy the original animal."

(iii) *Strictures on Pictures* (June), to the contents of which I refer elsewhere.

(iv) *Passages from the Diary of the late Dolly Duster, with Elucidations, Notes, etc., by various editors* (October and November), which was a review of a book called *Lady Carry-the-Candle's Diary*.

(v) From November, 1837, until August in this year the *Yellowplush Correspondence* appeared, seemingly without attracting any great amount of attention. These papers are referred to in a later chapter.

The Correspondence between Charles Yellowplush, Esq., and Oliver Yorke, Esq., editor of *Fraser's Magazine* appeared:—

THE LAST STROKE OF FORTUNE.
The Yellowplush Papers.

(i) *Fashnable Fax and Polite Annygoats* (November, 1837).

(ii) *Miss Shum's Husband* (January, 1838).

(iii) *Dimond cut Dimond* (February, 1838).

(iv) *Skimmings from "The Diary of George IV."* (March, 1838).

(v) *Foring Parts* (April, 1838).

(vi) *Mr. Deuceace at Paris* (May, June, 1838).

(vii) *The End of Mr. Deuceace's History* (July, 1838).

(viii) *Mr. Yellowplush's Ajew* (August, 1838).

It is almost needless to add that these papers were carefully revised before their republication.*

When, in after days, Thackeray wrote, "I suppose we all begin by being too savage. I know *one who did*," it was of these early papers he must have been thinking— chiefly, no doubt, of his personal and satirical attacks on Lytton (then simply Edward Bulwer) in *Fraser*.

In 1861 a common friend of Thackeray and Lord Lytton wrote to the latter: "I saw Thackeray at Folkestone. He spoke of you a great deal, and said he would have given worlds to have burnt some of his writings, especially some lampoons written in his youth. He wished so much to see you and express his contrition. His admiration, as expressed to me, was boundless; also his regret to have given vent to his youthful jealousy, etc. I tell you all this because I feel certain he meant me to repeat it." And shortly after this Lord Lytton received the following letter (which his son thought worthy of insertion in the *Life and Letters*) from Thackeray himself:—

*The *Correspondence* was published in book form late in 1838 by Messrs. Carey & Hart, of Philadelphia. This is the first volume ever issued of any of Thackeray's writings.

"Looking over some American reprints of my books, I find one containing a preface written by me when I was in New York, in which are the following words:* 'The careless papers written at an early period, and never seen since the printer's boy carried them away, are brought back and laid at the father's door, and he cannot, if he would, disown his own children. Why were some of the little brats brought out of their obscurity? I own to a feeling of anything but pleasure in reviewing some of these juvenile, misshapen creatures which the publisher has disinterred and resuscitated. There are two performances especially (among the critical and biographical works of the erudite Mr. Yellowplush) which I am sorry to see reproduced, and I ask pardon of the author of *The Caxtons* for a lampoon, which I know he himself has forgiven, and which I wish I could recall. I had never seen that writer but once in public when this satire was penned, and wonder at the recklessness of the young man who could fancy such personality was harmless jocularity, and never calculated that it might give pain.'

"I don't know whether you were ever made aware of this cry of '*Peccavi*,' but with the book in which it appears just fresh before me, I think it fair to write a line to acquaint you of the existence of such an apology, and to assure you of the author's repentance of the past, and the present sincere good will with which he is

"Yours most faithfully,
"W. M. THACKERAY."

To me it seems that the parody of Bulwer's style is most admirable, and it is, I think, almost as good as any-

*This is to be found in the *Preface*, which Thackeray wrote in December, 1852, to Appleton's edition of his minor works. See Appendix.

LORD CRABS BESTOWS UPON THE LADIES HIS PARTING BENEDICTION

The Yellowplush Papers.

thing in the *Prize Novelists*. Like *Cabbages*, the passages in *Mr. Yellowplush's Ajew* were prompted by Thackeray's sense of the overstrained sentiment which is so prevalent, especially in Lytton's earlier works, and as I feel certain that the parody was written entirely "without prejudice," I quote a couple of paragraphs, for the fun is too good to miss.

This is the speech in which Bulwer dissuades the footman from joining the world of letters: " 'Yellowplush,' says he, seizing my hand, 'you *are* right. Quit not your present occupation; black boots, clean knives, wear plush all your life, but don't turn literary man. Look at me. I am the first novelist in Europe. I have ranged with eagle wing over the wide regions of literature, and perched on every eminence in turn. I have gazed with eagle eyes on the Sun of Philosophy, and fathomed the mysterious depths of the human mind. All languages are familiar to me, all thoughts are known to me, all men understood by me. I have gathered wisdom from the honeyed lips of Plato, as we wandered in the gardens of the Academes,—wisdom, too, from the mouth of Job Johnson, as we smoked our "baccy" in Seven Dials. Such must be the studies, and such is the mission in this world, of the poet-philosopher. But the Knowledge is only emptiness; the initiation is but misery; the initiated a man shunned and banned by his fellows.' 'Oh,' said Bulwig, clasping his hands, and throwing his fine I's up to the chandelier, 'the curse of Pwometheus descends upon his wace. Wath and punishment pursue them from genewation to genewation! Wo to Genius, the Heaven-scaler, the fire-stealer! Wo and thrice bitter desolation! earth is the wock on which Zeus, wemorseless, stwetches his withing victim—men, the

vultures that feed and fatten on him. Ai, ai! it is agony
eternal—gwoaning and solitawy despair! And you,
Yellowplush, would penetwate these mystewies: you
would waise the awful veil, and stand in the twemendous
Pwesence. Beware as you value your peace, beware!
Withdwaw, wash neophite! for Heaven's sake—oh, for
Heaven's sake!'—here he looked round with agony—
'give me a glass of bwandy and water for this clawet is
beginning to disagwee with me.' "

Not less amusing is the speech "And pray for what,"
is he to be made a baronet:—

"What faw?" says Bulwig, "ask the Histowy of
Litewature what faw? Ask Colburn, ask Bentley, ask
Sawnders and Otley, ask the Gweat Bwitish Nation what
faw? The blood in my veins comes puwified thwough
ten thousand years of chivalwous ancestry; but that is
neither here nor there: my political pwincipals—the
equal wights which I have advocated—the gweat cause of
fweedom that I have celebwated, are known to all. But
this, I confess, has nothing to do with the question.
No; the question is this—on the thwone of litewature I
stand unwivalled, pwe-eminent; and the Bwitish government, honowing genius in me, compliments the Bwitish
nation by lifting into the bosom of the heweditawy
nobility, the most gifted member of the Democwacy,'
(the honrabble genlmn here sank down amidst repeated
cheers).''

Thackeray's work gradually became known among
his fellow-workers, and Mr. N. P. Willis, the editor of
the *New York Corsair*, secured his services for the paper
in which (August 24th, 1839) he printed the following
appreciative passages:—

"I have been delighted to find that the authors of

Mr. Dawkins advises with Mr. Blewett upon a difficult point at Ecarté.

THE YELLOWPLUSH PAPERS.

the two best periodical series of papers that have appeared for twenty years are one and the same person. One of my first enquiries in London was touching the authorship of the *Yellowplush Papers*, next the *Reminiscences of Major Gahagan*—the only things in periodical literature, except the *Pickwick Papers*, for which I looked with any interest or eagerness. The author, Mr. Thackeray, breakfasted with me yesterday, and the readers of the *Corsair* will be delighted, I am sure, to hear that I have engaged this cleverest and most gifted of the magazine writers of London to become a *regular* correspondent of the *Corsair*. He left London for Paris the day after, and having resided in that city for many years, his letters from thence will be pictures of life in France, done with a bolder and more trenchant pen than has yet attempted the subject. He will present a long letter every week, and you will agree with me that he is no common acquisition. Thackeray is a tall, athletic man of about thirty-five, with a look of talent that could never be mistaken. He has taken to literature after having spent a very large inheritance, but in throwing away the gifts of fortune he has cultivated his natural talents very highly, and is one of the most accomplished draughtsmen in England, as well as the cleverest and most brilliant of periodical writers. He has been the principal critic for the *Times*, and writes for *Fraser* and *Blackwood*. You will hear from him by the first steamer after his arrival in Paris, and thenceforward regularly."

To the *Corsair* Thackeray contributed eight *Letters from London, Paris, Pekin, Petersborough, etc. By the author of the "Yellowplush Correspondence," the "Memoirs of Major Gahagan," etc., etc.*, and seven of these letters, rewritten and renamed, were published in the

Paris Sketch Book.   On September 28 Mr. Willis printed the paper *Captain Rook and Mr. Pigeon*, and openly declared it by William Thackeray, author of the *Yellow-plush Correspondence*, though the letters continued to be signed T. T. as before.

During 1839 Thackeray also wrote an article on *Lord Brougham's Speeches* for the *British and Foreign Review* (April), in which, in the very first passage, he shows his insight into the ex-Minister's character:

"To discuss each speech properly," he wrote, "perhaps the reviewer should write a volume where the orator has produced only a few pages: for, vast as the latter's genius and labours are, great as have been his services, and keen as are often his views regarding the events and circumstances of his own time, we suspect that there are very few who would be disposed to take his ideas for their own and to believe implicitly in his story. Lord Brougham's exploits in literature, law, and politics have been chiefly those of a partisan; and as he has had, to our thinking, too strong a wit and too weak a character to allow him to enter the foremost rank of great men of his time, he has likewise too great a vanity and too small a principle to be its historian. You may hope from such a person much brilliancy of remark, and occasional truth; for his genius is great and his heart good and generous in the main; but the entire truth cannot be expected from him. Much of it he cannot see, and much he does not choose to tell. Ceaseless puffs of spleen ruffle the surface of his mind, and distort the proportion of the images reflected in it. His vanity is employed in making perpetual excuses for his principle, and thus it continually thwarts his genius. While the one is wide and kindly, the other is meanly unreasoning and jealous; as is commonly the case, of the two adverse principles the latter is the more active; and as we have often seen in marriages how a wise man will give himself abjectly over to the guidance of a shrew, Lord Brougham's wisdom is perpetually at the feet of his vanity, which in the contests between them is pretty sure to have the last word.''

He sent to Cruikshank's *Comic Annual, Stubbs' Calendar, or the Fatal Boots*, and to *Fraser*, in June, *A Second Lecture on the Fine Arts*,* and *The Great Kossack Epic of Demetrius Rigmarolovicz. Translated by a Lady* (the *Legend of St. Sophia of Kioff* of the *Ballads*); in September *The French Plutarch;* (1) *Cartouche's Highways and Byways*, and (2) *Little Poinsinet;* in October *The Fêtes of July*, and in December *The French School of Painting*.

I am inclined to include in this list of Thackeray's writings for 1839 both *Paris Pastimes for the Month of May*, and *Paris Revels of the 12th of May* (*Fraser*, June and August) written in the form of letters to ''Dear Fraser,'' and signed ''You know who,''—the fact that they are not signed *Titmarsh* being no argument against my contention, since, as he was writing so much for the magazine, it may have been advisable to use another nom-de-plume.

Thackeray was undoubtedly anxious to increase his income, which, when all the claims upon his purse were

---

*A good many of Thackeray's contributions to *Fraser's Magazine* were in the form of letters, and his headings to these are often very amusing. I give a couple of examples: The *Strictures on Pictures* is from Mr. Michael Angelo Titmarsh to Monsieur Anatole Victor Isodore Hyacinthe Achille Hercule de Bric-a-brac, *peintre d'histoire, Rue Mouffleard, à Paris;* while the *Second Lecture on the Fine Arts* is written by the same gentleman to another Mr. Bricabrac, evidently some relation of the first-mentioned owner of the name. This one is to Citoyen Brutus Napoleon Bricabrac, Refuge d'avril, Blessé de mai, Condamné de juin, Decoré de juillet, etc. Hôtel Dieu, à Paris.

settled, must have been a very meagre competence, and he endeavoured (Charles Mackay said) during this year to obtain the post of sub-editor to the *Morning Chronicle*—fortunately, without success. It was also about the same time that Mr. Cole, of the South Kensington Science and Art Department, recommended him for service in the Anti-Corn-Law-League, to Cobden. "The artist," so ran the letter, "is a genius both with his pen and his pencil. His vocation is literary. He is full of humour and feeling. Hitherto he has not had occasion to think much on the subject of Corn Laws, and therefore wants the stuff to work upon. He would like to combine both writing and drawing, when sufficiently primed, and then he would write illustrated ballads, or tales, or anything. I think you would find him a useful auxiliary."

Cobden suggested, as a subject for illustration, the Poles on one side of a stream, offering bread to starving people, standing on the other; a demon in the centre preventing the exchange. Cole carried the idea to Thackeray, who returned him a rough sketch with a letter.

"Dear Sir," he wrote, "I shall be glad to do a single drawing, series, or what you will, for *money*, but I think the one you sent me would not be effective enough for the Circular, the figures are too many for so small a sized block, and the meaning mysterious—the river, to be a river, should occupy a deuce of a space" [here he introduced a loose sketch]—"even this fills up your length almost. What do you think of a howling group with this motto: *Give us this day our Daily Bread*. The words are startling. Of course I will do the proposed design if you wish."

At this time Thackeray was trying a new method of engraving (invented by a Mr. Schönblung, of Hatton Garden) which, from Thackeray's next letter, dated June 29, 1839, did not seem to be an unqualified success.

"MY DEAR SIR,—I am very sorry to tell you of my misfortunes. I have made three etchings on the Schönblung plan, of the Anglo-allegory, and they have all failed; that is, Schönblung considers they are not fit for his process; that is, I fear the process will not succeed yet. I shall, however, do the drawing to-morrow on a wood-block, and will send it to you *sans faute*, unless I hear you are not inclined to deal with a person who has caused so much delay.

"Yours ever,
"(*Signed*) W. M. THACKERAY."

He eventually contributed two wood-cuts to the Anti-Corn-Law-Circular: the first, *Poles Offering Corn*, appeared in No. 8 (July 23), and the second, *The Choice of a Loaf*, in No. 18 (December 10).

And now to refer again to the most important of all these articles, reviews, and tales—the first of his more ambitious attempts—*Catherine*, which appeared in *Fraser* during May, June, July, August, November, 1839, and January, 1840.

Mr. Sala has related somewhere that the public soon forgot that *Catherine* was a professed satire on the Newgate novels, and became absorbed and fascinated by a wonderfully realistic fiction; while some of the critics spoke of the tale as "one of the dullest, most vulgar, and immoral works extant." Of course, Thackeray was delighted at the abuse, and expressed himself very

"pleased with the disgust which his work has excited."
And well he might be, for he had obtained exactly
what he wanted.   Still, satire and irony are very dangerous weapons, since often, by virtue of their very
intensity, they are read as serious earnest; and the people who were disgusted with *Catherine*, probably, some
years later, thought Thackeray an admirer of Barry
Lyndon, Esq., and had always held Henry Fielding to
be a staunch sympathiser with Mr. Jonathan Wild.

Catherine, clever as it undoubtedly is, did not at the
time much advance Thackeray's reputation or increase
his popularity—he was still regarded only as a useful
writer of magazine articles, and a fairly competent art
critic.

In 1840 Macrone—who had brought out Dickens's
earliest volume, *Sketches by Boz*—published Thackeray's
first book, *The Paris Sketch Book*, in two volumes; but
the *Sketch Book*, which was dedicated to a tailor who had
once done Thackeray a kindness, and consisted of a collection of articles and tales, about half of which had
already appeared in the magazines, was not well received
by the public—and certainly it contains nothing of any
astonishing merit, though there is much that is well
written and interesting.*

During the year he sent to *Fraser*, *Epistles to the
Literati XIII., Ch——s Y—U—wpl—sh to Sir Edward
Lytton Bulwer, Bart., John Thomas Smith, Esq.*, to

The Paris Sketch Book contains the following articles and stories,
of which the first eight were reprints: *An Invasion of France, The
Fêtes of July, On the French School of Painting, Cartouche, The
Story of Mary Ancel, Little Poinsinet, The Devil's Wager, Madame
Sand and the New Apocalypse, A Caution to Travellers, The
Painter's Bargain, On Some French Fashionable Novels, A Gambler's
Death, Napoleon and His System, Beatrice Merger, Caricatures and
Lithography in Paris, The Case of Peytel, French Dramas and
Melodramas,* and *Meditations at Versailles.*

Rex.

Ludovicus.
THE PARIS SKETCH-BOOK.

Ludovicus Rex.

C——s Y——h, *Esq.* (January), and a *Pictorial Rhapsody* (June, July). The July paper ended abruptly. A note was added nominally by "Oliver Yorke"—"He has not been heard of since the first day of June. He was seen on that day pacing Waterloo Bridge for two hours; but whether he plunged into the river, or took advantage of the steamboat, and went down in it only, we cannot state." After making inquiries from the waiter at Morland's Hotel, where Titmarsh had been staying, he unravelled the mystery. "This is conclusive," he then continued. "Our departed friend had many faults, but he is gone, and we need not discuss them now. It appears that on the first of June the *Morning Post* published a criticism upon him, accusing him of ignorance, bad taste, and partiality. His gentle and susceptible spirit could not brook the rebuke; he was not angry; he did not retort; but *his heart broke*. Peace to his ashes! A couple of volumes of his works, we see by our advertisements, are about immediately to appear."

This is the criticism to which the laughing reference is made:

"Among other papers in the magazine is what is called *A Pictorial Rhapsody* upon the Royal Academy, in which great personal favouritism and general bad taste in the criticism is boldly and unscrupulously indulged. The absurdities of this notice are plenty, and *parmi les autres*, the writer defends Mulready and the postage cover."

The Bedford Row Conspiracy, which was adapted from a story by Charles de Bernand, was printed in the *New Monthly Magazine* for January and March; while to the *Comic Annual* he sent *Barber Cox, and the Cutting of his Comb*, on which has been founded the well-known Dutch comedy *Janus Tulp*. An essay on *The Genius of*

George Cruikshank, which appeared in the *Westminster Review,* sign — was a kindly service to an artist whom the public were forgetting. It was immediately reprinted separately, and published.

For some time past Thackeray had had the rather morbid desire to see a man hanged. Years before, at Paris, he had gone to see an execution, but had missed the dismal spectacle. Now, however, he eagerly accepted an invitation, dated July 2nd, 1840, to be present at the death of Curvoisier.

"MY DEAR MILNES,—I shall be very pleased to make one at the Hanging, and shall expect you here.
"Yours ever,
"W. M. THACKERAY."

It was customary, then, when the hanging took place at five or six o'clock in the morning, for the intending spectators to "make a night of it," and to go eastwards after a very late supper, and evidently Monckton Milnes wrote to suggest that this should be done, for on the next day Thackeray wrote to him again. "You must not think me inhospitable in refusing to sit up. I must go to bed, that's the fact, or I shall never be able to attend to the work of to-morrow properly. If you like to come here and have a sofa, it is at your service, but I most strongly recommend sleep as a preparative to the day's pleasure."

Thackeray's experiences were told in *Fraser* in the article entitled *Going to see a man hanged.* In this he spoke his mind in no measured terms.

"There is some talk of the terror which the sight of this spectacle inspires. . . . I fully confess that I came away . . . that morning with a disgust for murder, but it was for *the murder I saw done*. . . .

"This is the twentieth of July, and I may be permitted, for my part, to declare that, for the last fourteen days, so salutary has the impression of the butchery been upon me, I have had the man's face continually before my eyes; that I can see Mr. Ketch at this moment, with an easy air, taking the rope from his pocket; that I feel myself ashamed and degraded at the brutal curiosity which took me to that brutal sight; and that I pray to Almighty God to cause this disgraceful sin to pass from among us, and to cleanse our land of blood."

Four years later, at Cairo, when he was invited to witness a similar spectacle, he only replied, "Seeing one man hanged is quite enough in the course of a life. *J'y ai été*, as the Frenchman said of hunting."

In *The Irish Sketch Book* he repeated the sentiments expressed in the *Fraser* article:—

"I confess, for my part, to that common cant and sickly sentimentality, which, thank God! is felt by a great number of people nowadays, and which leads them to revolt against murder, whether performed by a ruffian's knife or a hangman's rope; whether accompanied with a curse from the thief as he blows his victim's brains out, or a prayer from my lord on the bench in his wig and black cap." But nevertheless, there is reason to believe that he eventually changed his opinion in this matter, for when one day Mr. Bedingfield told him that he had just read the "Hanging" article with admiration, he remarked, "I think I was wrong. My feelings were overwrought. These murderers are such devils, after all.''

Still, if he ceased to advocate the abolition of the death-sentence, he always insisted that the ceremony should be performed in private, and not before audiences of forty to fifty thousand persons, many of whom were children of tender years.

CHAPTER VIII

THE TRAGEDY OF HIS MARRIED LIFE

CHAPTER VIII

THE TRAGEDY OF HIS MARRIED LIFE

THE best-remembered work of this year (1840) is *The Shabby Genteel Story*, which appeared in *Fraser* in June, July, August, and October—by which time nine chapters had been printed—when it was suddenly and abruptly brought to a conclusion without a word of explanation.

When, however, the fragment was reprinted in the *Miscellanies* (published in 1857) a note was prefixed by the author—which to those who knew of his misfortune was very touching. "It was my intention," so it ran, "to complete the little story of which only the first part is here written. . . . The tale was interrupted at a sad period of the writer's own life. The colours are long since dry; the artist's hand is changed. It is best to leave the sketch as it was when it was first designed seventeen years ago. The memory of the past is renewed as he looks at it.

> 'Die Bilder froher Tage
> Und manche liebe Schatten steigen auf.'"

The explanation of the abrupt conclusion of the *Shabby Genteel Story* is indeed very sad.

In May, his third child, Harriet Marion—afterwards Mrs. Leslie Stephen—was born, and his wife became very ill. The illness eventually affected her mind, and Thackeray, who regarded this as only a natural sequence

of the illness, which would pass away in time, when her
health was restored, threw all business aside, sent his
children to their grandparents at Paris, and for many
months travelled with his wife from watering-place to
watering-place, as the doctors as a last resource had
recommended, hoping against hope that the cloud on
her intellect would dissolve.

Writing to Mrs. Brookfield some ten years later, he
recalled this period: "As I am waiting . . . I find
an old review containing a great part of an article I
wrote about Fielding in 1840 in the *Times*. . . . My
wife was just sickening at that moment; I wrote it at
Margate where I had taken her, and used to walk out
three miles to a little bowling green, and write there in
an arbour—coming home and wondering what was the
melancholy oppressing the poor little woman. The
Times gave me five guineas for the article. I recollect
I thought it rather shabby pay, and twelve days after it
appeared in the paper, my poor little wife's malady
showed itself. How queer it is to be carried back all of
a sudden to that time and all that belonged to it, and
read this article over; doesn't the apology for Fielding
read like an apology for somebody else, too? God help
us! what a deal of cares and pleasures and struggles and
happiness I have had since that day in the little sunshiny
arbour, where, with scarcely any money in my pocket,
and two little children (Minnie was a baby two months
old), I was writing this notice about Fielding. Grief,
Love, Fame, if you like—I have had no little of all since
then (I don't mean to take the fame for more than its
worth or brag about it with any peculiar elation)."

At last Thackeray was compelled to realise the truth—
that his poor wife would never recover sufficiently to

undertake the duties of a mother and a wife. She was unable to manage her life, though she took interest in any pleasant things around her, especially in music; but it was essential that she should be properly cared for, and, with this object, she was placed with Mr. and Mrs. Thompson at Leigh, in Essex. She outlived her husband by so many years that it was with a shock, having already been dead to the world for nearly forty years, that the announcement of her death, in January, 1894, at the age of seventy-five, was read. She was interred in the same grave at Kensal Green cemetery as her husband.

How sad, how awful, it was! The man with his great heart, with his yearning for love and affection that, from this time forth, breathes through all his letters and all his books!

"I cannot live without the tenderness of some woman," he wrote, with the mixture of tears and laughter that is the characteristic of all his later works, "and expect when I am sixty, I shall be marrying a girl of eleven or twelve, innocent, barley-sugar-loving, in a pinafore." To be separated from the woman he had chosen for his companion through life, and who had cheered him when his fortunes were at a very low ebb, and his reputation was not yet made! How hard it was she should be taken from him before she could enjoy the great fame and good fortune! How much he loved her, and how much he felt the blow that had shattered his happiness and his home, he never divulged; he was not a man to parade his domestic sorrows in public—he might think of them in solitude, but if a visitor entered he would immediately look up with a smile and a joke—both forced. Still, from one source and another, it has been possible to glean something of the deep and sacred grief which Thackeray felt on his return alone, and worse than alone, to the desolate house in Great Coram Street.

"I was as happy as the day was long with her," he told one of his cousins; and one day when Trollope's groom said to him, "I hear you have written a book upon Ireland, and are always making fun of the Irish; you don't like us," Thackeray's eyes filled with tears as he thought of his wife—born in County Cork—and he replied, turning away his head, "God help me! all that I have loved best in the world is Irish."

Again in after years, referring to *The Great Hoggarty Diamond*, which was composed during this period of great unhappiness, he remarked that it "was written at a time when the writer was suffering under the severest personal grief and calamity," "at a time of great affliction, when my heart was very soft and humble. Amen. Ich habe auch geliebt."

Well might Thackeray echo the lines of poor broken-hearted Thekla's swan-song:—

"Ich habe genossen das irdische Glück,
Ich habe gelebt und geliebet."

Yet even in his bitterest moments he did not cry, with Thekla:—

"Das Herz ist gestorben, die Welt ist leer,
Und weiter giebt sie dem Wunsche nicht mehr,"

for, even in his most bitter grief, Thackeray remembered his children and his parents; and the man who, on hearing of a certain noble lady who, it was said, had died of grief at her husband's death, only remarked, "Ah! had she been Mrs. X——, the washerwoman, with sixteen children to provide for, she would not have died," set himself resolutely to work to make money so that when his children were old enough he could provide a comfortable home for them, dower them well, and, when he died, leave them, at least, a competency. From this time, more than ever, the thought of his children was the mainspring of most of his actions. "I sat up with the children and talked to them of their mother," he told Mrs. Brookfield. "It is my pleasure to tell them how humble-minded their mother was." We see him taking them to the Colosseum on their birthday; or to the Zoölogical Gardens, where they all amuse themselves in finding likenesses to their friends in many of the animals. ("Thank *Evns!*" is Thackeray's expression of gratitude, "both of the girls have plenty of fun and humour"); or, when he is very tired, having been at the opening of the Great Exhibition, he goes with them to the play "in recompense for their disappointment in not getting to the Exhibition, which they had hopes of seeing."

It was for the sake of his children that he battled with his constitutional timidity, and nerved himself to deliver the two series of lectures—he, to whom public speaking was misery; and solely on their account he made his trips to America, hating the separation from them, and longing all the time of his absence for the day of his return.

It is a painful subject to dwell upon—even for those who never knew or even saw Thackeray; a picture of fearful sadness to conjure up — this dreadful domestic affliction.

His fortune lost, his talents unrecognised except in a very small circle, his second child dead, his beloved wife taken from him! Is it marvellous that Thackeray was able to see the existence of evil as well as of good in the world? The wonder is that he did not become a second Swift, lashing the world and himself with a savage satire, blaspheming at God, cursing at man, sneering at good and evil alike, in some new *Gulliver's Travels*. Instead, however, the great sorrow chastened his soul, and made his later writings more sympathetic than his earlier; and the only use he made of his grand power of sarcasm was to chide, nearly always with gentle hand, the follies of his fellow-men, in the endeavour to show to them the path of honour, virtue, goodness, and mercy, which he himself endeavoured to follow.

What words can so fitly close this brief account of the terrible tragedy of Thackeray's married life as his own?

"Canst thou, O friendly reader, count upon the fidelity of an artless heart or tender or true, and reckon among the blessings which Heaven hath bestowed on thee, the love of faithful women? Purify thine own heart, and try to make it worthy of theirs. All the prizes of life are nothing compared to that one. All the rewards of ambition, wealth, pleasure, only vanity and disappointment, grasped at greedily and fought for fiercely, and over and over again found worthless by the weary winners."

CHAPTER IX

CLUB LIFE

CHAPTER IX

CLUB LIFE

WHEN deprived of his home, Thackeray, who was still under thirty, of necessity lived a bachelor life, went everywhere, saw everything, and met everybody; but he never forgot his self-respect, or the peculiar position in which he was placed. He did his best to be happy, and made the best of his life as his philosophy taught him; but there was no vice in him, and, in spite of his enemies (made chiefly by criticisms and satirical writings) no word of scandal was ever breathed against him.

He became a frequenter of clubs. He had long been a member of the Garrick, which then had its club-house in King Street, Covent Garden, the new building in Garrick Street not being completed until a year after his death. This was his favourite resort. "We, the happy initiated, never speak of it as the Garrick; to us it is the G., the little G., the dearest place in the world," he declared in a speech at a Shakespeare Birthday Dinner, then an annual event at the Club. The immense influence he obtained here was shown nearly twenty years later, when he quarrelled with Mr. Yates.*

*There was a member of the Garrick whose presence and speech seemed to irritate him, and who found pleasure in exercising his power as gadfly on a thoroughbred horse. One night in the smoke-room, Thackeray was in the middle of a most interesting story, when his enemy suddenly entered. To every one's surprise Thackeray hesitated and stopped, on which his persecutor, assuming an air of the most gracious patronage, blandly encouraged him with, " Proceed, sweet warbler; thy story interests me."—*The Memories of Dean Hole.*

137

He was elected a member of the Reform Club in April, 1840, being proposed by Mr. Martin Thackeray, and seconded by Mr. Henry Webbe. There is an interesting description of Thackeray at this Club in *Cassell's Magazine* (June, 1897) by Sir Wemyss Reid, in an article called *Some Club Ghosts*.

"In the morning-room the chair at which he used to sit when writing his letter is still pointed out; and again and again I have heard descriptions of how he used to stand in the smoking-room, his back to the fire, his legs rather wide apart, his hands thrust into the trouser-pockets, and his head stiffly thrown backward, while he joined in the talk of the men occupying the semi-circle of chairs in front of him. No man has made more use of the Reform Club in his writings than Thackeray has done. It is described minutely in *Brown's Letters to his Nephew;* it figures in many of his novels; it made its own contribution to the *Snob Papers*.

"One of the most amusing legends concerning the great writer is connected with the place. Going into the coffee-room of the Reform Club one afternoon, he chanced to see on the *menu* of the day 'beans and bacon.' He was to dine with some eminent personage that night, but 'beans and bacon' were more than he could resist. Straightway he betook himself to the morning-room and penned a note to his host, telling him that he could not have the pleasure of dining with him, as he had just met a very old friend whom he had not seen for years, and from whom he could not tear himself. Then he went back to the coffee-room and dined satisfactorily off his beloved dish in a corner. So runs the tale. Let us hope that it is true. . . . But we have no Thackeray now. To some of us, at least, the Club is endeared by the thought that he was once one of ourselves; that he sat in these chairs, dined at these tables, chatted in these rooms, and with his wise, far-seeing eyes surveyed the world from these same windows."

Later, on February 12, 1846, Thackeray was put up at the Athenæum Club, by the Rev. W. Harrenn, and seconded by Charles Buller, junr. The ballot took place in January, 1850, when, to the general surprise, the author of *Vanity Fair* and *Pendennis* was *black-balled.** All his supporters were furious, and Dean Milman immediately wrote to Abraham Hayward a letter that no doubt he intended should be shown to Thackeray.

"CLOISTERS, *January* 30, 1850.

"MY DEAR HAYWARD,—I cannot say how much I am annoyed by the failure of my attempt to bring in Thackeray at the Athenæum. But there is no counting on the stubborn stupidity of man. One voice, you know excludes, and among eighteen committee-men that there should not be one self-conceited—I must not fill up this sentence. We are bound not to reveal the secrets of our Conciliabulum, but I may say it was curious to see Macaulay and Croker row together in my boat with Martin, etc., etc. If I had not thought myself sure of my success, I should not have subjected Thackeray to the chance of rejection. Pray assure him of my regret and disappointment.

"Ever truly yours,
"H. H. MILMAN."

*"He" [Thackeray] "had the honour of being rejected at the 'Travellers' (1856); and the ruling majority (the ballot is by the members, not by the committee) gave as a reason that they were afraid of seeing themselves in some novel of the future."—JOHN HOLLINGS-HEAD, *My Lifetime.*

"Every man whose opinion Mr. Thackeray would value was with him."*

Thackeray took his rejection in very good part. "I was," he wrote to Hayward, "quite prepared for the issue of the kind effort made at the Athenæum on my behalf; indeed, as a satirical writer, I rather wonder that I have not made more enemies than I have. I don't mean enemies in a bad sense, but men conscientiously opposed to my style, art, opinions, impertinences, and so forth. There must be thousands of men to whom the practice of ridicule must be very offensive; doesn't one see such in Society, or in one's own family? persons whom nature has not gifted with a sense of humour. Such a man would be wrong not to give me a blackball, or whatever it is called, a negatory nod of his honest, respectable, stupid old head. And I submit to this without the slightest feeling of animosity against my judge. Why? Dr. Johnson would certainly have black-balled Fielding, whom he pronounced 'a dull fellow, sir, a dull fellow'! . . . Didn't I tell you once before that I feel frightened almost at the kindness of people regarding me? May we all be honest fellows, and keep our heads from too much vanity."

But even the honest, respectable old committee-man came in time to his senses—or perhaps he died. Any-way, on February 25, in the following year, the Club made amends. The Committee elected Thackeray under rule ii, which provides that the annual introduction of a certain number of "persons of distinguished eminence in science, literature, or for public services, shall be secured without recourse to ballot."

Thackeray's name appears on the roll of the Club as

*A Selection from the Correspondence of Abraham Hayward, Q.C.

a "barrister," but he was elected as the author of *Vanity Fair*, *Pendennis*, and other well-known works of fiction.

In later years—about November, 1861—he joined "Our Club," which had been founded by Douglas Jerrold. This was a social and literary meeting, and included among its members some of the best known of Thackeray's contemporaries — Mark Lemon, Leech, Horace Mayhew, and Shirley Brooks, from *Punch;* Samuel Lucas and Davidson, respectively the chief literary and the musical critic of the *Times;* Hepworth Dixon, of the *Athenæum;* the publishers, Robert Chambers, Evans (of Bradbury & Evans), Macmillan, and Hazlitt; as well as James Hannay, David Masson, Charles Knight, George Jessel, and Charles Lamb Kenney. The Club, with its guinea subscription, was next door to Evans's, and the members dined in a room on an upper floor of Clunn's Hotel; and the annual dinner in June was held either at Blackwall, Greenwich, Richmond, or Hampton Court. Mr. Jeffreson says that both Thackeray (who had a nature of almost womanly softness) and Jerrold were devoted to Frederick Hamstide, the hon. secretary, a little hunch-back, who in childhood had been crippled by a fall from his nurse's arms.

Mr. Jeffreson, the historian of "Our Club," gives, in his autobiography, a pleasant picture of Thackeray. "I cannot conceive him to have ever been seen to greater advantage than when he was sitting with a party of his congenial comrades at 'Our Club,' gossiping tenderly about dead authors, artists, and actors, or cheerily and in the kindliest spirit about living notabilities," he writes. "It was very pleasant to watch the white-haired veteran, and also to hear him (though at best he sang indiffer-

ently) whilst he trotted forth his favourite ballads touching Little Billie and Father Martin Luther. Better still
it was to regard the radiant gratification of his face,
whilst Horace Mayhew sang *The Mahogany Tree*, perhaps the finest and most soul-stirring of Thackeray's
social songs, or was throwing his soul into the passionate
Marseillaise.''

No list of Thackeray's haunts would be complete that
did not make mention of another place where he was
frequently to be seen at work, and where, like so many
men of letters, both distinguished and unknown, he felt
perfectly happy and quite at home—I refer to the read-
ing-rooms in the library of the British Museum.

''Most Londoners—not all—have seen the British
Museum Library,'' he paid tribute in a *Roundabout Paper*,
''I speak *à cœur ouvert*, and pray the kindly reader to
bear with me. I have seen all sorts of domes of Peters
and Pauls, Sophia, Pantheon—what not?—and have
been struck by none of them as much as by that catholic
dome in Bloomsbury, under which our million volumes
are housed. What peace, what love, what truth, what
beauty, what happiness for all, what generous kindness
for you and me, are here spread out! It seems to me
one cannot sit down in that place without a heart full of
grateful reverence. I own to have said my grace at the
table, and to have thanked Heaven for this my English
birthright, freely to partake of these bountiful books,
and to speak the truth I find there.''

In the summer of 1858, Motley, the historian, met
Thackeray there, and wrote of him to his wife.

''I believe you have never seen Thackeray,'' runs his
letter; ''he has the appearance of a colossal infant—
smooth white shiny ringletty hair, flaxen, alas! with

advancing years, a roundish face, with a little dab of a nose, upon which it is a perpetual wonder how he keeps his spectacles, a sweet but rather piping voice, with something of the childish treble about it, and a very tall, slightly stooping figure—such are the characteristics of the great snob of England.   His manner is like that of every one else in England—nothing original, all planed down into perfect uniformity with that of his fellow-creatures.   There was not much more distinction in his talk than in his white choker, or black coat and waistcoat.   .   .   .   After breakfast I went down to the British Museum.   I had been immersed half an hour in my manuscript, when, happening to turn my head round, I found seated next to me, Thackeray, with a file of old newspapers before him, writing the ninth number of *The Virginians*.   He took off his spectacles to see who I was, then immediately invited me to dinner the next day (as he seems always to do, every one he meets), which invitation I could not accept; and he then showed me the page he had been writing, a small, delicate legible manuscript.   After that we continued our studies.''

There is, in the Manuscript Department of the British Museum Library, a letter written by Thackeray to Mr. (afterwards Sir) Anthony Panizzi, when that gentleman was principal Librarian.   The letter, which I believe has never yet been printed, is undated, but it must have been written early in 1860, since it evidently refers to the select Committee of the House of Commons, which was ordered on April 24, 1860, ''to enquire into the necessity for the extension of the British Museum.''   I have examined the minutes of the Committee, before which Panizzi, Sir Charles Eastlake, Austin Layard, Professors Owen and Huxley, Sir Benjamin Brodie, Henry Cole, and Richard Westmacott, among others, were examined, but I cannot find that Thackeray gave evidence. The letter I have permission to insert here.

"KENSINGTON, *Thursday*.

"MY DEAR PANIZZI,—I'm writing my number for dear life; only got your number 2 letter last night, the greater part of which I passed over my book, and intended upon my word to answer you this very afternoon as soon as I came to a halt. Don't be angry with me; I'm half crazy with my work and other annoyances at this minute.

"I'll gladly come and say in behalf of the B. M. what little I know—that I've always found the very greatest attention and aid there—that I once came from Paris to London to write an article in a review about French affairs—and that I went to the Bibliothèque du Roi, I could only get a book at a time, and no sight of a catalogue. But then, I didn't go often, being disgusted with the place, and entering it as a total stranger, without any recommendation.

"If this testimony can be afforded by letter, I should like it much better, (it is some years old now), and, if by word of mouth, for Heaven's sake don't put me before a House of Commons' Committee at the end of the month.

"And don't be angry with me, my dear old fellow, for not writing, indeed I thought until the receipt of number 2 last night, that there was no hurry for an answer, and that I might put it off till my confounded month's work was done.

"Yours always truly, my dear Panizzi,
"W. M. THACKERAY."

Thackeray was also a frequent visitor to places of a very different type. He loved Bohemia, and left an admirable description of that land in the *Adventures of Philip*.

"A pleasant land, not fenced with drab Stucco like Tyburnia or Belgravia; not guarded by a huge standing army of footmen; not echoing with noble chariots; not replete with polite chintz drawing-rooms and neat tea-tables; a land over which hangs an endless fog, occasioned by much tobacco; a land of chambers, billiard rooms, supper rooms, oysters; a land of song; a land where soda-water flows freely in the morning; a land of tin dish-covers from taverns, and frothing porter; a land of lotus-eating (with lots of cayenne pepper), of pulls on the river, of delicious reading of novels, magazines, and saunterings in many studios; a land where men call each other by their Christian names; where most are old, where almost all are young, and where, if a few oldsters enter, it is because they have preserved more tenderly and carefully than others their youthful spirits, and the delightful capacity to be idle. I have lost my way to Bohemia now, but it is certain that Prague is the most picturesque city in the world."

Mr. Vizetelly has recorded that, in spite of Thackeray's love for "Prague," there was at least one of the customs of the inhabitants that he disapproved of. "I remember," he says, "when several smart young writers— whose success had emboldened them to turn their backs on Bohemia and most of its free and easy ways, but who were still somewhat regardless of their personal appearance—were frequent guests at Thackeray's dinner-table, where every courtesy was shown them by their distinguished host. After one of these entertainments I heard him remark—in the hope, no doubt, that the hint would be conveyed to those for whom it was intended, 'They are all capital fellows, but wouldn't be a whit the worse for cleaner shirts.' "

Mr. T. H. S. Escott mentions, in his *Platform and Press*, that Thackeray frequently dropped in, after the play, to a tiny establishment in the Strand kept by two elderly maiden ladies, respectable to primness, for fish suppers and other light refreshments. Mr. G. A. Sala recorded how he first met Thackeray at a small club on the first floor of a little old-fashioned tavern in Dean Street, Soho, kept by one Dicky Moreland, supposed to have been the last landlord in London who wore a pig-tail and top-boots, and how Thackeray that night sang *The Mahogany Tree*.

Thackeray was an original member of the Fielding Club, the title of which was chosen by him. The Club succeeded the C. C. C. (Cyder Cellars Club) and was established in 1852, owing to the impossibility of getting supper at the Garrick Club. Among the members were Andrew Arcedeckne (the *Foker* of *Pendennis*), Arthur Smith, Sir Charles Taylor, Monsieur Jullien, George Henry Lewes, Dr. Russell (the war correspondent), Tom Macdonald (the "Laughing Tom is laughing yet" of the *Bouillabaisse*), Tom Taylor, Pigott (after, Examiner of Plays), Shirley Brooks, Charles Lamb Kenney, Frank Talfourd, Baron Huddleston, Sergeant Ballantine, John Leech, Leigh Murray,—lastly, Albert Smith, who wrote a descriptive poem of the members, the last verse (xvi) of which runs:—

"And then there came a mighty man who, 'tis but fair to state,
Among the small is Affable, though Great amongst the great—
The good Pendennis."

There still remain to be mentioned three favourite haunts of Thackeray, which, had I been observing strict chronological order, should have been mentioned first. To these places, the "Coal Hole," the "Cyder Cellars," and "Evans's," Thackeray first went soon after he came of age, and continued his visits until his children began to grow into companions for him.

The "Coal Hole," owned by John Rhodes, was situated in a court off the Strand, near Fountain Court. "We became naturally hungry at twelve o'clock at night," Pendennis writes in *The Newcomes*, "and a desire for Welsh rabbits and good old glee singing led us to the 'Cave of Harmony.'"

"One night Colonel Newcome, with his son Clive, came here 'to see the wits.' A timely warning to the landlord from Jones of Trinity that a boy was in the room, and a gentleman who was quite a greenhorn, and the songs were so carefully selected that 'a ladies' school might have come in and, but for the smell of the cigars and brandy and water, have taken no harm by what occurred.' The Colonel was delighted, especially when Nadab the improvisatore, devoted a verse to him and to his son, and he sang a ditty himself, 'Wapping Old Stairs.' Unfortunately for the peace of the evening, however, Captain Costigan entered, very drunk, and insisted upon singing one of his most ribald songs.

" 'Silence!' Colonel Newcome roared at the end of the second verse of drunken Captain Costigan's song at the 'Cave of Harmony.' ' "Go on!" ' cries the Colonel, in his high voice, trembling with anger. 'Does any gentleman say "Go on?" Does any man who has a wife and sisters, or children at home, say "Go on" to such disgusting ribaldry as this? Do you dare, sir, to call yourself a gentleman, or to say you hold the King's commission and to sit down amongst Christians and men of honour, and defile the ears of young boys with this wicked balderdash?'

" 'Why bring young boys here, old boy?' cries a voice of the malcontents.

" 'Why? Because I thought I was coming to a society of gentlemen,' cried out the indignant Colonel. ' Because I never could have believed that Englishmen could meet together and allow a man, and an old man, so to disgrace himself. For shame, you old wretch! Go home to your bed, you hoary old sinner! And for my part, I'm not sorry that my son should see, for once in his life, to what shame and degradation and dishonour drunkenness and whisky may bring a man. Never mind the change, sir!—curse the change!' says the Colonel, facing the amazed waiter. 'Keep it till you see me in this place again, which will be never—by George, never!' And shouldering his stick, and scowling round at the company of scared bacchanalians, the indignant gentleman stalked away, his boy after him.

"Clive seemed rather shamefaced, but I fear the rest of the company looked still more foolish. 'Aussi, que diable venait-il faire dans cette galère?' says King of Corpus to Jones of Trinity; and Jones gave a shrug of his shoulders, which were smarting perhaps; for that uplifted cane of the Colonel's had somehow fallen on the back of every man in the room.' '*

*This episode in *The Newcomes* has something in common with the following reminiscence told by Mr. Francis St. John Thackeray in *Temple Bar*, 1893: "He" [Thackeray] "took me to the Garrick Club, where I remember his checking some one in the act of blurting out an oath, the utterance of which he would not tolerate in my presence." This illustrates what he once wrote in *Punch*: "We have a love for all little boys at school, for many thousands of them read and

There is nothing in the above passage but what any believer in Christianity might write; it is full of an overpowering love and awe, such as man feels under such circumstances when certain emotions are aroused.

The Pyramids, however, had quite another effect. This is his description of the marvels:—

"Looking ahead in an hour or two, we saw the Pyramids. Fancy my sensations, dear M——; two big ones and a little one:

! ! !

"There they lay, rosy and solemn in the distance— those old majestic, mystical, familiar edifices. Several of us tried to be impressed; but breakfast supervening, a rush was made at the coffee and cold pies, and the sentiment of awe was lost in the scramble for victuals. Are we so *blasés* of the world that the greatest marvels in it do not succeed in moving us? Have Society, Pall Mall Clubs, and a habit of sneering, so withered up our organs of veneration that we can admire no more? My sensation with regard to the Pyramids was that I had seen them before; then came a feeling of shame that the view of them should awaken no respect. Then I wanted (naturally) to see whether my neighbours were any more enthusiastic than myself—Trinity College, Oxford, was busy with the cold ham, Downing Street was particularly attentive to a bunch of grapes; Figtree Court behaved with decent propriety; he is in good practice, and of a conservative turn of mind, which leads him to respect from principle *les faits accomplis;* perhaps he remembered that one of them was as big as Lincoln's Inn Fields. But the truth is, nobody was seriously

The "Cyder Cellars," which is better known by name to the present generation, was owned by William Rhodes, the brother of the "Coal Hole" proprietor, and on his death it was successfully managed by his widow. It was situated in Maiden Lane, next to the stage door of the Adelphi Theatre—the site is now covered by a Jewish synagogue. Porson, the Greek Professor, used to come here, and for years his portrait hung upon the wall, and in Thackeray's time Dr. Maginn, and most of the *Fraser* set, were among the *habitués*.

It was here, too, that, in the days of his youth, Thackeray heard Sloman sing his improvisations, and referred to him in the verses to Braham in the *National Standard:*—"Sloman repeats the strains his father sang," to which was appended a satirical note: "It is needless to speak of this eminent vocalist and improvisatore. He nightly delights a numerous and respectable audience at the Cyder Cellars."

Here also, in October, 1848, he went, at least twice, "to hear the man sing about going to be hanged." The song was called *Sam Hall*, and the singer was the well-known comedian, Ross. "The chant," Mr. Hollingshead has recorded, "was that of a chimney-sweep before he was to be hanged for murder. He was a defiant, blasphemous chimney-sweep—a coarse Agnostic—with a determination to father his crimes on those who made him. . . . Ross sat astride upon a chair, leaning over the back, with his face glaring at the audience. He

love *Punch*. May he never write a word that shall not be honest and fit for them to read!"

Indeed, it may be gathered from any of his works that, while saying "Children, respect your parents and your elders," he persistently preached the quite as important, and much more often forgotten, "Parents, respect your children," "Men, respect the boys."

told his hearers how he had robbed both great and small, and at the end of each verse he damned his own eyes, until his very straightforward phrase became the catchword and refrain of the convivial early morning.'' This immensely popular song was usually given with tremendous effect about two o'clock in the morning, and as many of the guests had imbibed more liquor than was good for them, the songs became so equivocal in character as to quite justify Thackeray's attack in *The Newcomes.*

Albert Smith described the place in *The Medical Student,* and *The Adventures of Mr. Ledbury;* and Thackeray wrote of it as the ''Back Kitchen'' in *Pendennis,* in a passage that is well worth quoting:

''Healthy country tradesmen and farmers in London for their business came and recreated themselves with the jolly singing and suppers at the Back Kitchen; squads of young apprentices and assistants—the shutters being closed over the scene of their labours—came hither for fresh air, doubtless; dashing young medical students, gallant, dashing, what is called loudly dressed, and, must it be owned? somewhat dirty, came here, smoking and drinking and vigourously applauding the songs; young University bucks were to be found here, too, with that indescribable simper which is only learned at the knees of Alma Mater; and handsome young guardsmen and florid bucks from the St. James's Street clubs; nay! senators—English and Irish—and even members of the House of Peers.''

But more famous than either of the last-mentioned places, and more congenial to Thackeray, was Evans's Supper Rooms at the western corner of the Covent Garden Piazza. ''Evans's, late Joy's,'' was the punning inscription on the lamp, though in Thackeray's time the proprietor was John ("Paddy") Green. This was a great resort for men about town, and among the frequenters were Sergeant Ballantine, Douglas Jerrold, Albert and Arthur Smith, James Hannay, G. A. Sala, Lionel Lawson, Horace Mayhew, and (sometimes) Leech.

The principal entertainers here, in opposition to Ross's "Sam Hall," and the great bass singer (much appreciated by Thackeray) Hodgsen with his song, *The Bodysnatcher*, at the Cyder Cellars, were the tenor, John Binge; the basso, S. Jones; "Paddy" Green himself (he had been a chorus singer at the opera); and a German who sang jödling songs; while the comic element was supplied by Sam Cowell, singer and actor, and Sharpe, who was a great success at Vauxhall and Cremorne as well, but who took to drink and was found dead from starvation in a country lane. The ribald songs which were at first an element of the performances were soon abandoned; and in their place were choruses sung by trained choir-boys, whose fresh young voices in the old glees and madrigals of Purcell, Niedermayer, and Pearsall, were a source of delight to Thackeray.

"Thackeray's liking for Evans"—I again quote from Mr. Hollingshead's book—"was more cultivated than mine, and based upon his passionate love for the last century. Evans's belonged to the seventeenth nearly as much as it belonged to the eighteenth century. It was the connecting link between the old Covent Garden coffee-houses—the Wills and Buttons—and the music halls of the present. As a mansion it dates back to William the Third's time, and has a carved staircase of 1691, which cannot be matched in England. Its most celebrated resident perhaps was Admiral Lord Orford.

. . . In Hogarth's picture of *Morning*, the architectural frontage, unaltered for three centuries, appears. . . . These and a hundred other antiquarian memories served to endear the place to Thackeray, for it was a material link between the days of the old Garrick Club and the more beloved days when Queen Anne lived and reigned. . . ."

CHAPTER X

MISCELLANEOUS AUTHORSHIP—*PUNCH*

CHAPTER X

MISCELLANEOUS AUTHORSHIP—*PUNCH*

SHORTLY after his wife's break-down, Thackeray was constantly in Paris, where his children were staying with his grandmother; and it was during a visit there, in the autumn of 1840, that, from a room opening upon a garden in the Champs Élysées he witnessed the Second Funeral of Napoleon—that is, the ceremony of conveying the remains of the great warrior to their last resting-place at the Hôtel des Invalides. A description of this in the form of three letters to Miss Smith of London, together with the addition of a poem entitled *The Chronicle of a Drum** was published early in the following year by Hugh Cunningham of St. Martin's Place,† the successor of Macrone, who published *The Paris Sketch Book;* but it met with very little success,

---

*It is interesting to notice that this poem and Mrs. Browning's *Crowned and Buried* conclude with the same sentiment:

W. M. THACKERAY.

" And somewhere now, in yonder stars,
Can tell, mayhap, what greatness is."

E. B. BROWNING.

" But whether
The crowned Napoleon or the buried clay
Be better, I discern not—Angels may."

†"Have you read Thackeray's little book, *The Second Funeral of Napoleon?*" Edward Fitzgerald wrote to W. H. Thompson on February 18, 1841. "If not, pray do, and buy it, and ask others to buy it: as each copy sold puts 7½d. in Thackeray's pocket: which is not very heavy just now, I take it."

155

though it was brought out at the low price of half-a-crown. Now £33 10s. is paid for a copy. There is an interesting advertisement at the end of the volume, which announces that there is "preparing for immediate publication *Dinner Reminiscences, or the Young Gourmandizer's Guide at Paris, by Mr. M. A. Titmarsh*"; but, probably discouraged by the reception accorded to *The Second Funeral of Napoleon*, Thackeray abandoned his intention, and instead of the *Guide* he used part of the collected material for an article, *The Memorials of Gourmandizing*, which appeared in *Fraser* in June, 1841.

This book (*The Second Funeral*) is probably *the* book most characteristic of its author. He appreciated Napoleon, but thought the whole affair humbug; and he said so, though he knew he was running counter to the feelings of two nations. For this the *Times* reviewer blamed him, and, while praising the book, accused its author of flippancy and conceit. To this charge Thackeray replied in the article, *Men and Pictures* (*Fraser*, July, 1849), in the half-serious, half-bantering manner he affected towards adverse criticism.

"Oh, you thundering old *Times!* Napoleon's funeral was a humbug, and your constant reader said so. The people engaged in it were humbugs, and this even Michael Angelo hinted at. There may be irreverence in this, and the process of humbug-hunting may end rather awkwardly for some people. But surely there is no conceit. The shamming of modesty is the most pert conceit of all, the *précieuse* affectation of deference where you don't feel it, the sneaking acquiescence in lies. It is very hard that a man may not tell the truth as he fancies it, without being accused of conceit: but so the world wags. As has already been prettily shown in

that before-mentioned little book about Napoleon, that
is still to be had of the Publisher, there is a Ballad in the
Volume which, if properly studied, will be alone worth
two-and-sixpence to any man.

"Well, the Funeral of Napoleon *was* a humbug, and
being so, what was a man to call it? What do we call a
rose? Is it disrespectful to call it by its own innocent
name? And, in like manner, are we bound, out of
respect for society, to speak of humbug only in a cir-
cumlocutory way—to call it something else, as they say
some Indian people do their devil—to wrap it up in rid-
dles and charades! Nothing is easier. Take, for
instance, the following couple of sonnets on the subject :—

> "The glad spring sun shone yesterday, as Mr.
>   M. Titmarsh wandered with his favourite lassie
>   By silver Seine, among the meadows grassy—
> Meadows, like mail-coach guards new clad at Easter.
>   Fair was the sight 'twixt Neuilly and Passy;
> And green the field, and bright the river's glister.
>
> "The bird sang, sang salutation to the spring;
>   Already buds and leaves from branches burst:
>   'The surly winter time hath done its worst,'
> Said Michael; 'Lo, the bees are on the wing!'
> Then on the ground his lazy limbs did fling.
>   Meanwhile the bees pass'd by him with my *first*.
> My *second* dare I to your notice bring,
>   Or name to delicate ears that animal accurst?
>
> "To all our earthly family of fools
>   My *whole*, resistless despot, gives the law—
>   Humble or great, we kneel to it the same
> O'er camp and court, the Senate and the schools,
> Our grand Invisible Lama sits and rules
>   By Ministers that are its men of straw.
>
> "Sir Robert utters it—place of wit
>   And straight the Opposition shouts 'Hear, hear!'
>   And oh! but all the Whiggish benches cheer
> When great Lord John retorts it, as is fit.

In you, my *Press*, each day throughout the year,
  On vast broad sheets we find its praises writ.
Oh! wondrous are the columns that you rear
  And sweet the many hymns you roar in praise of it!

"(The reader can easily accommodate the line to the name of his favourite paper.   Thus:—

"In you, my $\frac{Times}{Post}$ each day throughout the year"

"In you, my $\frac{Herald}{'Tiser}$ daily through the year"

or, in France:—

"In you, my *Galignani's Messagère;*—

"a capital paper, because you have there the very cream of all the others.   In the last line for, 'Morning' you can read 'Evening' or 'Weekly' as circumstances prompt.)

"Sacred word! It is kept out of the Dictionaries, as if the great compilers of those publications were afraid to utter it.   Well then, the Funeral of Napoleon was a humbug, as Titmarsh wrote, and a still better proof that it was a humbug was this, that nobody bought Titmarsh's book, and of the 10,000 copies made ready by the publisher, not above 3,000 went off.   It was a humbug, and an exploded humbug.   Peace be to it.   *Parlons d'autres choses.*"

It was not until a quarter of a century had elapsed that the article was reprinted.   Then, in January, 1866, it was printed in the pages of the *Cornhill Magazine*, with an introductory note by the Editor:—

"Mr. Thackeray once more appears in the pages of the *Cornhill Magazine*. We are able to give our readers some sketches of his, which have, indeed, been printed before, but that was when he was writing for a generation so astonishingly dull as to see no merit in *Barry Lyndon;* while we in our days wonder sometimes whether even Thackeray himself ever surpassed that little book, so wonderfully vigourous and keen. But he wrote many things then that were neglected and were soon altogether forgotten. One of them was *The Second Funeral of Napoleon*, of which probably not one in ten thousand of the readers of this Magazine ever heard. And yet it was published in due form and in decent duodecimo, by Mr. Hugh Cunningham, a bookseller whose shop was at the corner of St. Martin's Place: he who also first published *The Paris Sketch Book*. It was illustrated by some woodcuts of no great merit, and thereto was added the famous *Chronicle of the Drum*—which the 'leading Magazines' had all refused to print. And as the able editors of the time rejected the ballad, so the intelligent public of the time refused to read the account of *The Second Funeral of Napoleon*, though it had all the allurement of being written at the time, and in the presence of the event it commemorates. The gentleman who sends us the original MS., from which we reprint the long-forgotten narrative, says:—

"The *Letters on the Second Funeral* were a failure. I had the pleasure of editing the tiny volume for Mr. Thackeray, and ran it through the press. And after a while, on the dismal tidings from the publisher that the little effort made no impression on the public, Mr. Thackeray wrote to me from Paris a pretty little note commencing: 'So your poor Titmarsh has made another fiasco. How are we to take the great stupid public by the ears? Never mind; I think I have something which will surprise them yet. . . .' This was evidently an allusion to *Vanity Fair*, which he had begun at that time."

In 1841 Thackeray also published, through Hugh
Cunningham, of St. Martin's Place, two volumes of
reprints under the title of *Comic Tales and Sketches.
Edited and illustrated by Mr. Michael Angelo Titmarsh*,
with a preface dated "Paris, April 1, 1841," the greater
part of which is well worth inserting here:—

"A custom which the publishers have adopted of late
cannot be too strongly praised, both by authors of high
repute, and by writers of no repute at all,—viz., the
custom of causing the writings of unknown literary characters to be edited by some person who is already a
favourite of the public.   The labour is not so difficult as
at first may be supposed.   A publisher writes—'My dear
Sir,—Enclosed is a draft on Messrs. So-and-So; will
you edit Mr. What-d'ye-call-em's book?'   The well-
known author writes—'My dear Sir,—I have to acknowledge the receipt of so much, and will edit the book with
pleasure.'   And the book is published; and from that
day until the end of the world, the well-known author
never hears of it again, except he has a mind to read it,
when he orders it from the circulating library.

"This little editorial fiction is one which can do harm
to nobody in the world, and only good to the young
author so introduced; for who would notice him in such
a great, crowded, bustling world unless he came forward
by a decent letter of recommendation?   .   .   .   .

"When there came to be a question of republishing
the tales in these volumes, the three authors, Major
Gahagan, Mr. Fitzroy Yellowplush, and myself, had a
violent dispute upon the matter of editing; and at one
time we talked of editing each other all round.   The
toss of a half-penny, however, decided the question in
my favour; and I shall be very glad, in a similar manner,

LONDON H. CUNNINGHAM, 1 St MARTINS PLACE, TRAFALGAR SQUARE.
1841.

to 'edit' any works, of any author, on any subject, or in any language whatever.

"Mr. Yellowplush's *Memoirs* appeared in *Fraser's Magazine*, and have been reprinted accurately from that publication. The elegance of their style made them excessively popular in America, where they were reprinted more than once. Major Gahagan's *Reminiscences* from the *New Monthly Magazine* were received by our American brethren with similar piratical honours; and the Editor has had the pleasure of perusing them likewise; but Doctor Strumpff, the celebrated Sanskrit Professor in the University of Bonn, has already deciphered the first ten pages, has compiled a copious vocabulary and notes, has separated the mythic from the historical part of the volume, and discovered it is like Homer, the work of many ages and persons. He declares the work to be written in the Cocknaic dialect; but, for this and other conjectures, the reader is referred to his essay.

"*The Bedford-Row Conspiracy* also appeared in the *New Monthly Magazine;* and the reader of French novels will find that one of the tales of the ingenious M. Charles de Barnard is very similar to it in plot. As M. de Barnard's tale appeared before the *Conspiracy*, it is very probable that envious people will be disposed to say that the English author borrowed from the French one; a matter which the public is quite at liberty to settle as it chooses.

"The history of *The Fatal Boots* formed part of *The Comic Almanack* three years since, and if the author has not ventured to make designs for it, as for the other tales in the volume, the reason is, that the *Boots* have been already illustrated by Mr. George Cruikshank, a gentleman upon whom Mr. Titmarsh does not wish to provoke criticism.

"On the title-page the reader is presented with three accurate portraits of the author of these volumes. They are supposed to be marching hand-in-hand, and are just on the very brink of Immortality."

The fact that *The Professor, a Tale*, which was included in this book, is not mentioned in the preface, has led more than one writer into the error of stating that it was then published for the first time. As a matter of fact it is the story of the same name contributed to *Bentley's Miscellany*, then under the editorship of *Boz*, and at the time when *Oliver Twist* was appearing in its pages.

From Kenny Meadows, who at this time was publishing a series of *Heads of the People*—Douglas Jerrold and Marryat were among the contributors — Thackeray accepted a commission to write three sketches: *Captain Rook and Mr. Pigeon*, and *The Fashionable Authoress* (by William Thackeray), and *The Artist* (by *Michael Angelo Titmarsh*). He also wrote for *Fraser* the already mentioned *Memorials of Gourmandizing* (June), the title of which explains itself—in this article first appeared one of his imitations of Horace, *To his Serving Boy; On Men and Pictures*, in which, as I have said, he defended his *Second Funeral of Napoleon;* and *Men and Coats* (August), an amusing paper on clothes; while to Cruikshank's *Omnibus* he contributed *Little Spitz, A Lenten Anecdote from the German Professor of Spass* (October), and the humourous *King of Brentford's Testament* (December).

But 1841 is especially memorable for the production of the best of his earlier writings. "The best thing I ever wrote," he himself said six years later, on the eve of the publication of *Vanity Fair*, which, after being rejected by *Blackwood*, came out from September to December in *Fraser—The History of Samuel Titmarsh and the Great Hoggarty Diamond, edited and illustrated by Sam's Cousin, Michael Angelo.*

The excellencies of this story were quite overlooked by the general reading public, who, no doubt, found it clever and amusing, but had not sufficient discernment to see *how* good it was, or to note in it the promise of the future greatness of its author. There were, however, a few critics who were less blind than the public, and amongst these was John Stirling, who wrote to his mother: "I have seen no new books, but am reading your last. I got hold of the two first numbers of *The Hoggarty Diamond*, and read them with extreme delight. What is there better in Fielding or Goldsmith? The man is a true genius, and with quiet comfort might produce masterpieces which would last as long as any we have, and delight millions of unborn readers. There is more truth in nature in one of those papers, than in all Dickens' novels put together." All of which letter says a great deal for the critical faculty of the writer, but unfortunately was of little avail in raising Thackeray's literary status.

This year, too, saw the commencement of Thackeray's long connection with *Punch*.

This is not the place to record the origin of this famous paper, but it is worth while noting that it was seriously intended by Thackeray and others to start a journal on very much the same lines about a year earlier. Mr. Henry Vizetelly is the historian of this unfulfilled intention. "A scheme was proposed," he wrote, "to produce a satirical journal on the lines of Phillipon's Paris *Charivari*, excepting that the proposed new venture was to be a weekly instead of a daily publication." As no capitalist could be found willing to risk his money "it was determined to start the *London Charivari* on the co-operative principle. . . . After considerable negotiation the following list of proprietors . . . was decided upon: Authors: Jerrold, Thackeray, Laman Blanchard, and Percival Leigh; . . . Artists: Kenny Meadows, Leech, and . . . Alfred Crowquill; Engraver: Orrin Smith; Printers: Jobbin, lithographic—J. Vizetelly, letter-press; publisher, R. Tyas. Specimen pages of the text were put into type, . . . when, by some means or other, Thackeray got hold of the idea that each co-partner in the proposed publication would not only be liable for its debts, but also for the private debts of his co-partners; and as none of the latter possessed sufficient legal knowledge to point out the fallacy of this assumption, and some were suspicious of the soundness of their proposed colleagues, the continuation of the *London Charivari* was forthwith abandoned, and on the 17th July, 1841, the first number of *Punch* appeared."

Soon after, to quote Shirley Brooks, "on a good day for himself, the journal, and the world, Thackeray found *Punch*." When Edward Fitzgerald heard of this, he wrote on May 22nd to a friend, "Tell Thackeray not to go into *Punch* yet." Thackeray disregarded this advice—fortunately as it happened—but there is no doubt the monitor was right, for the paper, originally owned by three people, had been so ridiculously under-capitalized, that they were compelled to sell the journal to its present proprietors in order to meet their liabilities. Messrs.

Bradbury & Evans, however, by their capital and business experience, soon put the paper on a more reputable footing.

Within a few weeks of Fitzgerald's warning, in the same number that introduced John Oxenford's work to the *Punch* reader, Thackeray's first contribution appeared—*The Legend of Jawbrahim-Heraudee.* *Miss Tickletoby's Lectures on English History*—which are usually considered his earliest work for this paper, did not appear until a fortnight later, at the beginning of the second volume for 1842. These *Lectures*, no doubt, suggested to Beckett and Leech the idea of *The Comic History of England*, and *The Comic History of Rome*, but they were not considered a success, and, indeed, were discontinued after the eleventh week.

"I am sorry to learn that you were dissatisfied with my contribution to *Punch*," Thackeray wrote from Halvertown on September 27 to the proprietors. "I wish my writing had the good fortune to please every one. . . . I shall pass the winter either in Paris or in London where, very probably, I may find some other matter more suitable to the paper, in which case I shall make another attempt upon *Punch*."*

He soon caught the tone of the paper, and was able to suit his writings to its requirements. For ten years he poured all his best work into it. He had a free hand and was able to employ all his talents—he contributed, with a fine indifference, duologues, sketches, love-letters, thumb-nail drawings, criticisms, political skits, social satires, poems, parodies, caricatures—even illustra-

The History of Punch. It is singular to notice now inaccurate the painstaking and laborious Trollope can be, when he takes to biographical work. He states that Thackeray began to write on *Punch* in 1843 and ceased writing in 1852; both of which dates are wrong.

tions to other writers' works. The paper would accept anything, if only it were amusing, and soon he became the principal literary supporter of the worthy Mr. Punch. To Number 137 (Christmas, 1843), which is still famous as having contained *The Song of the Shirt*, he contributed a *Singular Letter from the Regent of Spain*, and three cuts illustrating sailors who had found a bottle in the sea: "Sherry perhaps" — "Rum, I hope" — "*Tracts, by Jove!*" With this number he took his place at the Dinner, as a substitute for Albert Smith.*

Before this, he had contributed *Mr. Spec's Remonstrance,*† a *Turkish Letter concerning the Divertisement "Les Houris,"* a *Second Turkish Letter*, and with Jerrold had created *Jenkins* to typify the *Morning Post*.

His other papers, under the pseudonyms of *Titmarsh, Policeman X., Our Eastern Contributor, Our Fat Contributor, Solomon Pacifico, Fitzroy Clarence, Punch's*

---

*The plan (which I copy from the *History of Punch*) of the *Punch* dinner-table in 1855 was

William Bradbury,

Douglas Jerrold,	John Leech,
Tom Taylor,	W. M. Thackeray,
Gilbert A. Beckett,	Shirley Brooks,
Horace Mayhew,	Mark Lemon,
Percival Leigh,	John Tenniel,

F. M. Evans.

And in 1860:—

William Bradbury,

W. M. Thackeray,	John Leech,
(when he comes),	
Tom Taylor,	Henry Silver,
Horace Mayhew,	Charles Keene,
Shirley Brooks,	John Tenniel,
Percival Leigh,	Mark Lemon,

F. M. Evans.

†The pseudonym "Spec" seems to have been used about two years before, when Cunningham published *Sketches by Spec. No. 1, Britannia Protecting the Drama*. Only this No. 1 was published, and of this the only known copy is in the possession of Mr. C. P. Johnson, who had it reproduced in facsimile by the Autotype Company in 1885.

"SHERRY, PERHAPS."

"RUM, I HOPE."

Commissioner, Jeames, Paul Pindar, etc., will be mentioned later.

The account of *Punch* has made me anticipate a little, and it is now necessary to go back to 1842.

In that year Thackeray's published writings were:— *Sultan Stork, being the One Thousand and Second Night. By Major G. O'G. Gahagan, H.E.I.C.S.* (*Ainsworth*, February, May), a continuation of the *Arabian Nights* in the warrior's best style; *Dickens in France* (*Fraser*, March), a most amusing account of *Nicholas Nickleby, ou Les Voleurs de Londres*, then being performed at the Ambigu-Comique Theater on the Boulevard; *An Exhibition Gossip* (*Ainsworth*, June), a letter to Monsieur Guillaume, peintre, criticising contemporary English artists; *Fitz-Boodle's Confessions* (*Fraser*, June); *Professions, by George Fitz-Boodle, being appeals to the Unemployed Younger Sons of the Nobility* (*Fraser*, June)—only the first two of the three professions suggested here have been republished; and *Miss Löwe* (*Fraser*, October).

In June, 1842, Thackeray visited Ireland, where he made a sort of grand tour, seeing everything and everybody and going everywhere — to Dublin, Waterford, Cork, Killarney, Galway, Connemara, Wicklow, Belfast, The Giants' Causeway, and many other places. Perhaps the most interesting event of the trip was the visit paid to Charles Lever, who was then living at Templerogue, which lies four miles southwest of Ireland.

The two novelists had many conversations, and perhaps the principal result of this intercourse was that Lever's works, which had been essentially Irish before this time, became more cosmopolitan in character. Thackeray endeavoured to persuade him to quit Dublin, where he was surrounded by third-rate writers, and to come to London, where he would be able to make much more money without any more trouble. So much advantage, indeed, did Thackeray think his fellow-novelist would derive from his change of residence, that he backed his advice by offers of pecuniary and other assistance, if such were needed. Lever, however, for various reasons, declined this proposal, and afterwards told a friend that Thackeray was the most good-natured man in the world, "but that help from him would be worse than no help at all. . . . He (Thackeray) was like a man struggling to keep his head above water, and who offers to teach his friend to swim." Lever also added that Thackeray "would write for anything and about anything, and had so lost himself that his status in London was not good."*

The result of this visit to the sister isle was the *Irish Sketch Book*,† published in two volumes by Messrs. Chapman & Hall—the first book of Thackeray's brought out by this firm. The *Sketch-Book* was signed, like most of his work at this time, with the familiar *Michael Angelo Titmarsh;* but in the dedication (dated London, April 27, 1843) to Charles Lever, his real name first appeared—"laying aside for the moment the travelling title of Mr. *Titmarsh*, let me . . . subscribe myself, my dear Lever, most sincerely and gratefully yours, W. M. Thackeray."

Lever was much blamed by some of his countrymen for accepting the dedication of a book that they declared

---

* "Thackeray had a sincere regard for Charles, and would say anything to him."—MAJOR D.

†This work was to have come out under the Titmarshian title of *The Cockney in Ireland,* but the publishers, preferring the delightful ambiguity of "Sketch-Book," so ticketed the book.—VIZETELLY, *Glances Back Through Seventy Years.*

"TRACTS, BY JOVE!"

to be full of blunders and exaggerations—though Edward Fitzgerald wrote from Dublin: "It is all true. I ordered a bath here, and when I got in the waiter said it was heated to 90 degrees, but it was scalding; he next locked me up in the room, instead of my locking him out."

Lever, however, reviewed the book himself in the *Dublin University Magazine*, which he was then editing; and it is certain that Thackeray did not mean to annoy the Irish, for in after years he paid the whole nation a great compliment—a very unusual thing for him to do—in the *English Humourists*, when he declared: "No, the Dean was no Irishman—no Irishman ever gave but with a kind word and a kind heart."

Mr. Henry Vizetelly, in conjunction with Mr. Andrew Spottiswoode, had just set up the *Pictorial Times* in opposition to Ingram's *Illustrated London News* (with which until recently he had himself been associated), and he was gathering for his staff as many promising young men as he could find.

"I next saw Mr. Thackeray," he has related in his autobiography. "On calling at the address given me—a shop in Jermyn Street, eight or ten doors from Regent Street, and within a few doors of the present Museum of Geology—and knocking at the private entrance, a young lodging house slavey, in answer to my enquiries, bade me follow her upstairs. I did so, to the very top of the house, and after my card had been handed in I was asked to enter the front apartment, where a tall, slim individual between thirty and thirty-five years of age, with a pleasant, smiling countenance, and a bridgeless nose, and clad in dressing-gown of decided Parisian cut, rose from a small table standing close to the near window

to receive me. When he stood up the low pitch of the
room caused him to look even taller than he really was,
and his actual height was well over six feet. . . .
The apartment was an exceedingly plainly furnished
bedroom, with common rush-seated chairs, and painted
French bedstead, and with neither looking-glass nor
prints on the bare, cold, cheerless-looking walls. On the
table from which Mr. Thackeray had risen a white cloth
was spread, on which was a frugal breakfast tray—a cup
of chocolate and some dry toast; and huddled together
at the other end were writing materials, two or three
numbers of *Fraser's Magazine*, and a few slips of manuscript. I presented Mr. Nickisson's letter, and explained
the object of my visit, when Mr. Thackeray at once
undertook to write upon art, to review such books as he
might fancy, and to contribute an occasional article on
the Opera, more with reference to its frequenters than
from a critical point of view. So satisfied was he with
the three guineas offered him for a couple of columns
weekly, that he jocularly expressed himself willing to
sign an agreement for life upon these terms. I can only
suppose, from the eager way in which he closed with my
proposal, that the prospects of an additional hundred
and sixty pounds to his income was, at that moment,
anything but a matter of indifference. The humble
quarters in which he was installed seemed at any rate to
indicate that, from some reason or other, strict economy
was just then the order of the day with him.''

Thackeray's interview with Vizetelly led to the *Letters
on The Fine Arts*, which appeared in the *Pictorial Times*
during March and April. They were six in number, and
included a letter on Art Unions, notices of the Academy

and Water Colour Exhibitions, and reviews of Macaulay's newly collected essays, and Disraeli's *Coningsby*—the last in particular an exquisite performance. Then Thackeray went Eastward Ho! and the letters ceased. Before leaving the *Pictorial Times*, it may be mentioned that, by some error, Thackeray had not been paid for the *Coningsby* review, and on his return to England, he wrote to Vizetelly the following amusing note: "Why doesn't the P. T. pay up? Rate Keys" [the publisher] "for not sending on my cheque. I had more than half a mind to post the holder of Queen Victoria's patent" [Spottiswoode, the Crown printer] "as a defaulter at the top of Cheops' pyramid for the information of future gadders-about. The vigilant old centuries, which look down so inquisitively, would have blinked their weary eyes at the exposure."

During 1843 the continuation of the *Fitz-Boodle Papers—Dorothea* (January); *Ottilia*, in which are the two *Willow Tree* poems (February); and the *Men's Wives* series: *Mr. and Mrs. Frank Berry* (March), *The Ravenswing* (April, May), *Denis Haggarty's Wife* (October), *The ———'s Wife** (November), were his principal contributions to Fraser. But in addition Mr. *Titmarsh* printed *Jerome Paturot, with considerations on Novels in General* (September) and *Bluebeard's Ghost* (October) while Mr. *Fitz-Boodle* sent a review of Grant's *Paris and its people* for the December number.

The following is a letter first printed in the *Bookworm* (May, 1890) from Thackeray to the then proprietor of *Fraser's Magazine*.

The letter explains itself.

*This has not been reprinted.

"13, Great Coram Street, *April* 8, 1843.

"My dear Nickisson,—I was at no loss, in reading the amusing *Illustrations of Discount* in the Magazine, to discover the name of the Author.   Mr. Deady Keane shook me by the hand only a fortnight since, and at the very same time no doubt was writing the libel on me which appeared, to my no small surprise, in that very Article.

"I have advisedly let a week pass without deciding upon the course I ought to pursue.   Few people (none that I have seen) know that the attack in question is levelled at myself, nor indeed have I any desire to make the public acquainted with that fact.   But, as in a private house or an Inn, if any person with no other provocation but that of drunkenness or natural malice should take a fancy to call me by foul names, I should have a right to appeal to the host and request him to have the individual so offending put out of doors—I may similarly complain to you that I have been grossly insulted in your Magazine.

"Having written long in it; being known to you (please God) as an honest man and not an ungenerous one; I have a right to complain that a shameful and an unprovoked attack has been made upon me in the Magazine and as an act of justice to demand that the writer should no longer be permitted to contribute *to Fraser*.

"If Mr. Deady Keane continues his contributions in any form, mine must cease.   I am one of the oldest and I believe one of the best of your contributors.   A private individual, I have been grossly abused in the Magazine, and must perforce withdraw from it unless I have your word that this act of justice shall be done me.

"I make this demand not in the least as an act of

retaliation against Mr. Keane, but as an act of justice I owe to myself and which is forced upon me. At the present at least it cannot be said that my anger is very revengeful or that his attack has rendered me particularly vindictive. It would be easy to fight him with the same weapons which he uses did I descend to employ them; but I feel myself, and I hope one day he will discover, that they are unworthy of an honest man. If he only take care to let it be publicly known that it is his intention to abuse in the public Prints any private individuals whose personal appearance or qualities may be disagreeable to him, it is surprising how popular he will become, how his society will be courted, and his interests in life advanced.

"But I am sure you will no longer allow him to exercise his office of Satirist in your Magazine, and hope (without the least wish to imply a threat) that for both our sakes he will make no more attacks in print upon my person or my private character.

"Faithfully yours, dear Nickisson,

"W. M. THACKERAY.

"I have no copy of this letter, but if you send it to Mr. Keane will you please make one?"

In the early summer of 1844 Messrs. Chapman & Hall announced a *Monthly Series*, which was to be a collection of original works of biography and fiction, to be published in 8vo volumes of 350 to 420 pages. "The first biography," so ran the advertisement, "will be a Life of Talleyrande by W. M. Thackeray"—which would have been the first work published in his own name. He had written from the Reform Club to the firm on July 16:—

"My dear Sirs,—I will engage to write the volume, the Life of Talleyrande, and to have the MSS. in your hands by December 1, health permitting, and will sign an agreement to that effect, if you will have the goodness to prepare one.

"Faithfully yours, dear Sirs,
"W. M. Thackeray."

However, the agreement was never signed, and the reason of this appeared in the preface to the *Notes of a Journey from Cornhill to Grand Cairo*, (published in 1846) part of which I quote here:—

"On August 20, 1844, the writer of this little book went to dine at the '—— Club,' quite unconscious of the wonderful event which fate had in store for him. Mr. William was there, giving a farewell dinner to his friend Mr. James (now Sir James). These two asked Mr. Titmarsh to join company with them, and the conversation naturally fell upon the tour Mr. James was about to take. The Peninsular and Oriental Company had arranged an excursion in the Mediterranean, by which in the space of a couple of months as many men and cities were to be seen as Ulysses surveyed and noted in ten years. Malta, Athens, Smyrna, Constantinople, Jerusalem, Cairo, were to be visited, and everybody was to be back in London by Lord Mayor's Day. The idea of beholding these famous places inflamed Mr. Titmarsh's mind, and the charms of such a voyage were eloquently impressed upon him by Mr. James. 'Come,' said that kind and hospitable gentleman, 'and make one of my family party; in all your life you will never probably have a chance again to see so much in so short a time. Consider—it's as easy as a journey to Paris or to

Baden.' Mr. Titmarsh considered all these things, but also the difficulty of the situation; he had but thirty-six hours to get ready for so portentous a journey—he had engagements at home—finally, could he afford it? In spite of these objections, however, with every glass of claret the enthusiasm somehow rose, and the difficulties vanished. But when Mr. James, to crown all, said he had no doubt that his friends the Directors of the Peninsular and Oriental Company would make Mr. Titmarsh the present of a berth for the voyage,* all objection ceased on his part; to break his outstanding engagements—to write letters to his amazed family, stating they were not to expect him to dinner on Saturday fortnight, as he would be at Jerusalem on that day—to purchase eighteen shirts and lay in a sea stock of Russia ducks—was the work of twenty-four hours. And on August 22 the *Lady Mary Wood* was sailing from Southampton with the subject of the present memoir quite astonished to find himself one of the passengers on board.''

So Thackeray went to the East, and the *Life of Talleyrand* is only to be mentioned as among his unwritten works.

*When the *Notes* was published, Carlyle was very angry that Thackeray had accepted a free passage for this trip from the P. and O. directors. Sir Charles Gavan Duffy says that he compared the transaction to the practice of a blind fiddler going to and fro on a penny ferry boat in Scotland and playing tunes to the passengers for halfpence. Sir Charles adds "Charles Buller told Thackeray of this, and when he complained thought it necessary to inform him frankly, it was undoubtedly his opinion that, out of respect for himself and his profession, a man like him ought not to have gone fiddling for halfpence or otherwise in any steamboat under the sun."
This is all very well, but I cannot see the necessity for all this virtuous indignation and anxiety for the dignity of Thackeray and the literary profession; for not only did Thackeray not puff the Company, but the free passage was not really given to him by the Company, but by a friend, who had used his influence to obtain it from the directors, with whom he was on intimate terms.

"Titmarsh at Jerusalem will certainly be an era in Christianity," Fitzgerald said; but Jerusalem did not arouse feelings of mockery in Thackeray; there was no false sentiment to excite his satire—indeed, his own words show clearly that he was moved at the sight of this city of many traditions.

"From this terrace," he wrote about Jerusalem, "whence we looked in the morning, a great part of the city spread before us—white domes upon domes, terraces of the same character as our own. Here and there, from among these white-washed mounds round about, a minaret rose, or a rare date tree; but the chief part of the vegetation near was that odious tree, the prickly pear—one huge green wart growing out of another, armed with spikes, as odious as the aloe, without shelter or beauty. To the right the Mosque of Omar rose; the rising sun behind it. Yonder steep, tortuous lane before us, flanked by ruined walls on either side, has borne, time out of mind, the title of Via Dolorosa, and tradition has fixed the spots where the Saviour rested, bearing His cross to Calvary. But of the mountain, rising immediately in front of us, a few grey olive trees speckling the yellow sides here and there, there can be no question. That is the Mount of Olives. Bethany lies beyond it. The most sacred eyes that ever looked on this world have gazed on those ridges; it was there He used to walk and teach. With shamed humility one looks towards the spot where that inexpressible Love and Benevolence lived and breathed; where the great yearning heart of the Saviour interceded for all our race; and whence the bigots and traitors of His day led Him away to kill Him."

moved, . . . and why should they, because of an exaggeration of bricks ever so enormous? I confess for my part that the Pyramids are very big.''

There are two extracts from the *Notes* I cannot refrain from including here—they are so full of beautiful paternal love and tenderness. The first is the concluding verse of the famous *White Squall* ballad:—

> "And when, its force expended,
> The harmless storm was ended,
> And as the sunrise splendid
>   Came blushing o'er the sea,
> I thought as day was breaking,
> My little girls were waking
> And smiling and making
>   A prayer at home for me."

The second passage is even more charming, and I make no apology for giving it in its entirety: "But that Alexandrian two-pair front of a Consulate was more welcome and cheering than a palace to most of us. For there lay certain letters, with postmarks of *Home* upon them, and kindly tidings, the first heard for two months;—though we had seen so many men and cities since, that Cornhill seemed to be a year off at least, with certain persons dwelling (more or less) in that vicinity. I saw a young Oxford man seize his despatches, and slink off with several letters written in a light, neat hand, and sedulously crossed; which any man can see, without looking further, were the handiwork of Mary Anne, to whom he is attached. The lawyer received a bundle from his chambers, in which his clerk eased his soul regarding the state of Snooks *v.* Rogers, Smith *ats.* Tomkins, etc. The statesman had a packet of thick envelopes decorated with that profusion of sealing wax in which official recklessness lavishes the resources of the country; and your humble servant got just one little modest letter, containing another, written in pencil characters varying in size between one and two inches, but how much pleasanter to read than my Lord's despatch, or the clerk's account of Smith *ats*. Tomkins—yes, even than the Mary Anne correspondence! . . . Yes, my dear Madam, you will understand me, when I say that it was from little Polly at home, with some confidential news about a cat, and the last report of her new doll. It is worth while to have made the journey for the pleasure; to have walked the deck on long nights, and thought of home. You have no leisure to do so in the city. You don't see the heavens shine above you so purely there, or the stars so clearly.''

CHAPTER XI

NOVELIST AND CRITIC

CHAPTER XI

NOVELIST AND CRITIC

THE event of the year (1844)—it, in fact, marks an epoch in Thackeray's literary life—was the publication in *Fraser's Magazine* monthly, from January to December (October excepted) of *The Luck of Barry Lyndon, A Romance of the Last Century. By Fitz-Boodle.* This story, of which the later part was written during his journey to and from the East, seems to have given him more trouble to write than any of his earlier ones, and it was with a great sense of relief that he brought it to a close. Mrs. Ritchie gives three extracts from his diary that are well worth recording. "Malta, November 1.—Wrote *Barry*, but slowly and with great difficulty." "November 2.—Wrote *Barry* with no more success than yesterday." "November 3.—Finished *Barry* after great throes, late at night." The story met with no great success during its publication, but the discerning few who appreciated the merits of *The Great Hoggarty Diamond* were now satisfied that they had discovered a mighty man of genius, who must leave an impression upon the pages of Victorian literature.

Thackeray must have worked harder than ever this year, especially before he left England in August, for his literary output was enormous. Besides *Barry Lyndon* he sent to *Fraser:*—

(i) *A Box of Novels* (February), containing criticisms

of *Tom Burke, Harry Lorrequer, L.S.D.* (by Lever), *The Miser's Son, The Burgomaster of Berlin*, and Dickens's *Christmas Carol*.

(ii) *Little Travels and Roadside Sketches: From Richmond in Surrey to Brussels in Belgium* (May)—*Ghent to Bruges* (October)—*Waterloo* (January, 1845).

(iii) *May Gambols, or Titmarsh in the Picture Galleries* (June).

(iv) *Carmen Lilliense*, dated Lille, September 2, a delightful little poem, narrating an incident that had occurred to the author during his stay at Lille, when his purse was stolen and he was absolutely without money until he could receive remittances from England. The refrain of the song runs:—

> "My heart is weary, my peace is gone,
>   How shall I e'er my woes reveal?
> I have no money, I lie in pawn,
>   A stranger in the town of Lille."

But happiness comes to him after days of misery:—

> "What see I on my table stand?
>   A letter with a well-known seal!
> 'Tis grandmamma's! I know her hand:
>   'To Mr. M. A. Titmarsh, Lille.'
> I feel a choking in my throat,
>   I pant and stagger, faint and reel!
> It is—it is—a ten-pound note,
>   And I'm no more in pawn at Lille!"

[He goes off by the diligence that evening and is restored to the bosom of his happy family.]

The New Monthly Magazine received two tales from *Launcelot Wagstaff*—a relation, it may be, of *Théophile Wagstaffe* of *Flore et Zephyr* fame—*The Partie Fine* (May) and *Greenwich — Whitebait* (July); the *Morning Chronicle* (April 2), a review of a book by R. H. Horne, entitled *A New Spirit of the Age;* and *Punch, The History of the next French Revolution* (in nine parts), and *The Wanderings* and *Travelling Notes,* both by *Our Fat Contributor,* which were continued in the following year.

About this time Thackeray obtained the assistant editorship of the *Examiner,* to which paper he was a contributor, and he held the post until 1848, when he resigned, because it took up more time than he could afford to give for four guineas a week. *A propos* of his great prolixity, Edward Fitzgerald wrote in May (1844) to Frederick Tennyson: "I see in *Punch* a humourous catalogue of supposed pictures; Prince Albert's favourite spaniel and bootjack, the Queen's Micaw with a muffin, etc., by Landseer, etc., in which I recognize Thackeray's fancy. He is in full vigour, play, and pay in London, writing in a dozen reviews, and a score of newspapers, and while his health lasts he sails before the wind. . ."

In 1845 he wrote more than ever. This was probably due to the beneficial results of the voyage upon his health. *The New Monthly Magazine* printed in July two more stories by Mr. *Wagstaff—The Chest of Cigars* (in which he prints a story related to him by General Sir Goliah Gahagan, H.E.I.C.S.); and, in the next month, *Bob Robinson's First Love.*

To Cruikshank, for his *Table Book,* he sent *A Legend of the Rhine,* which is a clever burlesque of the elder Dumas's *L'Othon l'Archer;* but *Punch* received a whole list of contributions—*Punch in the East, Meditations on Solitude, Beulah Spa, Brighton, A Brighton Night's Entertainment, Meditations Over Brighton, The Georges, A Doe in the City, A Lucky Speculation,* with the famous *Jeames of Buckley Square, Jeames on Time Bargings,* and the commencement of the immortal *Jeames's*

Diary, which was largely quoted in the papers at the time, and has since been dramatised.

Fraser had *Picture Gossip* (June), his annual criticism on the May exhibitions; *Barmecide Banquets* (November), a review of the *Practical Cook;* and *About a Christmas Book*.

Thackeray's art criticisms were not at all pleasant reading to the painters of the day, as a single perusal will convince any one, and there is rather an amusing passage about the way the artists felt towards Thackeray in a letter written in June by Edward Fitzgerald to Frederick Tennyson about *Picture Gossip:* "If you want to know something of the Exhibition, however, read *Fraser's Magazine* for this month; there Thackeray has a paper on the matter full of fun. I met Stone in the street the other day; he took me by the button, and told me in perfect sincerity and with increasing warmth how, though he loved old Thackeray, yet these yearly out-speakings of his sorely tried him; not on account of himself (Stone), but on account of some of his friends, Charles Landseer, Maclise, etc. Stone worked himself up to such a pitch under the pressure of forced calmness that he at last said Thackeray would get himself horse-whipped one day by one of those infuriated Appellesses. At this I, who had partly agreed with Stone that ridicule, though true, need not always be spoken, began to laugh, and told him two could play at that game. These painters cling together and bolster each other up to such a degree that they really have persuaded themselves that any one who ventures to laugh at one of their drawings, exhibited publicly for the express purpose of criticism, insults the whole corps. Thackeray laughs at all this, and goes on in his own way; writing hard for half a day.

Reviews and newspapers all the morning; dining, drinking, and talking of a night; managing to preserve a fresh colour and perpetual flow of spirits under a wear and tear of thinking and feeding that would have knocked up all the other men I know two years ago, at least."

In this same year (1845) Thackeray figures for the first, and I believe, the only time, as an *Edinburgh Reviewer*.

The two following letters of Thackeray may fitly be inserted here. They are taken from the *Macvey-Napier Papers* in the British Museum Library. The first letter has, I believe, not been published before, while the second is of distinct literary value as giving Thackeray's opinion of Eugene Sue as a writer of fiction.

"REFORM CLUB, *Sunday, 6 April,* [1845.]

"MY DEAR SIR,—I hardly know what subject to point out as suited to my capacity—light matter connected with art, humourous reviews, critiques of novels— French subjects, memoirs, poetry, history from Louis XV. downwards and of an earlier period—that of Froissart and of Monstrelet—German light literature and poetry—though of these I know but little beyond what I learned in a year's residence in the country 14 years ago. Finally, subjects relating to society in general, where a writer may be allowed to display the humourous *ego*, or a victim is to be gently immolated. But I am better able to follow than to lead, and should hope to give satisfaction in my small way.

"Very faithfully yours, dear Sir,

"W. M. THACKERAY.

"To T. LONGMAN, ESQ."

[This letter is endorsed: "T. L. has written to Mr. Thackeray as requested by Mr. Napier. Apr. 7—'45."]

On July 16 Thackeray wrote direct to Macvey Napier as follows, suggesting an article for the *Edinburgh*.

"88, St. James St., 16 *July*, 1845.

"DEAR SIR,—I am glad to comply with your request that I should address you personally, and thank you for the letter which you have written to Mr. Longman regarding my contribution to the *Edinburgh Review*.

"Eugène Sue has written a very great number of novels—beginning with maritime novels in the *Satanic* style so to speak—full of crime and murder of every description. He met in his early work with no very great success. He gave up the indecencies of language and astonished the world with *Mathilde* three years since, which had the singular quality among French novels of containing no improprieties of expression. In my mind it is one of the most immoral books in the world. *The Mysteries of Paris* followed, with still greater success, and the same extreme cleverness of construction, and the same sham virtue. It has been sold by tens of thousands in London in various shapes, in American editions, and illustrated English translations. The book just translated is an old performance—it is called *Latreaumont* in the French original.

"To go through a course of Sue's writings would require, I should think, more than a short article—and the subject has been much dealt with in minor periodicals here.

"The *Glances at Life* is a very kindly and agreeable little book by a Cockney philosopher—could it be coupled in an article with N. P. Willis's *Dashes at Life*, which Messrs. Longman now advertise?

"A pleasant short paper might be written, I fancy, commenting upon the humours of the pair. Should the subject meet with your approval perhaps, you will give me notice; and state what space the *Review* can afford. Should you not approve I will look through Lady Hester Stanhope and hope to be able to treat it to your satisfaction. I am bringing out a little book about the Mediterranean which I hope shortly to have the pleasure of sending you.

"Dear Sir, Your very obedient Servant,
"W. M. THACKERAY.
"PROFESSOR NAPIER."

In the Correspondence of Abraham Hayward a letter is printed that Mr. Hayward received from Macvey Napier, then the Editor of the *Review:*—

"Will you tell me confidentially, of course, whether you know anything of a Mr. Thackeray, about whom Longman has written me, thinking he would be a good hand for light articles? He says that this Mr. Thackeray is one of the best writers in *Punch*. One requires to be very much on one's guard in engaging with mere strangers. In a Journal like the *Edinburgh*, it is always of importance to keep up in respect of names."

It was immediately on receipt of Hayward's answer, which must have been satisfactory—though I have not been able to find a copy of it—that Mr. Napier communicated with Thackeray.

Mr. Napier probably hesitated at entrusting a very long article to a new man, and chose the alternative—the Willis Review—which appeared in the October number, but very much mutilated; and it is to this that Thackeray refers in a charming and graceful letter to Mr. Napier, dated St. James Street, October 16, 1845:—

"MY DEAR SIR,—I have just read and acknowledge
with many thanks your banker's bill. From them or
from you, I shall always be delighted to receive communications of this nature. From your liberal payment
I can't but conclude that you reward me, not only for
labouring, but for being mutilated in your service. I
assure you I suffered cruelly by the amputation which
you were obliged to inflict upon my poor dear paper.
I mourn still—as what father can help doing for his
children?—for several lovely jokes and promising facetiæ
which were born and might have lived, but for your scis-
sors urged by ruthless necessity. I trust, however, that
there are many more which the future may bring forth,
and which will meet with more favour in your eyes. I
quite agree with your friend who says Willis was too
leniently used. O, to think of my pet passages gone
for ever!   "Very faithfully yours,
                          "W. M. THACKERAY."*

"The little book about the Mediterranean" appeared
some months later, and its full title is *Notes of a Journey
from Cornhill to Grand Cairo by way of Lisbon, Athens,
Constantinople, and Jerusalem, performed in the steamers
of the Peninsular and Oriental Company. By Mr. M. A.
Titmarsh, Author of " The Irish Sketchbook," etc.* Chapman & Hall published the volume, which bore a dedication dated December 24, 1845, to Captain Lewis.

In 1846 his writings were in the main confined to
Fraser and *Punch*. To the Magazine he sent the poem
Ronsard to his Mistress (January), *A Brother of the Press
on the History of a Literary Man, Laman Blanchard, and
the Chances of the Literary Profession* (March); *On Some*

*The Macvey-Napier Papers; Selections from the Correspond-
ence of the late Macvey Napier.*

Illustrated Children's Books (April); and *Proposals for a Continuation of "Ivanhoe" in a letter to Monsieur Alexandre Dumas* (August and September), which later, recast and expanded, appeared as *Rebecca and Rowena*.

Titmarsh versus Tait and *Jeames on the Gauge Question*, came out in *Punch*, in which paper, on February 28, appeared the first number of a long series of articles that of itself would have made the lasting reputation of many a less famous man—*The Snobs of England*. These papers were so much liked and so well received that they were continued, week after week, without any interruption, for a whole year, the last number appearing in the issue for February 27, 1847.

While these papers were being written, Thackeray gave up the chambers at 88, St. James Street, he had occupied for the last two years, and in 1846 made for himself a home at 13 (now 16) Young Street. It was when passing by this residence in after years, with Fields, the American publisher, that Thackeray exclaimed, with mock gravity, "Down on your knees, you rogue, for here *Vanity Fair* was penned; and I will go down with you, for I have a high opinion of that little production myself."

To him here in the late autumn his children were brought from Paris by Mrs. Smyth, who, however, soon returned to her husband, when her place was taken by *her* mother, who remained with the children until her death in 1848.

He was very busy, writing hard every day, and very poor nevertheless. Even *Vanity Fair*, though it brought him fame, did not increase his income. Like his father before him, he had many luxurious tastes, which he did

not always refrain from indulging,* and he never heard
a tale of distress without putting his hand in his pocket
to relieve the sufferer as far as lay in his power.

He knew he could always make money by his pen,
and, though he must have received considerable sums, he
never saved (except the proceeds of the two courses of
Lectures, which he invested for his children) until the
last years of his life.   But though he may have been
anxious about the future, he allowed nothing to interfere
with the pleasure that the arrival of his "little girls"
brought in its train.   He had them constantly with him;
and whenever he could snatch an hour or an afternoon
from his work, they went for those little outings that he
enjoyed as much as they.   He was never again separated
from them, except when they paid a visit to his parents
and when he went to America, and from this time forth
they shared all the pleasures of his life, until it pleased
God to take him from them.

*"He was a man of sensibility; he delighted in luxuriously fur-
nished and well lighted rooms, good music, excellent wines and
cookery, exhilarating talk, gay and airy gossip, pretty women and
their toilettes, and refined and noble manners, 'le bon goût, le ris,
l'aimable liberté.'   The amenities of life, and the traditions, stimu-
lated his imagination."—F. LOCKER-LAMPSON.

CHAPTER XII

THACKERAY AND THE PUBLIC

CHAPTER XII

THACKERAY AND THE PUBLIC

THE letter headed *Barmecide Banquets*, dated October 25, 1845, commences as follows:—

"MY DEAR LIONEL,—There is a comfort to think that, however, other works and masterpieces bearing my humble name have been received by the public, namely with what I cannot but think (and future age, will I have no doubt, pronounce) to be unmerited obloquy and inattention, the present article, at least, which I address to you through the public prints, will be read by every one of the numerous readers of this magazine. What a quantity of writings of the same hand have you, my dear friend, pored over! How much delicate wit, profound philosophy (lurking hid under harlequin's vermilion)— how many quiet wells of deep gushing pathos have you failed to remark as you hurried through those modest pages, for which the author himself here makes an apology!—not that I quarrel with my lot, or rebel against that meanest of martyrdoms, indifference, with which a callous age has visited me—not that I complain because I am not appreciated by the present century—no, no!— he who lives at this time ought to know better than to be vexed by its treatment of him—he who pines because Smith, or Snooks, doesn't appreciate him, has a poor, puny vein of endurance, and pays those two personages too much honour."

In this passage, apparently written in a jocular strain, I think Thackeray described his feelings. He was disappointed that the merits of his writings had not been discovered, and rather hurt that in 1846 people only said of him, as Mr. Willis had written seven years earlier: "He is one of the cleverest and most gifted of the magazine writers in London." "I can suit the magazines, but I can't suit the public, be hanged to them!" he exclaimed, with some bitterness, after the failure of *The Irish Sketch Book* to attract notice.

Now every one is well aware of his "delicate wit," "profound philosophy," and "quiet wells of gushing pathos," and Thackeray himself felt that his day must come sooner or later (only it seemed more likely to be late than early), for he was confident of his genius, though perhaps ignorant of its extent. His lightest sketches, even his airy criticisms, have a ring about them that shows he knew his powers, and in *Barry Lyndon* there cannot be detected a trace of mistrust in his capabilities. Throughout the whole romance one feels the hand of the artist working at his first great masterpiece, with absolute confidence in the ultimate success of his labours. His magazine articles were for the most part, I think, regarded by him as "pot-boilers"—even as late as 1844 he wrote: "Poor fellows of the pen and pencil! we must live. The public likes light literature, and we write it. Here am I writing magazine jokes and follies, and why? Because the public likes such, and will purchase no other."

Ainsworth published *Rookwood* when he was twenty-nine; Disraeli was famous as the author of *Vivian Grey* at two-and-twenty, and had written *The Young Duke*, *Contarini Fleming*, *The Revolutionary Epick*, *Alroy*,

Henrietta Temple, and *Venetia*, before he was eleven years older; Albert Smith was only twenty-eight when he made his mark with the *Adventures of Mr. Ledbury;* Dickens had written *Sketches by Boz* when he was four-and-twenty, *Pickwick* a year later, and *Oliver Twist*, *Nicholas Nickleby*, *The Old Curiosity Shop*, *Barnaby Rudge*, and *American Notes*, before he was thirty. Yet Thackeray, in his thirty-sixth year, was unknown outside his circle. In this chapter I shall endeavour to show how it was success came to him so (comparatively) late in life. It has been said that this was due to the fact that his genius took longer to mature than that, let us say, of his contemporary Dickens; but I am confident that this statement is unsound, even though Dickens wrote *Pickwick* when he was twenty-five, and at the same age Thackeray had written nothing of any importance—the *Great Hoggarty Diamond* not being written until he was thirty, or *Barry Lyndon* until three years after. This admission might induce the superficial observer to jump to conclusions and admit the plausibility of the argument; but there are weighty reasons beneath the surface which upset such hasty judgments. Dickens was, almost from his childhood, connected with journalism, and, not unnaturally, at a very early age tried his hand at short stories, which, meeting with success, induced him to attempt something more ambitious, which became *Pickwick!* Thackeray's life was very different. Dickens was almost entirely self-educated, and was probably a reporter while Thackeray was still at Cambridge, or on his travels. Then, be it remembered, Thackeray was entered at the Middle Temple when he came of age, and though he may not have studied hard, yet as he was a man of means he had no need to turn

to Literature for bread.   Even when he lost his fortune,
it was to Art, and not to Literature, that he looked for
a living; and almost as late as the publication of *Pickwick*, Edinburgh Reviewer Hayward well remembered
seeing him "day after day, engaged in copying pictures
in the Louvre, in order to qualify himself for his profession."

S'asseoir entre deux selles, le cul à terres, is a proverb
of by no means recent origin; and if Art and Letters
stand for the two stools it is easy to find at least one
reason why Thackeray did not write *Barry Lyndon* when
he was five-and-twenty.

See how Anthony Trollope, in the biographical introduction to the volume in the "Men of Letters" series,
on "Thackeray," has endeavoured to solve the problem.
He tells how Thackeray had a marked want of assurance,
("I can fancy," Trollope says, "that as the sheets went
from him every day, he told himself, with regard to
every sheet, that it was a failure.   Dickens was quite
sure of his sheet"); that he was "unsteadfast, idle,
changeable of purpose, aware of his own intellect, but
not trusting it"; and lastly, that "no man ever failed
more than he to put his best foot foremost."   Now, this
explanation is, on the face of it, most unconvincing, and,
what is far worse, misleading.   Though Dickens, and
Trollope also, we may be certain, felt quite sure of their
sheets, it does not seem to me to have anything to do
with the question—though if it has, or even if it has not,
it is something Thackeray never overcame.

But then, perhaps this dissatisfaction with his work
was because, besides being a novelist, Thackeray was an
artist to his finger-tips, and that, while lesser men might
turn away from their completed work with a self-satisfied

smile, Thackeray would glance at his mournfully, re-read it perhaps, and think, not whether the public would like it, but how far from perfect in *his* eyes were the pages he had written. Indeed, all his life long he was conscious that his work might be improved, and it was with a sigh that he sent the sheets from him to the printer.

The other charges of idleness, etc., may be left alone for the moment, while I do my best to explain the reason that deferred the popular acknowledgment of his genius until he was thirty-seven years old.

The reason is startling: *Thackeray had not given the public a fair chance to discover him*—I hope I can prove it convincingly.

Remember the number of pseudonyms he used. Had he elected always to write over *Titmarsh* this would have been perfectly immaterial. *Titmarsh* would have been as much appreciated as "Thackeray" should have been. But, besides his contributions to *Punch* over various fantastic signatures, and the anonymous work for the magazines and journals, while *Michael Angelo Titmarsh* wrote most of the reviews in *Fraser*, *The Great Hoggarty Diamond*, *The Sketch Book*, and a host of short stories, it was *Ikey Solomon* who wrote *Catherine*, *Yellowplush* who wrote the *Correspondence* and *Diary*, *Major Gahagan* who wrote his own *Tremendous Adventures*,* *The Professor*, and *Sultan Stork*, and who supplied Mr. *Wagstaff* with material for one of the four stories credited to that gentleman. *Fitz-Boodle* wrote his own *Confessions*, *Professions*, *Men's Wives*, and *The Luck of Barry Lyndon;* and Thackeray, under his own name, only *Captain*

*It is true that when republished in the *Comic Tales and Sketches* Mr. *Titmarsh* edited these two stories.

Rook and Mr. Pigeon, *The Fashionable Authoress*, and *Going to see a Man Hanged*.

This rendered it difficult even for the initiated to recognise all his work, and to the average reader each name suggested a different author.

Thackeray himself has explained the necessity that drove him to the use of so many *noms-de-plume*. "It may so happen to a literary man," he wrote in *Brown on the Press*, "that the stipend which he receives from one publication is not sufficient to boil his family pot, and that he must write in some other quarter. If Brown writes articles in the daily papers, and articles in the weekly and monthly periodicals too, and signs the same, he surely weakens his force by extending his line. It would be better for him to write *incognito* than to placard his name in so many quarters—as actors understand, who do not perform in too many pieces on the same night, and as painters, who know it is not worth their while to exhibit more than a certain number of pictures."

He also realised that this was not the high-road to fame. "It cannot be denied," he says in the same article, "that men of signal ability will write for years in papers and perish unknown—and in so far their lot is a hard one, and the chances of life are against them. It is hard upon a man, with whose work the whole town is ringing, that not a soul should know or care who is the author who so delights the public."

Then, too, it must be remembered that the only *books* he had published before *Vanity Fair* were *The Paris Sketch Book* and *Comic Tales and Sketches*, which were reprinted magazine articles of not the greatest value; *The Irish Sketch Book* and *From Cornhill to Grand Cairo*, both interesting, intelligent, and cleverly written; and

the notoriously unpopular *Second Funeral of Napoleon.*
Now all these books are very excellent reading—for
though Thackeray's magazine articles might be hack-
work, they were undoubtedly very superior hack-work—
but they scarcely showed that a new genius had arisen;
and even to-day these early books are among the least
read of Thackeray's works.

Of course, I know it will be objected that no mention is made of the best of Thackeray's early writings—
*The Great Hoggarty Diamond, The Luck of Barry Lyn-
don,* and *The Snobs of England*—and I have purposely
avoided naming these, for the first two had only appeared,
and the last was *still* appearing in the *periodicals,* and I
do not think it can be denied that even we, who know
their value, would fully appreciate the beauty of the two
tales, had we first so read them then, one in four, the
other in a dozen doses, there being a month's interval
between the doses. This objection, however, is somewhat
discounted in the case of the *Snob Papers,* as *they* might,
without losing their charm, indeed with advantage, be
read singly, being really only so many units, bound
together at the fountain head. But this does not
destroy my reasoning, for who, among the public, knew
that the "Snobographer" was Mr. *Titmarsh?*

This very simple explanation is, in my opinion, the
true solution of the somewhat complex problem.

But there may be some readers who may not yet be
convinced. For them let me adduce additional argu-
ments.

Let us suppose that the public, with wonderful discernment, had recognised all his writings, and let us
further suppose that, recognising them, the public had
had every chance to read them, and *had* read them—how

much would the position be changed? Not very much, I think. He would have been more appreciated by the few, perhaps, but just as much neglected by the many.

One important reason for this is that while most of his contemporaries, in spite of (or perhaps because of) this fine quality, appealed to the gallery, and on occasions were not above playing to it. Thackeray, so far from lowering himself to the level of the public, held it the duty of the artist to educate it to his own intellectual level — a performance painfully slow and not at all remunerative to the tutor.*

Apart from the high intellectual level of Thackeray's writings, nothing would induce him to abate one jot of his prejudices to suit the taste of the public, though no one knew better than he what would suit the majority of novel-readers.

"I suppose," he said in one of his lectures on the *Humourists*, "I suppose as long as novels last, and authors aim at interesting their public, there must always be in the story a virtuous and gallant hero, a wicked monster, his opposite, and a pretty girl who finds a champion: bravery and virtue conquer beauty, and vice, after seeming to triumph through a certain number of pages, is sure to be discomfited in the last volume, when

---

*There is another similar instance in the case of the popularity of the greatest of our living novelists—the only name of our day that may without absurdity be mentioned in the same breath with Thackeray. Mr. George Meredith published his first volume of poems when *The Newcomes* was still lisping in numbers: his earliest masterpiece, *The Ordeal of Richard Feverel*, when he was thirty-one (in 1859); and even this remained practically unknown to the reading public until the last few years. Even to-day, after the *Egoist* and *Diana of the Crossways* have appeared, the circle of his readers is absurdly small, and Mr. Meredith is unappreciated, unknown even beyond the little world of those who see the "Master's" genius. And the only reason for the lack of popularity is, the public is not yet educated up to Mr. Meredith's standard of intellect.

justice overtakes him, and honest folks come by their own. There never was perhaps a greatly popular story but this simple plot was carried through it: mere satiric wit is addressed to a class of readers quite different to those simple souls who laugh and weep over the novel. I fancy very few ladies indeed could be brought to like *Gulliver* heartily, and (putting the coarseness and difference of manners out of the question) to relish the wonderful satire of *Jonathan Wild*."

Yet, knowing this, and anxious as he was to obtain the approbation of his female readers, he bravely and deliberately wrote on in his own way, preaching his own philosophy, and indulging in his own satiric humour; even the finest work he produced before *Vanity Fair* must be included in the same class as *Jonathan Wild*—a work which has never been popular with the general reader. When a critic accuses him—as some few still do—of having preached his cynical philosophy for profit, let them consider how much more profitable it would have been for him to write in the style of Bulwer, or Lever, or Disraeli, as he so clearly showed he could have done. To give an example: What success would probably have rewarded the *Second Funeral of Napoleon* had he written to please the public, instead of presenting the work to a hero-loving nation in a form that he *knew* ran counter to the feelings of the book-buyers. Read an extract from the volume:—

"I feel that you are angry. I can see from here the pouting of your lips, and know what you are going to say. You are going to say, 'I will read no more of this Mr. Titmarsh. There is no subject, however solemn, but he treats it with flippant reverence, and no character, however great, at whom he does not sneer.'

"Ah, my dear! you are young now and enthusiastic, and your Titmarsh is old, very old, sad, and grey-headed. I have seen a poor mother buy a halfpenny wreath at the gate of Montmartre burying-ground, and go with it to her little child's grave, and hang it there over the humble little stone; and if ever you saw me scorn the mean offering of the poor, shabby creature, I will give you leave to be as angry as you will. . . . Something great and good must have been in this man" [Napoleon], "something loving and kindly, that has kept his name so cherished in the popular memory, and gained him such lasting reverence and affection.

"But, madam, one may respect the dead without feeling awestricken at the plumes of the hearse; and I see no reason why one should sympathise with the train of mutes and undertakers, however deep may be their mourning."

But that was Thackeray all over. As he said in the *Charity and Humour* lecture:—

"The author of this work" [*Vanity Fair*] "has lately been described by the London *Times* newspaper as a writer of considerable parts, but a dreary misanthrope, who sees no good anywhere, who sees the sky above him green, I think, instead of blue, and only miserable sinners around him. So we are, as is every writer and reader I ever heard of, so was every being who ever trod this earth, save One. I cannot help telling the truth as I view it, and describing what I see. To describe it otherwise than it seems to me would be falsehood in that calling in which it has pleased Heaven to place me; treason to that conscience which says that men are weak; that truth must be told; that faults must be owned; that pardon must be prayed for; and that Love reigns supreme over all."

There is Thackeray's confession of literary faith.

But I can further support my statement that Thackeray would not have been a popular writer, even if his writings had been more widely known, with the sweeping assertion that all his earlier work, in spite of its cleverness, in spite of its wit and wisdom, and in spite of, or more probably because of, its very truth, is most unpleasant and painful reading.*

Let me briefly discuss these writings—I take the appearance of the *Snob Papers* as bringing to a close the first part of his literary life. This is no arbitrary decision, for it is the rightly drawn boundary-line that separates the clever and brilliant, but unrecognised, writer of magazine articles and short stories from the successful novelist. They are best divided into (I) art-criticisms and literary reviews, and (II) tales and sketches.

The former will be treated in later chapters. The articles themselves are shrewd, sensible, honest, and painstaking, and undoubtedly deliberately amusing for the most part. But, though they are well worth reading, both for the views advocated and for the style, they are not such as to make or mar a man's reputation, and no great appreciation would be awarded to the author by the average reader.

It is with the latter we must concern ourselves. Leaving his shorter stories out of the question, let us devote our attention to those upon which his earlier reputation is based: *The Yellowplush Correspondence, Some*

---

* "I really don't know where I get all these rascals for my books. I have certainly never lived with such people," Thackeray said to Mr. J. E. Cooke.

Passages in the Life of Major Gahagan, Catherine, A Shabby Genteel Story, The Great Hoggarty Diamond, The Fitz-Boodle Papers, including *Men's Wives* and *The Luck of Barry Lyndon.*

Putting aside *Major Gahagan*, which is a delightful extravaganza, and far more amusing than *Munchausen*, there is not another quite pleasant story to be found.

They are wonderfully clever. Their literary merit is astonishing: the style is mature, the word-pictures are delightful, and there are some charming touches, and some beautiful passages that are Thackerayesque in their tenderness; but their predominant feature is intelligence, and when has the great reading public admired a book only because it is intellectual? It must be admitted that the public is right not to admire such, for it is a truism that a story suggesting chiefly the cleverness, or the wit, or the brilliancy of the writer is not a complete success— it shows there is a something wanting in the story itself. Readers ask more than this, and the taste that demands that the writer's genius shall not be thought of until the book is laid down, finished, is quite sound.

All the books are clever. *Catherine* is wonderful, Carlyle quite rightly said; and no one but Fielding and its author could have written the marvellous *Barry Lyndon:* but there is a want of heart, and lack of tenderness, and the books have really kept their position by virtue of the genius that created them: one is impressed by the author, one is depressed by the book.

There can be no doubt that for these early works Thackeray drew upon his own unhappy experiences; and these, together with the cynicism that all clever young men affect, give his stories a certain harshness that makes them compare unfavourably with his maturer productions. His purpose was honest enough: he fought

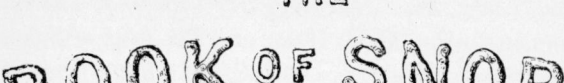

THE
BOOK OF SNOBS

By

W M Thackeray.

LONDON: PUNCH OFFICE, 85, FLEET STREET.

[Price 2s. 6d.]

against snobbishness and vulgarity; against gambling, against company-promoting swindlers, against the *Jack Sheppard* class of novels — indeed, against everything that did not appeal to him as simple and honourable. But he did not select his weapons carefully; he fought with the button off the foil, and *à l' outrance*. It may be taken as an axiom that all the principal characters in his early books are (more or less) swindlers, scoundrels, hypocrites, or fools. The briefest examination of these writings shown it to have been so.

Yellowplush, who is taken from the gutter, sees no reason why he should not listen at key-holes, or read his master's letters, pry into his private affairs, or do a hundred other dirty actions—he has no more than a swiftly passing pang of remorse when, for a bank-note, he sells the master, who, with all his faults, was too good to him. All the people he knows do things of this sort, and he sees no particular cause for shame.

The naturalness of the *Correspondence* is its greatest merit—perhaps its chief fault against nature is that so many unpleasant people could scarcely be found together.

In the farce there is the picture of the Shum family's wretched life, the cowardly husband, the bullying wife, the objectionable daughter, but out of the gloom comes Altamont, a good fellow, and the rather lovable Mary. Look at the actors in the tragedy — for tragedy it is undoubtedly: the scamp Yellowplush, the sharper Blewitt, the silly and snobbish Dawkins, the revengeful Lady Griffin, the insignificant Jemima, the terrible Earl, and Deuceace himself, card-sharper, swindler, fortune-hunter. Only the foolish Matilda remains, and for her loyalty much may be forgiven her: "My Lord, my place is with *him*."

In these *Papers* Thackeray meant to draw the moral that roguery comes to a bad end, but he overreached himself. Deuceace does come to a bad end, so far that is right enough, but the retribution that falls upon him is planned by his own father; this occasions a revulsion of feeling which causes the sympathy to be with the swindler until the end,—the most sensational Thackeray ever employed. There is nothing in all his writings so terrible.

In *Catherine*, the history of jail-birds, told by one of them, we do not look for virtuous people. Mrs. Cat, Brock, Galgenstein, Thomas Billings, John Hayes, Mrs. Scare, and Ensign Macshane, in their several ways, are as bad as bad can be—so vicious, indeed, that the sympathy is rather with the murderess; in such company she could hardly be other than she is.

The *Shabby Genteel Story*, which shows distinct signs of growing power, presents another group of objectionable people. It opens with a description of Margate lodging-house society, and concludes with a mock marriage, into which the family Cinderella, a loving, trusting girl, is trapped. Mr. Gann, a ruined tradesman, drunk three times a week with the liquor imbibed at the "Bag o' Nails"; Mrs. Gann and her two daughters by a first marriage; the Misses Macarty, shrews, with lady-like pretensions; the tuft-hunting scoundrel Brandon, Tuft-hunt himself, and the blackguard Cinqbars,—are the *dramatis personæ*, which is only partially brightened by the honest but vulgar Fitch. The most displeasing, though not the least clever, of all the tales.

It is quite a relief to turn to *The Great Hoggarty Diamond*, for that at least is more artistic than anything he had then written; and at last on his literary horizon good simple people begin to be sighted, though they are still outnumbered by hypocrites and snobs. There is a dreadful Aunt in the story, and a marvellous picture of a swindling company-promoter. But pathos and growing tenderness are to be noted, especially in the handling of Sam's mother and wife; and the death of a child is beautifully and reverently described. But humour is sadly lacking and, in spite of its many beauties—I state it trembling—I am afraid *The Great Hoggarty Diamond* is *dull*.

Fitz-Boodle, however, is undoubtedly a humourist. In his *Confessions* there are many touches that suggest the older Thackeray. He is a good-hearted scamp, and amusing enough. His love-affairs are well told, and though Minna Lowe is a mean little wretch—let us hope she was forced by her father and *fiancé*, scoundrels both—yet Dorothea, silly, sweet Dorothea, and that sketch for Blanche Amori, Ottilia—I wonder if they were both drawn from Carlyle's friend—are pleasanter and more interesting. They are all three very real. Most of us have met Dorothea and Ottilia, though perhaps our Ottilias have not over-eaten themselves—some of us have known Minnas too, perhaps. But Fitz cannot be forgiven for writing those scandalous chronicles of his friends' private lives—*Men's Wives*. Curiously enough, it is the last one of these, the ——'s [*Executioner's*] *Wife*, which has never been reprinted in his collected works, the story of a heartless coquette and of a brother's revenge, that seems to me the most admirable. The others are stories of mean lives without any redeeming sun-rays to enliven the surrounding gloom. The scoun-

drel Walker, the blackguard Boroski, the humbug Sir
George, the foolish Ravenswing herself (though *she*
improves with age), the dragon-like Mrs. Berry, and the
selfish, vain, snobbish, and terribly vulgar Mrs. Dennis
Haggarty—the history of Dennis is a tragedy second
only to that of Deuceace,—are so many people whom
we would rather not know, and of whom we would certainly rather not read.

And now, *Barry Lyndon!*—the greatest of all these
stories and the first in which the author's genius shines
unfettered.

"In that strange apologue" [*Jonathan Wild*], Thackeray wrote in one of the lectures on the *Humourists*, "the
author takes for a hero the greatest rascal, coward,
traitor, tyrant, hypocrite, that his wit and experience,
both large in this matter, could enable him to devise or
depict; he accompanies this villain through all the
transactions of his life, with a grinning deference and a
wonderful mock respect, and doesn't leave him till he
is dangling at the gallows, when the satirist makes him
a low bow and wishes the scoundrel good-day."

This is what Thackeray has done in *Barry Lyndon*,
only he lets his scoundrel die of *delirium tremens* in the
nineteenth year of his residence in the Fleet Prison.
The stroke of genius that induced him to make Barry tell
his own adventures in all good faith, places the story on
a literary plane higher even than that of Fielding's novel.
Not so good or so pure as *The Great Hoggarty Diamond*,
but how much grander a conception! The humour, the
satire, the remorseless irony—read the speech where
Barry defends cheating at cards—the pictures of life presented, the minor characters depicted, place it not very
far below *Esmond* itself in the list of Thackeray's works.

There is no short story in the language more artistically beautiful than the *Princess's Tragedy*.*

But just as *Jonathan Wild* is the most neglected of Fielding's works, so *Barry Lyndon* is the least read of all Thackeray's. Work of genius though it be, it is an unpleasant story, as its author fully realised.

"Wherever shines the sun, you are sure to find Folly basking in it. Knavery is the shadow at Folly's heels," Thackeray wrote in his character sketch of *Captain Rook and the Pigeon*. Yet it seems as if he had not quite grasped the fact that there are things other than folly or knavery to write about, and that a surfeit of rogues has an unpleasant after-effect.

"Oh! for a little manly, honest, God-relying simplicity, cheerful, unaffected, and humble!" Thackeray had prayed many years before, in one of his earliest reviews; but it was only with *Vanity Fair* that he began to *give* them.

*This was suggested by an episode in the book, now little known, entitled *L'Empire, ou dix ans sous Napoleon*.

CHAPTER XIII

"VANITY FAIR"

CHAPTER XIII

"VANITY FAIR"

L ET the cause be what it may, the undisputed fact remains that in 1846 Thackeray was unknown outside literary circles and his own intimate friends. Indeed, many years after this time he complained to Mr. Fields that he was nearly forty years old before he was recognised in Literature as belonging to a class of writers at all above the orginary magazinists of his day. "I turned off far better things then," he said, "than I do now, and I wanted money sadly (my parents were rich, but respectable, and I had spent all my guineas in my youth); but how little I got for my work! It makes me laugh at what the *Times* pays me now, when I think of the old days, and how much better I wrote for them then, and got a shilling where I now get ten."

Now Thackeray was thirty-five in 1846, and he was undoubtedly discontented with his lot; and, seeing his juniors and inferiors pass him in the race for popularity and fame, he thought that at last the time had come for him to exert his great powers to make *his* name a household word, to occupy his proper place at the head of his profession, and above all, to make money to lay aside for his wife and children. It was such thoughts as these that led, early in January, 1847, to the appearance of the first number of *Vanity Fair*.

On January 2 he wrote to his friend, Professor Aytoun:—

"I think I have never had any ambition hitherto, or cared what the world thought my work, good or bad; but now the truth forces itself upon me, if the world will once take to admiring Titmarsh, all his guineas will be multiplied by ten. Guineas are good. I have got children, only ten years more to the fore say, etc.; now is the time, my lad, to make your A when the sun at length has begun to shine. Well, I think if I can make a push at the present minute—if my friends will shout, Titmarsh for ever! hurrah for, etc., etc.,—I may go up with a run to a pretty fair place in my trade, and be allowed to appear before the public among the first fiddles. But my tunes must be heard in the streets, and organs must grind them. Ha! now do you read me?

"Why don't *Blackwood* give me an article? Because he refused the best story I ever wrote?" [*The Great Hoggarty Diamond.*]* "Colburn refused the present 'Novel without a Hero,' and if any man at Blackwood's or Colburn's, and if any man since—fiddle-de-dee. Upon my word and honour I never said so much about myself before; but I know this, if I had the command of Blackwood, and a humouristical person like Titmarsh should come up, and labour hard and honestly (please God) for ten years, I would give him a hand. Now try, like a man, revolving these things in your soul, and see if you

---

*Mrs. Oliphant has spoken of Thackeray in her book on *William Blackwood and His Sons*: "About the same time" [December, 1839] "there is talk in one of Alexander's letters of sending back a bundle of prose and verse mingled, written by Thackeray, who had published *The Yellowplush Papers*. I believe it was *The Irish Sketch Book*. The *Sketches* were not in those days considered good enough for the Magazine." But *The Irish Sketch Book* was not written until after the visit to Ireland in 1842. A friend subsequently wrote introducing him, and Thackeray offered to do some "gossiping" articles—a sort of *Roundabout Paper;* but his first communication was neglected, and he never wrote again.

VANITY FAIR:

PEN AND PENCIL SKETCHES OF ENGLISH SOCIETY.

BY W. M. THACKERAY.

Author of "The Irish Sketch Book:" "Journey from Cornhill to Grand Cairo:" of "Jeames's Diary"
and the "Snob Papers" in Punch : &c. &c.

LONDON:

PUBLISHED AT THE PUNCH OFFICE, 85, FLEET STREET.

J. MENZIES, EDINBURGH ; J. M'LEOD, GLASGOW ; J. M'GLASHAN, DUBLIN.

1848.

[Bradbury & Evans, Printers, Whitefriars.]

can't help me. . . . And if I can but save a little money, by the Lord I'll try and keep it.

"Some day, when less selfish, I will write to you about other matters than the present *ego*. . . . I have my children with me, and am mighty happy in that paternal character—preside over legs of mutton comfortably—go to church at early morning and like it—pay rates and taxes, etc., etc. Between this line and the above a man has brought me the *Times* on the *Battle of Life*. 'Appy Dickens! But I love Pickwick and Crummles too much to abuse this great man. *Aliquando bonus*. And you, young man, coming up in the world full of fight, take counsel from a venerable and peaceful gladiator who has stripped for many battles. Gad, sir, this caution is a very good sign. Do you remember how complimentary Scott and Goethe were? I like the patriarchal air of some people."*

Some ten days afterwards, however, Thackeray determined to have no friendly puff. Let *Vanity Fair* stand or fall on its own merits; his pride asserted itself in another letter to Aytoun.†

"I have been thinking of the other matter on which I unbosomed myself to you, and withdraw my former letter. Puffs are good and the testimony of good men; but I don't think these will make a success for a man, and he ought to stand as the public chooses to put him,

---

Memoirs of Professor Aytoun. By Sir Theodore Martin.

†Though Thackeray refused all extraneous aid for himself, he would nevertheless do all he could for others, as the following extracts from letters to Mr. Bedingfield show:—
   (i) December 21, 1843. "I shall give you a notice in *Fraser* in the February number; but I tell you it's no use."
   (ii) November —, 1847. "Don't be displeased at my not reviewing you. By Jove, I have not time to do half what I ought to do, and have books upon books on my table at this minute—all the works of private friends who want a criticism. Yours distractedly, W. M. T."

I will try, please God, to do my best, and the money will come, perhaps, some day! Meanwhile a man so lucky as myself has no cause to complain. So let all puffing alone, though, as you know, I am glad if I can have, and deserve your good opinion. The women like *Vanity Fair*, I find, very much, and the publishers are quite in good spirits regarding that venture. This is all I have to say—in the solitude of midnight—with a quiet cigar, and the weakest gin and water in the world, ruminating over a child's fall, from which I have just come, having gone as chaperon to my little girls. One of them had her hair plaited in two tails, the other had ringlets and the most fascinating bows of blue ribbon. It was very merry and likewise sentimental. We went in a fly quite genteel, and law! what a comfort it was when it was over. Adyou."*

"I wonder whether this will take, the publishers accept it and the world read it," Thackeray said when he began to write *Vanity Fair;* and though the publishers had accepted it, it still seemed doubtful if the world would read. The earlier numbers failed to attract attention, and even the advisability of stopping its publication was mooted; but fortunately, later in the year, the sale increasing with great strides, the success of the venture was assured.

There has been much speculation as to what caused the change from failure to such brilliant success, and many reasons have been suggested. Some will have it that the change in the public attitude was the result of an article in the *Edinburgh Review* for January, 1848; while others insist that the attention of the world to the merits of the work was attracted by *Currer Bell's* eulogistic

Memoirs of Professor Aytoun. By Sir Theodore Martin.

dedication to Thackeray prefixed to the second edition of *Jane Eyre*. Thackeray himself always insisted that it was the success of his first Christmas book, *Mrs. Perkyns' Ball*, that made him popular.

No doubt the review, the dedication especially, and the Christmas Book, each gave an impetus to the sale of the novel, but I think the most probable and simple explanation is that the book recommended itself by the greater interest that was to be found in its pages as it progressed; and I am to a certain extent supported in this belief by a letter written in May (1847) by Fitzgerald: "Thackeray is progressing greatly in his line: he publishes a novel in Nos.—*Vanity Fair*—which began dull I thought, but gets better every number." However, not every one found the earlier parts dull. A friend wrote to Thackeray, after two or three numbers had come out: "Don't get nervous or think about criticism or trouble yourself about the opinions of friends; you have completely beaten Dickens out of the inner circle already;" and Mrs. Carlyle wrote in September (1847) to her husband: "I brought away the last four numbers of *Vanity Fair*, and read one of them during the night. Very good indeed, beats Dickens out of the world."

People in 1847 were accustomed to buy their fiction in green-covered monthly parts, which overflowed with exaggerated humour and extravagant pathos; or in pink-covered numbers, containing brilliantly inaccurate and thoroughly enjoyable descriptions of Irish or army life; and not unnaturally they did not at first take kindly to the less exciting, though far more intellectual and artistic sketches of English society, that were offered in the yellow wrappers. Yet even during the time of the greatest success of *Vanity Fair*, only about six thousand copies of a number were sold, while the circulation of the parts of Dickens's novels was frequently as much as twenty or twenty-five thousand.

But though *Vanity Fair* may not have appealed to the general public as Dickens and Lever did, yet it is plain that among the literary class, and in what is known as "Society," Thackeray had now established a foremost place. Such high-class journals as the *Spectator* specially praised the novel as it was coming out in serial parts. The following interesting letter appeared in a recent issue of that journal (*Spectator*, January 14, 1899), and quite bears out what has been said as to the effect produced by *Vanity Fair* on the more educated and refined portions of the community :—

THACKERAY AND THE "SPECTATOR."
[TO THE EDITOR OF THE "SPECTATOR."]

SIR,—May I, as an old lady entitled to be reminiscent and garrulous, "bestow my tediousness upon you" in a little anecdote which relates to the *Spectator?* In 1847 we were living in Paris in the Rue Neuve de Berri. One morning I saw my father (Admiral—then Captain—Wormeley) putting the *Spectator* into his coat-pocket. "Oh! father," I cried, "please don't take it away. It only came this morning." "Yes, yes, my dear," he answered; "I must take it at once to Mrs. Carmichael Smyth. It has a nice review of her son's serial in it. Only yesterday she was lamenting to me that no notice seemed to be taken by the Press of William's book, while so much was being said of Dickens's new novel, and, for her part, she did not see that *Dombey and Son* was more worthy of notice than *Vanity Fair."* They were both coming out as serials,—*Vanity Fair* in yellow covers, *Dombey* in green.

I am, Sir, etc.,

E. W. LATIMER.

714, PARK AVENUE, BATIMORE, MARYLAND,
December 30th.

It is quite conceivable that *Currer Bell's* dedication, dated December 21, 1847, may have hastened the general recognition of the genius of the *Snobographer;* for although now *Vanity Fair* is held to be the greater work, yet we have it on the authority of Sara Coleridge that it was not so popular, even in 1847, as *Jane Eyre.*

The identity of *Currer Bell* had not then been revealed, and many were the guesses as to who the writer could be. In October, 1848, Thackeray wrote to Mrs. Brookfield, saying:—

"Old Dilke of the *Athenæum* vows that Procter (Barry Cornwall) and his wife between them wrote *Jane Eyre*, and when I protest ignorance, says, 'Pooh! you know who wrote it; you are the deepest rogue in England, etc.'; I wonder whether it can be true? It is just possible; and then, what a singular circumstance is the cross-fire of the two dedications (*Jane Eyre* to Thackeray, *Vanity Fair* to Barry Cornwall*").

I quote part of this dedication, which is very interesting still, even if only on account of the misdirected eulogy it contains:—

"There is a man in our own days whose words are not framed to tickle delicate ears: who, to my thinking comes before the great ones of society—much as the son of Imlah comes before the throned Kings of Judah and

Israel; and who speaks truth as deep, with a power as prophet-like and as vital—a mien as dauntless and as daring. Is the satirist of *Vanity Fair* admired in high places? I cannot tell; but I think if some of those amongst whom he hurls the Greek fire of his sarcasm, and over whom he flashes the levin brand of his denunciation, were to take his warnings in time, they or their seed might yet escape a fatal Ramoth-Gilead.

"Why have I alluded to this man? I have alluded to him, Reader, because I think I see in him an intellect profounder and more unique than his contemporaries have yet recognised; because I regard him as the first social regenerator of the day—as the very master of that working corps who would restore to rectitude the warped system of things; because I think no commentator on his writings has yet found the comparison that suits him, the terms which rightly characterise his talent. They say he is like Fielding: they talk of his wit, humour, comic powers. He resembles Fielding as an eagle does a vulture: Fielding could stoop on carrion, but Thackeray never does. His wit is bright, his humour attractive, but both bear the same relation to his serious genius that lambent steel lightning playing under the edge of the summer cloud does to the electric death-spark hid in its womb. Finally, I have alluded to Mr. Thackeray because to him—if he will accept the tribute of a total stranger—I have dedicated this second edition of *Jane Eyre.*"

In the *Correspondence of Abraham Hayward* it has been told how, when a few numbers of *Vanity Fair* had appeared, it was thought that Mr. Hayward might consent to review them in the *Edinburgh Review*. He was very good-natured about it, but happened to be busied about

other things, and fancied he could not undertake it.
Mrs. Procter, however, kindly undertook to mark the
passages which might be usefully quoted, and Hayward
thereupon consented and wrote a review upon the basis
furnished by Mrs. Procter, and "the review—because
praising a work really adorable and then only imperfectly
known to the general public—had an immense effect,
and accelerated the recognition of Mr. Thackeray's reputation and power."

Although I cannot speak from actual knowledge, I am
inclined to doubt the immense effect of the review, for
this effect would only be produced amongst the readers
of the quarterly, who are only to be found in the cultured class; and even the readers of the *Edinburgh
Review* itself are not legion. Again, the article appeared
in January, 1848, when more than half the book had
already appeared, and when, I think, the commercial
success of the novel had been established.

But even while objecting that too much stress has
been laid upon the great help that the article rendered
to the success of the book, I willingly admit the service
Mr. Hayward did for the reputation of the author, and
that the article is fair enough except in parts, where the
reviewer seems to have been afraid that his enthusiasm
would run away with his pen, and has endeavoured to
steady himself by setting to work to discover imaginary
faults. The review opened as follows: "Full many a
valuable truth has been sent undulating through the air
by men who have lived and died unknown. At the
present moment the rising generation are supplied with
the best of their mental aliment by writers whose names
are a dead letter to the mass; and among the most
remarkable of these is Michael Angelo Titmarsh, alias

William Makepeace Thackeray, author of *The Irish Sketch Book*, of *A Journey from Cornhill to Grand Cairo*, of *Jeames's Diary*, of *The Snob Papers* in *Punch*, of *Vanity Fair*, etc., etc.,'' all of which works the reviewer criticises, dealing with *Vanity Fair*, as far as it had gone (the first eleven numbers). And the article concluded: ''A writer with such a pen as Mr. Thackeray's is an acquisition of real and high value in our literature. High life, middle life, and low life are (or very soon will be) pretty nearly the same to him: he has fancy as well as feeling: he can laugh or cry without grimacing: he can skim the surface, and he can penetrate to the core. Let the public give him encouragement, and let him give himself time, and we can fearlessly prophesy that he will soon become one of the acknowledged heads of his own peculiar walk of literature.''

''*Vanity Fair*,'' said the Edinburgh Reviewer, ''is as sure of immortality as ninety-nine hundredths of modern novels are sure of annihilation.''

Even to this day a general belief exists that *Vanity Fair* was hawked round the town, and offered and rejected here, there, and everywhere, before Messrs. Bradbury & Evans, the proprietors and publishers of *Punch*, brought it out in twenty monthly parts.

This view is absolutely erroneous. All the evidence I have collected points to an entirely different conclusion. Mr. Trollope says, ''We are aware that the monthly nurses of periodical literature did not at first smile on the effort. The proprietors of magazines did not see their way to undertake *Vanity Fair*, and the publishers are said to have generally looked shy upon it.'' Mr. Marzials tells us that ''*Vanity Fair* itself, *Vanity Fair*, one of the unquestioned masterpieces of English literature, was rejected by *Colburn's Magazine*." Even Mrs. Ritchie says, in her Biographical Introduction to the novel, "One has heard of the journeys which the manuscript made to various publishers' houses before it could find one ready to undertake the venture, and how long its appearance was delayed by various doubts and hesitations."

On the other hand Mr. Vizetelly, who saw a great deal of Thackeray about this time, has told what I take to be the true tale. "The hawking about of *Vanity Fair*," he said, in the *Glances Back Through Seventy Years*, "of course presupposed that the manuscript was complete, and was submitted in this state to the half score fatuous fools who declined it with thanks, but I'm positive that, when arrangements were made with Messrs. Bradbury & Evans for the publication of the work, with no further knowledge on their part of its nature than could be gleaned from Mr. Thackeray during a brief interview, nothing beyond number one was written. I have no doubt whatever that the publishers of *Vanity Fair* bought it—like most works by known authors are purchased—solely on its writer's then reputation, which his *Snobs of England* in *Punch* had greatly extended." And then Mr. Vizetelly supports his statement by adding the following passage: "One afternoon, when he [Thackeray] called in Peterborough Court [at Vizetelly's offices] he had a small brown paper parcel with him, and opened it to show me his two careful drawings for the page plates to the first number of *Vanity Fair*. Tied up with them was the manuscript of the earlier part of the book, of which he had several times spoken to me, referring to the quaint character that Chiswick Mall—within a stone's throw of which I was then living—still retained. His

present intention, he told me, was to see Bradbury &
Evans, and offer the work to them. . . . In little
more than half an hour Thackeray again made his appearance, and, with a beaming face, gleefully informed me
that he had settled the business. 'Bradbury & Evans,'
he said, 'accepted so readily that I am deuced sorry I
didn't ask them for another tenner. I am certain they
would have given it.' He then explained that he had
named fifty guineas per part, including the two sheets of
letter-press, a couple of etchings, and the initials at the
commencement of the chapters. He reckoned the text,
I remember, at no more than five-and-twenty shillings a
page, the two etchings at six guineas each, while as for
the few initials at the beginning of the chapters, he threw
those in. Such was Mr. Thackeray's own estimate of his
commercial value as an author and engraver, A.D. 1846.
I know perfectly well that after the publication commenced much of the remainder of the work was written
under pressure for and from the printer, and not infre-
quently the first instalment of 'copy' needed to fill the
customary thirty-two pages was penned while the
printer's boy was waiting in the hall at Young Street."

This proves Mr. Trollope's statement to be entirely
inaccurate, and I will now give another extract from Mr.
Taylor, that corroborates Mr. Vizetelly and further
points out that Mr. Marzial's remark should be modified
(and this too in spite of the sentence in Thackeray's letter to Professor Aytoun).

"Some time before" [1846], Mr. Taylor wrote in his
Life of Thackeray, "he, Thackeray, had sketched some
chapters entitled *Pencil Sketches of English Society* which
he had offered to the late Mr. Colburn for insertion in
The New Monthly Magazine. It formed a portion of a

TAILPIECE.

From " Vanity Fair."

continuous story, of a length not yet determined, and
was rejected by Mr. Colburn after consideration. The
papers which Mr. Thackeray had previously contributed
to *The New Monthly* were chiefly slight comic sketches
and perhaps the least favourable specimens of his powers. They were indeed not superior to the common run
of magazine papers, and were certainly not equal to his
contributions to *Fraser*. In fact, as a contributor to *The
New Monthly*, he had achieved no remarkable success,
and his papers appear to have been little in demand
there. Happily the author of *Pencil Sketches of English
Society*, though suspending his projected work, did not
abandon it. He saw in its opening chapters—certainly
not the best part of the story when completed—the
foundations of a work which was to secure him at last a
fame among contemporary writers in his own proper
name. The success of Mr. Dickens's shilling monthly
parts suggested to him to make it the commencement of
a substantive work of fiction, to be published month by
month, with illustrations by the author.''

When he offered it to Colburn he had not even
thought of the now famous title, which suddenly occurred
to him in the middle of the night. ''I jumped out of
bed,'' he told Miss Perry, ''and ran three times round
my room, uttering as I went: '*Vanity Fair! Vanity Fair!
Vanity Fair!*' ''

Before *Vanity Fair* was finished Thackeray had
become a personage, and was in his proper place, as one
of the foremost men of the day. He was no longer
dependent on *Fraser* and *Punch* for his livelihood: he
stood forward as a great novelist, the equal of the great
humourists whom he so much admired.

Writing on May 4, Fitzgerald observed: "He is become a great man, and I am told goes to Holland House and Devonshire House, and for some reason or another will not write a word to me. But I am sure this is not because he is asked to Holland House." And a couple of months later he wrote: "Thackeray is a great man, goes to Devonshire House, etc., and his book (which is capital) is read by the great, and will, I hope, do them good." "Thackeray is winning great social success, dining at the Academy, Sir Robert Peel's, etc.," another old friend, Monckton Milnes, wrote in May, 1849. "I doubt whether he will be much the happier for it, though I think people generally are for satisfied ambition."

Now Thackeray was always of a sensitive disposition, and the applause was to him a glorious stimulant; just the thing that he had been wanting for thirteen years, and which, now he had obtained it, did not make him content to rest upon his laurels, but urged him on and on to struggle for yet greater honours. He became a lion, and remained a lion till the end of his life. He went everywhere, and saw everything. "There is no more dangerous or stupefying position for a man in life than to be a cock of small society," he has written. "It prevents his ideas from growing, it renders him intolerably conceited. A twopenny-halfpenny Cæsar, a Brummagem dandy, a coterie philosopher or wit, is pretty sure to be an ass; and, in fine, I lay it down as an axiom that it is good for a man to live where he can meet his betters, intellectual and social." He followed his own advice and went everywhere—Holland House, Sir Robert Peel's, Devonshire House, Lord Lansdowne's, Royal Academy banquets, Lady Waldegrave's,

Rothschild's, etc., to balls, dinners, and receptions, indiscriminately. He liked society; he felt quite at home in it, and, as a well-bred gentleman, liked to meet his peers; but he never became conceited or vain, and to the end of his life was amused in his quiet way at the idea of being a great man. "I was going to send you a letter the other day from a sculptor who wants to make my bust; think of *that*," he wrote to a friend of his. "Lady C——, beautiful, serene, stupid old lady: she asked, 'Isn't that the great Mr. Thackeray?' Oh, my stars! think of *that*," he wrote later. And in a letter to Mrs. Brookfield from Cambridge in 1850, he said, "I think William" [Brookfield] "is a little disappointed that I have not been made enough a lion of, whereas my timid nature trembles before such honours, and my vanity would be to go through life as a gentleman—as a Major Pendennis—you have hit it. I believe I never do think about my public character, and certainly didn't see the gyps, waiters, and under-graduates whispering in hall, as your William did, or thought he did."

Perhaps he wasted too much time in this way, and Carlyle was right enough when he surmised that the course Thackeray had got into, since he had taken to cultivating dinner-eating in fashionable houses, was not salutary discipline for work. But on the other hand, society was useful and necessary to him. "A social painter must be of the world which he depicts, and native to the manners he portrays," he wrote, when comparing the accuracy of Leech's drawings with the many mistakes of Gilray's. "If I don't go out and mingle in society, I can't write," he once wrote to Mr. Bedingfield's mother; and this was true enough, for just as Dickens portrays the lower classes, so was Thackeray

the novelist of the higher classes. Even in his letters
are numerous references to the use to which he put his
social opportunities. He makes a speech at the Library
Fund Dinner at which he breaks down. "Of what I
said I have not the smallest idea," he wrote, "The discomfiture will make a good chapter for *Pendennis*"; or
he goes to a "Sybarite repast," where he "saw a chapter or two of *Pendennis* in some of them" [the guests];
and so on.

Candid friends hinted that he was becoming a tuft-
hunter.

"Mr. Thackeray has said more, and more effect-
ively, about snobs and snobbism than any other man,"
Harriet Martineau has written; "and yet his frittered
life, and his obedience to the call of the great, are the
observed of all observers. As it is so, so it must be;
but 'O, the pity of it, the pity of it!' Great and unusual
allowance is to be made in his case, I am aware; but
this does not lessen the concern occasioned by the spectacle of one after another of the aristocracy of nature
making the Ko-to to the aristocracy of accident."

"Thackeray had grown a little *blasé*," Sir Frederick
Pollock wrote in 1849; and some years later: "Thackeray . . . after he became famous, liked no subject
so well" [as himself and his books], and this, too, after
Thackeray had complained—humourously, I admit—to
Mr. Brookfield that at a dinner at the "Star and Garter"
with the Strutts and Romillys they talked about *Vanity
Fair* and *Pendennis* almost incessantly, though he declared
he tried to turn the conversation at least ten times, but
they would not let him. Very probably these people
who complained of Thackeray's conversation turning on

his books were the very people who would not permit the subject to be changed.

Compare the following extract from Macaulay's diary (February 12, 1849): "I dined at Lady Charlotte Lindsay's with Hallam and Kinglake. I am afraid that I talked too much about my book. Yet really the fault was not mine. People *would* introduce the subject. I will be more guarded; yet how difficult it is to hit the right point! To turn the conversation might look ungracious and affected."

And now listen to old Isaac Disraeli: "Men of genius have often been accused of imaginary crimes. Their very eminence attracts the lie of calumny, which tradition often conveys beyond possibility of refutation."

Remember the old libel, that Thackeray had drawn *Currer Bell* in "Becky Sharp," and in revenge she had portrayed him in "Rochester." Well might he exclaim, in a *Roundabout Paper*, "Good gracious! how do lies begin?"

But to return to Thackeray and his friends.

Fitzgerald at first seems to have noticed no change in him. "I have seen Thackeray three or four times," he wrote. "He is just the same. All the world admires *Vanity Fair*, and the author is courted by dukes and duchesses and wits of both sexes." But in the following year he remarked: "Thackeray is in such a great world that I am afraid of him; he gets tired of me, and we are content to regard each other at a distance." But though, as the years passed, the friends saw less of each other, their love never diminished.

Thackeray had some enemies—who among the fortunate has not? Has ever a successful man of genius gone through the world without stirring up angry feelings, or unconsciously rousing feelings of jealousy?

"Who has no enemies shall know no friends,
  'A real good chap,' and there it ends."

Arcedeckne (supposed to be the prototype of "Foker") especially seems to have disliked him. At Epsom, on a Derby Day, he warned Jeaffreson: "As you ain't a swell you'd better steer clear of Thack for a little time, for when I saw him and gave him the 'Hullo, Thack!' he was walking with a lord." At this race-meeting Thackeray lost his gold repeater and Jeaffreson had his watch stolen, so Arcedeckne may have felt himself avenged.

But Thackeray never did desert his older friends, and the more strictly intellectual and artistic society of earlier days. We know how he dined at Macready's house to meet Sir T. Wilson, Panizzi, Landseer, and others, and at Foster's, where he saw Macready, Rintoul, Kenyon, Procter, Kinglake, Alfred Tennyson and Brookfield, and how Macready dined with Thackeray and met the Kenyons, the Procters, Reeve, Villiers, Evans, and Stanfield, and saw Miss Sartoris, S. C. Danse, White, and Goldsmith in the evening.

He was quite aware of the charge of tuft-hunting that was brought against him. "To know young noblemen and brilliant and notorious town-bucks and leaders of fashion has this great disadvantage," he wrote in *Mr. Brown on Friendship*, "that if you talk about them or are seen with them much, you offend all your friends of middle life. It makes men envious to see their acquaintance better off than themselves;" and of course Thackeray had to pay the inevitable price for his social popularity—the loss of some of his friends of early life. "I like what are called Bohemians and fellows of that sort," he told Mr. J. E. Cooke. "I have seen all sorts of society—dukes, duchesses, lords and ladies, authors, actors, and painters—and taken altogether I think I like painters the best, and Bohemians generally. They are more natural and unconventional: they wear their hair on their shoulders if they want, and dress picturesquely and carelessly.'' That is not like the language of a tuft-hunter, nor is the following language likely to come from an idolator of rank: "When I see these magnificent dandies yawning out of White's or caracolling in the Park, I like to think that Brummell was the greatest of them all, and that Brummell's father was a footman.''

But nevertheless he thoroughly admired the *je ne sais quoi* that marks the gentleman. "They" [the Kickle-burys] "are travelling with Mr. Bloundell, who was a gentleman once and still retains about him some faint odour of that time of bloom." "It is true . . . poor Plantagenet" [Gaunt] "is only an idiot . . . a zany, . . . and yet you see somehow that he is a gentleman.'' These are among the lines that Thackeray has written, expressive of the high value he placed on good breeding. "No doubt a man may be the descendant of eleven earls, and yet be a pitifully mean creature,'' he once said to Mr. Jeaffreson; "all the same for that, I am of opinion that it takes three generations to make a gentleman.'' But a man may like to be in the company of gentlemen without being a snob!

Thackeray had a spiteful enemy in Dr. Gordon Hake, who treated him very unjustly in his *Memoirs*. "He could never realise the independent feelings of those who happen to be born to fortune—a thing which a man of genius should be able to do with ease,'' the Doctor wrote. "Thackeray, as if under the impression that the party was invited to look at him, thought it necessary to make a figure and attract attention during the dessert, by telling stories and more than half acting them: the aristocratic party listening, but appearing little amused. Borrow knew better how to behave in good company, and kept quiet, though doubtless he felt his name.'' Borrow *may* have known how to behave in good company, but he certainly never learnt to behave elsewhere. For instance, he asked a simple, unpretending woman, who said to him, "Oh, Mr. Borrow, I have read your books with so much pleasure," "Pray what books do you mean, madam—my account books?" and when Miss Strickland expressed a wish to send him a copy of her *Queens of England*, "For Heaven's sake don't, madam; I shouldn't know what to do with them"; and then, turning to a friend, remarked, "What a damned fool that woman is!" No, I do not think, in spite of Dr. Hake, that Thackeray could have learnt much of the proprieties from Borrow.

Perhaps these dislikes may be explained away by the fact that Thackeray had some contempt for dull persons. "Stupid people," he wrote, "who do not know how to laugh, are always pompous and self-conceited, *i.e.* bigoted, *i.e.* cruel, *i.e.* ungentle, uncharitable, unchristian."

However, the contrary evidence is overwhelming. Major D—— declared that "perhaps no man was ever so improved by success"; Albert Smith insisted that Thackeray was a very jolly fellow, and no "High Art about him"; and similar testimony is borne by Dr. John Browne, J. E. Cooke, Mrs. Kemble, Fields, Reed, James Payn, Dr. Merriman, Bayard Taylor, and a great number of other men and women of all classes of those who met him.

"What I saw of Thackeray impressed me with his gentleness and charity," Mr. John Hollingshead has written. "Far from being a cynic, he was more like a good-natured schoolboy." "None of the little aside sermons which he preached in his books fell by any chance from his lips," Mr. Vizetelly said. "His placid temper and pleasant courtesy, in spite of the mild expressions in which he indulged, charmed all who came into contact with him. . . . Thackeray was reticent in expressing his opinion upon people whom he did not like, and very rarely said ill-natured things about any one."*

"There was, too, a diversity of opinion about his temper and principles," Dean Hole said. "Others who did not understand him have made some cruel mistakes. Whoever desires to know what sort of man he was, his love of goodness and contempt of evil, let him read *The Newcomes*."

"There were times," Blanchard Jerrold has told us, "when Thackeray could not break through his outward austerity, even when passing an intimate friend in the street. A mutual friend met him one afternoon in Fleet Street, ambling to Whitefriars on his cob, and a very

---

*Mr. Hollingshead gives a good instance of Thackeray's practical insight into human character.

"I was frankly brutal, and brutally frank, and might have been a Brummagem Carlyle in the way I addressed my future editor.

"'You write a very pure style,' said Thackeray, 'May I ask where you learnt it?'

"'Mostly, I am afraid, in the streets,' I replied, rather impudently, 'from costermongers and skittlesharps. My model may have been the first chapter of Genesis, which is composed chiefly, if I remember rightly, of words of one syllable: anyway, I rarely use long words, because I am not sure I always understand their meaning, and sometimes there might be a difficulty about the spelling.' This was hardly diplomatic language from a young correspondent to a great and able editor, but Thackeray was incapable of taking offence where none was meant. Speaking to the wild Irish Secretary afterwards, I believe he set it down to my constitutional nervousness and excitement. He was quite right. 'Cheek' is often the offspring of bashfulness."

extraordinary figure he made. He caught sight of us, and my companion was about to grasp his hand, but he just touched his hat with his finger, and without opening his lips, or relaxing the solemn cast of his features, he passed on. My companion stamped his foot on the pavement, and cried, 'Who would think we were up till four o'clock this morning together? He sang his *Reverend Dr. Luther*, and was the liveliest of us all.' But Thackeray was a sick man as well as a hard-worked one. He was threatened by several disorders of long continuance and against which he stoutly fought, turning his noble, placid face bravely upon the world—this great Achilles whom we knew, and who was most loved by those who knew him best.'' And Mr. George Hodder, who had every opportunity of knowing him well, said the same thing in words not very dissimilar.

Hear Mr. Locker Lampson: ''I had a sincere regard for Thackeray. I well remember his striking personality—striking to those who had the ability to recognise it—the look of the man, the latent power, and the occasional keenness of his remarks on men and their actions, as if he saw through and through them. Thackeray drew many unto him, for he had engaging as well as fine qualities. He was open-handed and kind-hearted. He had not an overweening opinion of his literary consequence, and he was generous as regarded the people whom the world chose to call his rivals.''

And lastly, read Mrs. Field's tribute to the great man: ''I seem to see one kindly face—large, full of humour, full of human sympathy. The face belongs to Thackeray, and I can recall his goodness to one who, although married already, was hardly more than 'a slip of a girl,' and very much afraid of him—afraid, let me say, rather of the idea of him, the great author and famous lecturer, who was making his crowded audiences laugh and cry at his simple word every evening; the great man of the moment whom everybody was 'running after,' yet of whom they said that he liked his friends so much better than all their noise about himself, that he was always trying to escape from it—and here he was!—coming to see—whom? Well, it appears it did not so much matter, for he was bent on kindnesses, and he took it all in at a glance, and sat down by the window, and drew me to him, and told me about his 'little girls' at home; how he walked down the wrong side of Piccadilly one day, and so lost what money he had had out of his pocket—money which belonged properly to these same dear girls of his; therefore it came about that he made up his mind though it was hard enough to come away from them to get something to take back to them in place of what he had lost; and how they were the dearest girls in the world and when I came to England I should find them more like old friends, and should have somebody, I am sure, he thought, to 'play with,' though, under the circumstances, he could not use just those words! And then, soon after, he went away, leaving a great train of sunshine and kindness behind him which has never faded. . . . I remember one other interview with Thackeray during his visit to America, in New York. He was coming down a long flight of steps into the street after one of the lectures. We were in front, and we were with Washington Irving. Thackeray startled the little group by overtaking us and striking Irving briskly on the shoulder (they were evidently very much at home together); then, turning to us, 'And here's the very little woman I was telling you of to-day!''

at which sally, since he evidently had not been telling anything very serious, we all laughed, and then he began to relate the experiences of the evening (his lecture). It was only a touch, a glance, a nothing, as one may say, but that warmth and sunlight of his nature always seemed to wake a new flowing of existence into being where it shone even for an instant. . . . It need not be told here that Thackeray loved the great world, and the strange, noble, and even ignoble creatures it contains, and liked to see them straight, as he says, somewhere; and would have said to his favourites, as Dr. Johnson said to Mrs. Thrale, 'Be brisk, be splendid, and be public'; but he loved, above all, his fireside corner, and his 'little girls,' and the friends they drew about them.''

I do not believe that Thackeray neglected his friends intentionally. That he did so is a view I hold to be entirely untenable—his whole character, his every action, shows the absurdity of this opinion.

We all know how it is—if a social equal or inferior pass us in the street without a word of recognition, it is because he does not see us; but if a person of a much higher rank do the same, *then* it is because he does *not wish* to see us. The same absurd sensitiveness, which can only arise from a feeling of uncertainty about one's own position, may be seen when a family has lost its money. They lose their friends, and then to the end of the chapter they grumble at the perfidy of wealthy people. But is it entirely the fault of the friends? I think not. Perhaps in most cases it is because the unfortunate family is on the look-out for slights and insults in a way that was quite unnatural to them in their days of prosperity. Thus was it with the friends of Thackeray who found him *blasé*, bored, or cold.

Thackeray in a letter to Mrs. Bayne, has defended himself:—

"When a man gets this character (of being haughty, and supercilious to old acquaintances) he never loses it. . . . This opinion once put forth against a man, all his friends believe it, accommodate themselves to the new theory, see coolness where none is meant. They won't allow for the *time* an immensely enlarged acquaintance occupies, and fancy I am dangling after lords and fine people because I am not so much in their drawing-rooms as in former days. They don't know in what a whirl a man plunges who is engaged in my business. Since I began this work [lecturing] besides travelling, reading, seeing people, dining—when I am forced out and long to be quiet—I write at the rate of five thousand letters a year. I have a heap before me now. Six of them are about lectures—one from an old gentleman whom I met on the railroad and who sends me his fugitive poems. I must read them, answer them, and compliment the old gentleman. Another from a poor widow, in bad spelling, asking for help. Nobody knows the work until he is in it. Of course with all this, old friends hint you are changed, you are forsaking them for great people, and so forth, and so forth."

CHAPTER XIV

"PENDENNIS"—CHARLOTTE BRONTË

CHAPTER XIV

"PENDENNIS"—CHARLOTTE BRONTË

THOUGH the success of *Vanity Fair* made Thackeray independent of the magazines, he did not cease to contribute to the periodical literature of the day, and if he severed his connection with *Fraser* it was only to enable him to send a greater quantity of work to *Punch*, which paper was far more congenial to him, and, it may safely be conjectured, a far better paymaster. His last contribution to *Fraser*, with the exception of the satirical *Mr. Thackeray in the United States*, some six years later, was *A Grumble at the Christmas Books*. In this paper, printed in January, 1847, he took a secret farewell of the unconscious readers in the following characteristic paragraphs on "the very last page of the very last sheet" he thought he would ever contribute to the magazine.

"Ha! what have we here? *M. A. Titmarsh's Christmas Book*—MRS. PERKYN'S BALL. Dedicated to the Mulligan of Ballymulligan. Ballymulligan! Ballyfiddlestick! What *you*, too, Mr. Titmarsh? You, you sneering wretch, setting up a Christmas book of your own! This, then, is the meaning of your savage feelings towards 'the minor fiddlers'! Is your kit, sirrah, any bigger than theirs? You, who in the columns of this very Magazine, have sneered at the works of so many painters, look at your own performances! Some of your folks have scarcely more legs than Miss Biffin: they have fins instead of hands—they squint, almost every one of them! . . . All this is quite true. But see where we have come to!—to the very last page of the very last sheet; and the writer is called upon to stop just at the very moment he was going to cut his own head off. So have I seen Mr. Clown (in that Christmas drama which has been foremost in my thought, during all the above meditations) set up the gallows, adjust the rope, try the noose curiously, and—tumble head over heels.''

Mrs. Perkyn's Ball, the Christmas Book for 1847—like its annual successors, *Our Street, Dr. Birch and his Young Friends, The Kickleburys on the Rhine*, it contained humourous letterpress, illustrated by many full-page illustrations by the author—was such a success that Thackeray determined to take advantage of its popularity by issuing in book-form, through Messrs. Bradbury & Evans, the *Snob Papers** and *The Great Hoggarty Diamond*. In both these volumes his own name was printed on the title-page; but he had still a sneaking fondness for his favourite pseudonym, and all his Christmas Books, including *The Rose and the Ring*, bore the superscription of *M. A. Titmarsh*.

Though he was publishing his novel with success, he did not dare to discontinue his other writings and devote himself entirely to novel-writing. Even late in 1848 he said, ''As if I had not enough to do I have begun to blaze away in the *Chronicle* again; it's an awful bribe—that five guineas an article.'' He was not yet satisfied with his prospects; he feared his popularity might diminish. He knew well that the earnings of a man of

*Seven of the original *Snob Papers* were omitted in this edition, for, Thackeray explained, ''on re-perusing these papers I have found them so . . . personal, so snobbish—in a word—that I have withdrawn them from this collection.''

letters are always more or less precarious, and at this
time he was determined to make money that could be
stored away for the time of necessity. With this object
in view he caused himself to be called to the bar by the
Honourable Society of the Middle Temple on May 26,
1848,* not with the intention of practising, but so as to
be able to accept, if fate would only give him the chance,
one of the many appointments for which a barrister is
eligible. Soon he was endeavouring to obtain a vacant
magistracy—his great model, Fielding, had sat at Bow
Street—but without success, as he told Monckton Milnes
in the following letter—a letter in which can be discerned
such a longing for rest from the never-ceasing writing
and revising which had become almost insupportable;
but while the pathos is marked, a smile must be given at
the idea of Thackeray, who is for all time, and who had
not then written *Esmond* or *The Newcomes*, being able to
live for six years in the literary world by trading on his
past reputation.

"You are a good and lovable adviser and M.P., but
I cannot get the Magistrate's place, not being eligible.
I was only called to the Bar last year; and they require
barristers of seven years' standing. Time will qualify
me, however, and I hope to be able to last six years in
the literary world; for though I shall write, I daresay,
very badly, yet the public won't find it out for some
time, and I shall live on my past reputation. It is a
pity to be sure. If I could get a place and rest, I think
I could do something better than I have done, and leave
a good and lasting book behind me; but Fate is overrul-
ing. I have written to thank L—— for his kind letter,

*At the time it seems that Thackeray had chambers at 10, Crown
Office Row, Temple.

and to beg him to remember me if an opportunity occurs of serving me. I wonder whether Lord Palmerston could? But I would rather be in London. Thank you for thinking of me, and believe me I am grateful."*

In this year, too, the assistant secretaryship at the post-office became vacant, and Lord Clanricarde, then postmaster-general, endeavoured to obtain the situation for Thackeray; but so much opposition was aroused in the service at the mere mention of the appointment of an outsider to a berth that required special experience, that the Marquis was obliged to abandon his intention.

Others besides Thackeray himself thought he required rest and quiet, and his friends continually urged him to work less. In 1849 Thackeray wrote to Mrs. Brookfield: "Big Higgins" [*Jacob Omnium*], "who dined with me yesterday, offered me, what do you think? 'If,' says he, 'you are tired, and want to lie fallow for a year, come to me for the money. I have much more than I want.' Wasn't it kind? I like to hear and tell of kind things."

Writing to the same correspondent a little later from Paris, during one of his numerous visits there, he said: "What brought me to this place? Well, I am glad I came; it will give me a subject for at least six weeks in *Punch*, of which I was getting so weary that I thought I must have done with it. . . . I went to see my old haunts when I came to Paris thirteen years ago, and made believe to be a painter—just after I was ruined, and before I fell in love, and took to marriage and writing. It was a jolly time. I was as poor as Job, and sketched away most abominably, but pretty contented; and we used to meet in each other's little rooms and talk

The Life and Letters of Monckton Milnes.

about art, and smoke pipes, and drink bad brandy and
water.   That awful habit still remains, but where is art,
that dear mistress whom I loved, though in a very indo-
lent, capricious manner, but with a real sincerity?   I see
her far, very far off.   I jilted her.   I know it very
well; but you see it was Fate ordained that marriage
should never take place, and forced me to take on with
another lady, two other ladies, three other ladies—I
mean the muse, and my wife, etc., etc."

How sad were the memories conjured up in the ballad
of *Bouillabaisse!*   How easy to see the true pathos, the
deep feeling, the sorrowing heart, the sad man!   Who,
knowing the story of the writer's life, does not feel a
little dull after reading the exquisite verse:—

> "Ah me! how quick the days are flitting!
>   I mind me of a time that's gone,
> When here I'd sit as now I'm sitting,
>   In this same sad place—but not alone.
> A fair young face was nestled near me,
>   A dear, dear face looked fondly up
> And sweetly spoke, and smiled to cheer me!
>   There's no one now to share my cup."

He had left London for the continent immediately the
last number of *Vanity Fair* was written (July, 1848),*
and it was at Spa that he began his next great novel,
*The History of Pendennis—His Fortunes and Misfortunes, and
his Friends and his Greatest Enemy*, the first instalment of
which was published by Messrs. Bradbury & Evans (who
had just issued *Vanity Fair* in two-volume form) in
November.   The publication of the new venture contin-

*Mr. Eyre Crowe has related how, when Thackeray and Mr. Torrens
McCullagh were lunching with his father in June, 1848, the latter said
to the novelist, "Well, I see you are going to shut up your puppets
in their box."   "Yes," Thackeray replied immediately, "and with
your permission I'll work up that simile."   How skillfully he did this
all readers of the preface *Before the Curtain* will remember.

ued regularly month after month, and the eleventh number had appeared in September, 1849, when the even tenour of its way was suddenly interrupted, and for the rest of the year *Pendennis* was at a standstill.   Thackeray was ill—so ill, indeed, during September, October, and November, that it seemed only too probable that he would never rise from the sick bed.   It was a time of dreadful anxiety to his family and to his friends.   Dr. Merriman attended him, and also Dr. Elliotson, to whom, thirteen months later, *Pendennis*, on its publication in book form, was dedicated.   It was not until December that his recovery was assured.   Fitzgerald saw him on the 7th, and wrote to Frederick Tennyson: "I saw poor Thackeray in London, getting slowly better of a bilious fever that had nearly killed him. . . . People in general thought *Pendennis* got dull as it got on; and I confess I thought so too: he would do well to take the opportunity of his illness to discontinue it altogether.   He told me last June he himself was tired of it, and must not his readers naturally tire too?"   Fortunately, Thackeray, after being rescued from illness, was saved from his friends, and the twelfth number of *Pendennis* appeared in January of the new year.   Fitzgerald, re-reading the novel years later, altered his opinion.   "I like *Pendennis* much," he then said; "and Alfred [Tennyson] said he thought it was quite delicious; 'it seemed to him so mature,' he said.   You can imagine Alfred saying this over one's fire, spreading his great hand out."

There is probably nothing more interesting to be related in the whole story of Thackeray's life than the account of his slight acquaintance with Charlotte Brontë, whom he first met about this time.   Even before

No. VII.

Price 1s.

THE HISTORY

OF

PENDENNIS.

HIS FORTUNES AND MISFORTUNES,
HIS FRIENDS AND HIS GREATEST ENEMY.

BY

W. M. THACKERAY,

Author of "Vanity Fair," the "Snob Papers" in Punch, &c. &c.

LONDON. BRADBURY & EVANS, 11, BOUVERIE STREET.

J. MENZIES, EDINBURGH; T. MURRAY, GLASGOW; AND J. M'GLASHAN, DUBLIN.

Bradbury & Evans.]   1849.   [Printers, Whitefriars.

he knew her name or sex he had sent her a copy of *Vanity Fair*, inscribed "With the grateful regard of W. M. Thackeray," and he was not a man to send indiscriminately inscribed copies of his works, even to the most famous writers. On the other hand, it has already been told how greatly the lady admired the works of the great novelist, and therefore, when the authoress of *Jane Eyre* came up to town in 1849, she eagerly accepted the offer of Mr. Smith, her publisher and host, to introduce Thackeray to her. When Miss Brontë met him she was much astonished. She had expected—as the dedication to the second edition of *Jane Eyre* showed—to find a fervent prophet, and Thackeray was simply a quiet, well-bred gentleman, with nothing in appearance to distinguish him from hosts of other men. He was an enigma to *Currer Bell;* she could not understand him; she was never certain whether he was speaking in jest or in earnest; and she told Mrs. Gaskell that "she had (she believed) completely misunderstood an inquiry of his, made on the gentlemen's coming into the drawing-room. He asked her 'if she had perceived the scent of their cigars,' to which she literally replied, discovering in a moment afterwards, by the smile on several faces, that he was alluding to a passage in *Jane Eyre*.

Miss Brontë also wrote at this time to friends: "All you say of Mr. Thackeray is most graphic and characteristic. He stirs in me both sorrow and anger. Why should he lead so harassing a life? Why should his mocking tongue so perversely deny the better feelings of his better moods? . . . Mr. Thackeray is a man of very quiet, simple demeanour; he is, however, looked up to with some awe and even distrust. . . . Thackeray is a Titan of mind. His presence and powers impress one deeply in an intellectual sense; I do not know him, or see him as a man. All the others are subordinate. . . . I was sufficiently at my ease with all but Thackeray; with him I was fearfully stupid.''

The truth is that she never understood Thackeray—read the extract from a letter written to a friend, after her first meeting with the giant.

''I have had a remarkable epistle from Thackeray, long, interesting, characteristic, but, unfortunately, concludes with the strict injunction, 'Show this letter to no one,' adding that if he thought his letters were seen by others he should either cease to write, or write only what was conventional. I have answered it at length; whether my reply will give satisfaction or displeasure remains to be ascertained. Thackeray's feelings are not such as can be gauged by ordinary calculation. Favourable weather is what I should ever expect from that quarter. Yet in correspondence, as in verbal intercourse, this would torment me.''

In June of the following year she came up to London again. ''He [Thackeray] made a morning call,'' she wrote, ''and sat about two hours. Mr. Smith only was in the room the whole time. He described it afterwards as a queer scene, and I suppose it was. The giant sat before me; I was moved to speak of some of his shortcomings (literary, of course); one by one the faults came into my head, and one by one I brought them out, and sought some explanation or defence. He did defend himself like a great Turk and heathen; that is to say, the excuses were often worse than the crime itself. The matter ended in decent amity; if all be well I am to dine at his house this evening (June 12).''*

*Mrs. Gaskell's *Life of Charlotte Brontë*.

In the *Life of Lord Houghton* Sir Wemyss Reid has written: "Before me, as I write, is a little note penned in the beautiful hand of Thackeray upon a card which in its interest is not surpassed by any other letter among the many thousands left behind him by Milnes. 'My dear Milnes,' it runs, 'Miss Brontë dines here to-morrow at seven. If you are by any wonder disengaged, come to yours truly, W. M. Thackeray.' The invitation is dated '13, Young Street, Tuesday.' It is, alas! the only record that remains of a meeting the interest of which it would be hard to exaggerate."

The *Life of Lord Houghton* was published in 1890, and since then a full account of the dinner-party, "as amusing as it is interesting," has been written by Mrs. Ritchie. Among the guests were Mrs. Crowe, Mrs. Brookfield, the Carlyles, Mrs. Eliot, Miss Perry, and Mrs. Procter and her daughter. Monckton Milnes could not go.

"It was a gloomy and a silent evening," Mrs. Ritchie has recorded; "every one waited for the brilliant conversation which never began at all. Miss Brontë returned to the sofa in the study, and murmured a low word now and then to our kind governess, Miss Truelock. The room looked very dark, the lamp began to smoke a little, the conversation grew dimmer and more dim, the ladies sat round still expectant, my father was too much perturbed by the gloom and the silence to be able to cope with it at all. Mrs. Brookfield, who was in the corner in which Miss Brontë was sitting, leant forward with a little commonplace, since brilliance was not to be the order of the evening. 'Do you like London, Miss Brontë?' she said; another silence, a pause, then Miss Brontë answered, 'Yes — No,' very gravely.

After Miss Brontë had left, I was surprised to see my father opening the front door with his hat on. He put his fingers to his lips, walked out into the darkness, and shut the door quietly behind him. When I went back to the drawing-room again, the ladies asked me where he was. I vaguely answered that I thought he was coming back. . . .

"Long years afterwards, Mrs. Procter, with a good deal of humour, described the situation—the ladies, who had all come expecting so much delightful conversation, and the gloom and constraint, and how, finally, over-whelmed by the situation, my father had quietly left the room, left the house, and gone off to his club. The ladies waited, wondered, and finally departed also; and as we were going up to bed with our candles, after every-body was gone, I remember two pretty Miss L——s, in shiny silk dresses, arriving, full of expectation. . . . We still said we thought our father would soon be back, but the Miss L——s declined to wait upon the chance, laughed, and drove away almost immediately."*

Once more did the man of genius and the gifted woman meet. It was in the early summer of 1851. Miss Brontë's letters tell the tale:—

"I came here [London] on Wednesday, being sum-moned a day sooner than I expected, in order to be in time for Thackeray's second lecture, which was deliv-ered on Thursday afternoon. This, as you may sup-pose, was a great treat, and I was glad not to miss it. . . . Thackeray called, too, separately. I had a long talk with him, and I think he knows me now a little better than he did; but of this I cannot yet be sure; he is a great and strange man. . . . As our party left

*Chapters from Some Unwritten Memoirs: A. I. Ritchie.

the [lecture] Hall, he [Thackeray] stood at the entrance; he saw and knew me, and lifted his hat; he offered his hand in passing, and uttered the words, 'Qu'en dites vous?'—a question eminently characteristic and reminding me, even in this his moment of triumph, of that inquisitive restlessness, that absence of what I considered desirable self-control, which were amongst his faults. He should not have cared just then to ask what I thought; or what anybody thought; but he *did* care, and he was too natural to conceal, too impulsive to repress his wish. Well! if I blamed his over-eagerness, I liked his *naiveté*. I would have praised him; I had plenty of praise in my heart; but, alas! no words on my lips. Who has words at the right moment? I stammered lame expressions; but was truly glad when some other people, coming up with profuse congratulations, covered my deficiency by their redundancy.''*

Indeed, though intensely appreciative, she proved so severe a critic, both of himself and his works, that Thackeray was not quite pleased with the various letters (printed in Mrs. Gaskell's *Life*) in which she had expressed her opinions, and he said as much in his *Last Sketch*, prefixed to *Emma* when, under his editorship, that fragment appeared in the *Cornhill Magazine*.

''I can only say of this lady, *vidi tantum*. I saw her first just as I rose out of an illness from which I had never thought to recover. I remember the trembling little frame, the little hand, the great honest eyes. An impetuous honesty seemed to me to characterise the woman. Twice I recollect she took me to task for what she held to be errors in doctrine. Once about Fielding we had a disputation. She spoke her mind out. She

*Mrs. Gaskell's *Life of Charlotte Brontë*.

jumped to conclusions (I have smiled at one or two passages in the *Biography*, in which my own disposition or behaviour form the subject of talk). She formed conclusions that might be wrong, and built up whole theories of character upon them. New to the London world, she entered it with an independent, indomitable spirit of her own; and judged of contemporaries, and especially spied out arrogance or affectation, with extraordinary keenness of vision. She was angry with her favourites if their conduct or conversation fell below her ideal. Often she seemed to be judging the London folks prematurely: but perhaps the city is rather angry at being judged. It fancied an austere little Joan of Arc marching in upon us, and rebutting our easy lives, our easy morals. She gave me the impression of being a very pure, and lofty, and high-minded person. A great and holy reverence of right and truth seemed to be with her always. Such, in our brief interview, she appeared to me.''*

*In *To-day* the following anecdote, entitled *A Crushed Ideal*, was inserted, I know not on what authority; but whether real or imaginary, it is amusingly true of Charlotte Brontë's attitude:—

It is of Thackeray's first meeting with Charlotte Brontë. The tiny, intense creature had idealised Thackeray, personally unknown to her, with a passion of idealisation. "Behold, a lion cometh out of the North!" she quoted under her breath, as Thackeray entered the drawing-room. Some one repeated to him. "Oh, Lord!" said Thackeray, "and I'm nothing but a poor devil of an Englishman, ravenous for my dinner!" At dinner Miss Brontë was placed opposite Thackeray, by her own request. "And I had," said he, "the miserable humiliation of seeing her ideal of me disappearing down my own throat, as everything went into my mouth and nothing came out of it; until at last, as I took my fifth potato, she leaned across, with clasped hands and tears in her eyes, and breathed imploringly, 'Oh, Mr. Thackeray! Don't!'"

CHAPTER XV

THACKERAY AND *PUNCH*

CHAPTER XV

THACKERAY AND *PUNCH*

DURING 1847 and the two following years Thackeray wrote and drew so much for *Punch* that it is only possible to enumerate a few of his contributions. *An Eastern Adventure of the Fat Contributor*, the immortal *Mahogany Tree*, the *Love Songs*, including the well-beloved *Cane-bottomed Chair*, the *Travels in London* (it was said that Frank Whitestock, in *The Curates' Walk*, was intended to be a sketch of the Rev. W. H. Brookfield), the *Bow Street Ballads* (*Ballads of Pleaceman X*), and *A Little Dinner at Timmins's*. Besides there were *Punch's Prize Novelists*, six in number, parodies of the styles of popular authors, which were so excellent that Lever, on reading *Phil Fogarty*, declared he might as well shut up shop, and actually altered the character of his novels, and that Disraeli never forgave the *Codlingsby*, but, in *Endymion*, travestied the style of *St. Barbe* (Thackeray) in *Topsy Turvey* (*Vanity Fair*) and *Scaramouch* (*Punch*).* These, together with the Ballad of *Bouillabaisse*, and *Brown's Letters*, must complete this list.

There is a pleasant episode to chronicle during 1848 in connection with Thackeray and *Punch*. In Edinburgh, Dr. John Brown, a great admirer of the humourist's writings, had seen a silver statuette of *Punch* in a

*He had intended to write parodies both of Dickens and of himself, but *Punch* refused to insert that on Dickens, and so both remained unwritten.

jeweller's window, and suggested to his friends that it should be bought and sent to Thackeray. The cash price was ten pounds, and so it was determined—to make the little testimonial more valuable—that eighty persons should subscribe for it. The subscribers included Lord Jeffrey and Sir William Hamilton; the inkstand was purchased, engraved with an inscription—

GULIELMO MAKEPEACE THACKERAY

ARMA VIRUMQUE

GRATI NECNON GRATAE EDINENSIS

L X X X

D   D   D

and forwarded with an explanatory note to Thackeray, who, delighted with the unexpected tribute, hastened to thank the donors through their spokesman, Dr. John Brown, the author of *Rab and His Friends*.

"13, YOUNG STREET, KENSINGTON SQUARE, *May* 11, 1848.

"MY DEAR SIR,—The arms and the man arrived in safety yesterday, and I am glad to know the names of two of the eighty Edinburgh friends who have taken such a kind method of showing their good will towards me. If you are grati, I am gratior. Such tokens of regard and sympathy are very precious to a writer like myself, who has some difficulty still in making people understand what you have been good enough to find out in Edinburgh, that under the mask satirical there walks about a sentimental gentleman who means not unkindly to any mortal person. I can see exactly the same expression under the vizard of my little friend in silver, and hope some day to shake the whole octagint by the hand gratos and gratas, and thank them for their friend-liness and regard. I think I had better say no more on the subject, lest I should be tempted into some enthusiastic writing of which I am afraid. I assure you these tokens of what I can't help acknowledging as popularity—make me humble as well as grateful—and make me feel an awful sense of the responsibility which falls upon a man in such a station. Is it deserved or undeserved? Who is this that sets up to preach to mankind and to laugh at many of the things which men reverence? I hope I shall be able to tell the truth always, etc., to see it straight, according to the eyes which God Almighty gives me. And if, in the exercise of my calling, I get friends and find encouragement and sympathy, I need not tell you how much I feel and am grateful for this support. Indeed, I can't reply lightly upon this subject, or feel otherwise than very grave when men praise me as you do. Wishing you and my Edinburgh friends all health and happiness,

"Believe me, my dear Sir, most faithfully yours,

"W. M. THACKERAY."

The year 1850 saw an event of much importance in his literary life.

"What do you think I have done to-day?" he wrote to Mrs. Brookfield. "I have sent in my resignation to *Punch*. There appears in the next *Punch* an article so wicked, I think, by poor ——, that upon my word I don't think I ought to pull any longer in the same boat with such a savage young Robespierre. The appearance of this incendiary article has put me in such a rage that I could only cool myself by a ride in the Park."

In the columns of the paper he also announced his determination: "Another member of Mr. *Punch's* cabinet, the biographer of *Jeames*, the author of the *Snob Papers*, resigned his functions on account of Mr. *Punch's* assault upon the present Emperor of the French nation, whose anger *Jeames* thought it unpatriotic to arouse.''*

It seems that at the time there was some misunderstanding as to the cause of his resignation. This Thackeray cleared up in a letter, dated March 20, 1855, addressed to F. M. Evans (*History of Punch*, pp. 323-24). ''I had had some difference with the Conduct of *Punch* about the abuse of Prince Albert and the Crystal Palace, at which I very nearly resigned, about abuse of Lord Palmerston, about abuse finally of L. Napoleon—in all of which *Punch* followed the *Times*, which I think and thought was writing unjustly at that time, and dangerously for the welfare and peace of the country. Coming from Edinburgh I bought a *Punch* containing the picture of a Beggar on Horseback, in which the Emperor was represented galloping to hell with a sword reeking with blood. As soon as ever I could after my return (a day or two after) I went to Bouverie Street, saw you and gave in my resignation.''

But even after his formal resignation he continued to write for the journal. In the *History of Punch* we are told that there are forty-one literary items and twelve cuts to his credit in 1851. It is known, too, that in April of this year he sent in his *May-day Ode* to the editor—which, for insertion in the next issue, should have been delivered not later than Saturday morning, but was not delivered until the evening, when Mark Lemon either could not or would not insert it until the following week. Thackeray was annoyed, and himself carried the manuscript to Printing House Square; the *Ode* appearing in the *Times* on the following Monday

*Richard Doyle had recently left the staff on account of the attacks on the Catholics.

morning (April 30). During the next three years he contributed only *The Organ Boy's Appeal*, which was printed in the twenty-fifth volume, and then, during June and July, 1854, *Letters from the East by Our Own Bashi Bazouk*, which was his swan song as far as *Punch* was concerned. "Wishing you all heartily well," he wrote in the letter just mentioned, "I wrote a few occasional papers last year—and not liking the rate of remuneration, which was less than that to which I had been accustomed in my time, I wrote no more. And you can say for me, as a reason why I should feel hurt at your changing the old rates of payment made to me— that I am not a man who quarrels about a guinea or two except as a point of honour; *and* that when I could have had a much larger sum than that which you gave me for my last novel—I preferred to remain with old friends, who had acted honourably and kindly by me. . . . And I think it now about time my old friends and publishers should set me right."

There is an interesting page in the *History of Punch* on which is given a tabular account of the amount written by each of the staff during the second half-year of 1844. Jerrold produced 139¾ columns, a Beckett 94¾, Leigh 39, Thackeray 24½, Mayhew 16¾, Taylor 6¾, the editor (including outside contributions) 20, Oxenford 1½, Laman Blanchard 1¾, and H. Wills 1 only. Each member was expected to fill a certain number of columns, for outside contributions have always been discouraged, and to Thackeray were allotted forty-six columns per half-year.

For ten years he had well and truly served the paper with both pen and pencil. His collected contributions would more than fill two large volumes, and this, too,

in spite of the fact that he did not find the task of production easy. "I must beg of you to excuse me," he
wrote once, after three hours' unproductive labour,
"for I've worked as hard for you as though I had done
something." His pencil, however, did not as a rule
give him so much trouble, and Mr. Swain has told us
how Thackeray would often produce a *Punch* drawing
"while you wait." He did not leave *Punch* in anger,
nor, as it has just been shown, did he desert the journal
to which he had rendered such signal service, and which
had been of so much assistance to him. "Ah, Swain,"
he said one day, "if it had not been for *Punch*, I wonder
where I should be!" And when in later years his help
was asked on behalf of the widow of one of the *Punch*
staff, he offered to do all in his power, "for," he wrote,
"it is through my connection with *Punch* that I owe the
good chances that have lately befallen me, and have had
so many kind offers of help in my own days of trouble,
that I would thankfully aid a friend whom death has
called away."

One misunderstanding he did have with the *Punch*
staff, though, but one only. In December, 1854, he
sent to the *Quarterly Review* an article on *John Leech's
Pictures of Life and Character*. In this he said, "There is
no blinking the fact that in Mr. *Punch's* cabinet John
Leech is the right-hand man. Fancy a number of *Punch*
without Leech's pictures! What would you give for it?
The learned gentlemen who write the work must feel
that without him it were as well left alone." Anthony
Trollope has related that for a week there existed at the
Punch office a grudge against Thackeray in reference to
this awkward question: "What would you give for your
Punch without John Leech?" Then he asked the con-

fraternity to dinner—*more Thackerayano*—and the confraternity came.

The passage was undoubtedly a blunder. Not that I think he was wrong in what he wrote—for I believe twenty people glance at the pictures in *Punch* for one who reads the letterpress; but the statement was certainly one of those things better left unsaid, and it was only used by Thackeray to show the great value he placed on Leech's work, forgetting entirely that it would read as disparagement of the various writers' handiwork. He, indeed, admitted this in a letter to "Professor" Percival Leigh, one of the oldest of the paper's contributors, and the author of the *Comic Latin* and *English Grammars*.

"Of all the slips of my fatal pen," he wrote, "there's none I regret more than the unlucky half-line which has given pain to such a kind and valued old friend as you have been, and I trust will be still to me. I ought never to have said, '*Punch* might as well be left unwritten but for Leech.' It was more than my meaning, which is certainly that the drawing is a hundred times more popular than the writing; but I had no business to write any such thing, and forget it so much that I was quite surprised when I first heard I had been accused of sneering at *Punch*. I knew when I came back from Paris, and read the line in the *Quarterly Review*, which I had forgotten as utterly as many another speech* which I have made and didn't ought. Jerrold has had his fire into me, and, do you know, I feel rather comforted."

*This is not the only case in which Thackeray complains of his memory, and in the Brookfield Letters are several mentions of his forgetfulness. In July, 1850, he wrote: "I've been working all the morning, and reading back numbers in order to get up names, etc., I'd forgotten." And in September of the previous year: "As for *Pendennis*, I began upon No. 7 to-day, and found a picture which was

To the last he would, from time to time, attend the weekly dinners, where a place was always kept for him; and when he died, it was in the columns of this journal that was chronicled the most sincere regret at the great loss suffered, not by the death of the novelist, but by the death of the comrade and friend, the *man*. On the sad Christmas Eve "Ponny" Mayhew brought the fatal news to the jovial *Punch* party. "I'll tell you what we'll do," he said, "we'll sing the dear old boy's *Mahogany Tree;* he'd like it." Accordingly they all stood up, and with such memory of the words as each possessed, and a catching of the breath here and there by about all of them, the song was sung.

In the obituary notice further honour was paid. "While generous tributes," it runs, "are everywhere being paid to the genius of him who has been suddenly called away in the fulness of his power and the maturity of his fame, some who have for many years enjoyed the advantage of his assistance and the delight of his society, would simply record that they have lost a dear friend. At an early period in the history of the periodical he became a contributor to its pages, and he long continued to enrich them; and though of late he has ceased to give other aid than suggestions and advice, he was a constant member of our council, and sat with us on the eighth day from that which has saddened England's Christmas. Let the brilliancy of his trained intellect, the terrible strength of his satire, the subtlety of his wit, the richness of his humour, and the catholic range of his calm

perfectly new, and a passage which I had as utterly forgotten as if I had never read or written it. This shortness of memory frightens me, and makes me have gloomy anticipations. Will poor Annie have to nurse an old imbecile of a father some day, who will ramble incoherently about old days, and people whom he used to love?"

wisdom, be themes for others; the mourning friends who inscribe these lines to his memory think of the affectionate nature, the cheerful companionship, the large heart and the open hand, the simple courteousness, the endearing frankness of a brave, true, honest gentleman, whom no pen but his own could depict as those who knew him most desire."

On the other hand, the true compliment Thackeray paid *Punch* was not less magnificent: "When the future inquirer shall take up your volumes, or a bundle of French plays, and contrast the performance of your booth with that of the Parisian theatre, he won't fail to remark how different they are, and what different objects we admire or satirise. As for your morality, sir, it does not become me to compliment you to your venerable face; but permit me to say that there never was before published so many volumes that contained so much cause for laughing, and so little for blushing, so many jokes, and so little harm. Why, sir, say even your modesty, which astonishes me more and more every time I regard you, is calculated, and not a virtue naturally inherent in you, that very fact would argue for the high sense of the public morality among us. We will laugh in the company of our wives and children; we will tolerate no indecorum; we like that our matrons and girls should be pure."

During his long connection with the paper, he regarded as his most important rival Douglas Jerrold— witty, brilliant Jerrold, who is little more than a name to most of us now. When, on receiving his early number of the journal, he would hastily tear off the wrapper, it was to see "what young Douglas has to say this week," and he would remain for some moments reading the chapter of the *Caudle Lectures*, or of *Miss Robinson Crusoe*, or whatever the contribution might be, before turning to the remaining contents.

It was of Jerrold, who posed as a democrat, that Thackeray, on noticing at the Earl of Carlisle's a presentation copy of one of his (Jerrold's) books, the inscription of which ran, "To the Right Hon. the Earl of Carlisle, K.G., K.C.B., etc., etc., etc.," remarked, "Ah! this is the sort of style in which your rigid, uncompromising radical always toadies the great."* Jerrold, for his part, did not understand Thackeray. "I have known Thackeray for eighteen years," he complained, "and I don't know him yet."

It was Jerrold, Mr. Cuthbert Bradley says, and not Arcedeckne, who laconically criticised Thackeray's first public reading of the *Humourists* to Mark Lemon: "Very good. But wants a piano." And after Thackeray had stood sponsor to a child, exclaimed, "Good Lord, Thackeray, I hope you didn't present the child with your own mug." A silly rumour got afloat about the period of what was called "Papal aggression," that Thackeray, the staunchest of Protestant Broad Churchmen, had a

*The following extract from Taine's *Notes on England* is interesting, as showing Thackeray's feeling on the subject of aristocracy-worship. I suspect, however, that the last sentence was said with a twinkle in his eye:—

"I had a conversation," Taine wrote, "with Thackeray, whose name I mention because he is dead, and because his ideas and his conversation are to be found in his books. He confirmed orally all that he had written about the snobbish spirit. I told him a trivial circumstance of which I was an eye-witness. At a charity meeting the speaker set forth to the audience the importance of the work undertaken by remarking that the Marquis of ——," a person in such a situation, "had kindly consented to take the chair." Thackeray assured me that platitudes like these are common, . . . and that great people are so habituated to see people on their knees before them, that they are shocked when they meet a man of independent demeanor. I myself," he added, "am now regarded as a suspicious character."

leaning towards the Church of Rome. "Why, they're Romanizing old Thackeray," said some one to Jerrold. "I hope," replied the caustic wit, "they'll begin at his nose."

They said many sharp and stinging words to one another and of one another, but I think a really good understanding existed between them. In one of his drawings Thackeray has represented Jerrold and himself in a railway carriage listening, with most amusing expressions on their faces, to the other two occupants discussing, with quite sublime ignorance, the members of the *Punch* staff—this does not show ill-feeling. And it was an overt act of friendship when Thackeray ran up to town one day from Leamington, where he was lecturing, and on his return announced to the astonished Mr. Hodder, "We've got the little man in"—and then, noticing his bewilderment, explained, "Why, Jerrold: we've elected him a member of the Reform Club." Some difficulties, known to the initiated as "blackballs," had been expected when Jerrold was balloted for, as his wit had made him enemies, and so Thackeray had gone up to town to use his influence to secure his election. Again, Thackeray was honestly pleased when he heard of the increased popularity to which *Lloyd's Newspaper* attained under Jerrold's editorship, and then characteristically declared, "I am quite pleased with myself at finding myself pleased at men getting on in the world." At Jerrold's death, too, he co-operated with Dickens to raise a fund for the widow and children, contributing for his share the lecture on *Weekday Preachers*, in which he made special and admirable reference to Jerrold and his writings. This lecture was delivered on July 22, 1857, the day after the declaration of the poll of the Oxford election in which Thackeray was defeated, and the audience were on the alert for some allusion to that event, and were not disappointed, for the opening words of the discourse, delivered with comical solemnity were, "Walking yesterday in the High Street of a certain ancient city. . . ." "So began the lecturer," says the *Times*, in its account of the lecture, "and was interrupted by a storm of laughter that deferred for some moments the completion of the sentence."

CHAPTER XVI

LECTURES IN ENGLAND AND AMERICA—THE
ENGLISH HUMOURISTS—ESMOND

CHAPTER XVI

LECTURES IN ENGLAND AND AMERICA—THE ENGLISH HUMOURISTS—ESMOND

THE discussion of Thackeray's connection with *Panch* made me drop the thread of my story of his life. I must now return to the year 1850, when he published *Rebecca and Rowena. A Romance upon Romance. By M. A. Titmarsh*—undoubtedly the finest burlesque of its kind in English literature. A few months later appeared the Christmas Book, *The Kickleburys on the Rhine*, which produced the now famous criticism in the *Times*, written probably by Samuel Phillips, the author of the now almost-forgotten novel *Caleb Stukely*.* The review was absurd in the highest degree, and the language inflated to the verge of imbecility. Take, for example, this one sentence, which is really a treasure—the italics are mine! "To our, perhaps, unphilosophical taste the aspiration towards sentimental perfection of another popular author are infinitely preferable to *these sardonic divings after the pearl of truth whose lustre is eclipsed in the display of the diseased oyster.*"

Thackeray, who with all his scorn for the ridiculous and the *outré*, usually ignored such criticism, for once let himself go, and replied in the preface to the second

---

*Mr. Sala has somewhere stated that Thackeray believed the review to have been written by Charles Lamb Kenny, but Mr. Vizetelly declared that the novelist always spoke of it in his hearing as being the work of Samuel Phillips.

edition of *The Kickleburys*, in so scathing and severe, though so intensely amusing, a manner, that it is difficult to believe it came from his pen.

"I remember," Mr. Vizetelly, who had engraved the drawings and printed the work, has written, "I remember Mr. Thackeray calling upon me, accompanied by his *fidus Achates*, Mr. J. Higgins (*Jacob Omnium*), of colossal stature like himself, but of more stalwart build, and handing me the memorable preface for the second edition, *An Essay on Thunder and Small Beer*, in reply to the recent *Times* criticism on the book. Thackeray was in high glee over the circumstance of a second edition being called for at the very moment the *Times* was launching its little thunderbolt; and in his excitement he read several sentences of the preface aloud in which he thought he had made his keenest thrusts. The whole was apparently a mere friendly passage-at-arms, as not long after the publication of Thackeray's amusing retort, which to the author's delight was copied in several papers, his *May-Day Ode*, on the opening of the 1851 Exhibition, came out in the *Times*." We know, however, that Thackeray had no intention, until *Punch* refused to print the Ode, of sending it to the *Times*, and it is exceedingly doubtful if the Thunderer ever did forgive him, for it "slated" *Esmond* in a most malicious and unjust way, gave a shorter notice of his death and funeral than any other paper, and was the only daily of any importance that did not insert a leading article on the great loss sustained by the world of letters.

"You must be thinking of coming back to Pimlico soon," Thackeray wrote on April 29, 1851, to Mrs. Brookfield, "for the lectures are to begin on the 15th.

AUTHORS' MISERIES, NO. 6.

Old Gentleman: *Miss Wiggets: Two Authors:*

Old Gentleman: "I am sorry to see you occupied, my dear Miss Wiggets, with that trivial paper, 'Punch.' A railway is not a place, in my opinion, for jokes. I never joke—never."

Miss W.: "So I should think, sir."

Old Gentleman: "And besides, are you aware who are the conductors of that paper, and that they are Chartists, Deists, Atheists, Anarchists, to a man? I have it from the best authority, that they meet together once a week in a tavern in Saint Giles's, where they concoct their infamous print. The chief part of their income is derived from threatening letters, which they send to the nobility and gentry. The principal writer is a returned convict. Two have been tried at the Old Bailey; and as for their artist—as for their artist...."

Guard: "Swin-dun! Sta-tion!"

[Exeunt two Authors.

I tried the great room at Willis's yesterday, and recited part of the multiplication table to a waiter at the opposite end, so as to try the voice. He said he could hear perfectly, and I daresay he could, but the thoughts somehow swell and amplify with that high-pitched voice and elaborate distinctness. As I perceive how poets become selfish,* I see how orators become humbugs, and selfish in their way, too, absorbed in that selfish pursuit, and turning of periods. It is curious to take these dips into a life new to me as yet, and try it and see how I like it, isn't it?''

The lectures referred to are, of course, the series on *The English Humourists of the Eighteenth Century*. Anthony Trollope has devoted two pages of his short biographical chapter to the discussion of the effect that these lectures might have had upon Thackeray's fame as a writer. He argued for and against the indignity of the proceedings, and finally concluded that the money made by the new venture was "earned honestly and with the full approval of the world around him." Well, perhaps it was! Even the author of *Vanity Fair* was not likely to imperil his dignity to any great extent by writing, or by reading to an audience, *The English Humourists* or *The Four Georges*, which (in spite of certain objections raised at the time against the latter) have both taken their place in the classical literature of our century.

---

*In this same letter, *à propos* of the *May-Day Ode*, he wrote: "I don't wonder at poets being selfish, such as Wordsworth and Alfred. I have been for five days a poet, and have thought and remembered nothing else but myself, and my rhymes, and my measure. If somebody had come to me and said, 'Mrs. Brookfield has just had her arm cut off,' I should have gone on with 'Queen of Innumerable Isles, tidumtidy, tidumtidy,' and not stirred from the chair. The children and nobody haven't seen me except at night, and now (though the work is just done) . . . I hardly see the paper before me, so utterly beat, nervous, bilious, and overcome do I feel."

The *raison d'être* of the lectures was the desire to make a good provision for his wife and daughters; and the subject selected seems only natural since his great fondness for the Queen Anne writers dates back to the early years of his life. Allusions to Steele and Addison and Pope and Swift, and Stella, Venessa, Dr. Johnson, Richard Savage, and others, real or unreal, may be found in some of his earliest writings, especially in *Catherine* and *Barry Lyndon*.

The first lecture was eventually postponed until the afternoon of May 22, and the others were delivered on May 29, June 12, 19, 26, and July 3. The price for a reserved seat for the whole course was two guineas, seven-and-sixpence was charged for an unreserved seat for a single lecture, and the audiences included many of the most famous persons in London. Hallam attended on each occasion. So did Macaulay, who referred to one of them in his Diary: "Margaret came to take me to Thackeray's [third] lecture. He is full of humour and imagination, and I only wish that these lectures may answer, both in the way of fame and money. He told me, as I was going out, that the scheme had done wonders for him; and I told him, and from my heart, that I wished he had made ten times as much." Carlyle and his wife went, Harriet Martineau too, and Monckton Milnes, Dickens, and Lord Carlisle, besides Charlotte Brontë.

Thackeray, always averse to public speaking, very naturally dreaded the ordeal, and his nervousness during the half-hour previous to the delivery of the first lecture was really painful. "Going thither before the time for his beginning," Mrs. Kemble afterwards wrote in her

Reminiscences, "I found him standing like a forlorn, disconsolate giant in the middle of the room, gazing about him. 'Oh, Lord,' he exclaimed, as he shook hands with me, 'I'm sick at my stomach with fright.' I spoke some words of encouragement to him, and was going away, but he held my hand like a scared child, crying, 'Oh, don't leave me!' 'But,' said I, 'Thackeray, you mustn't stand here. Your audience are beginning to come in,' and I drew him from the middle of his chairs and benches, which were beginning to be occupied, into the retiring-room adjoining the lecture-room, my own readings having made me perfectly familiar with both. Here he began pacing up and down, literally wringing his hands in nervous distress. 'Now,' said I, 'what shall I do? Shall I stay with you till you begin, or shall I go, and leave you alone to collect yourself?' 'Oh,' he said, 'if I could only get at that confounded thing [his MS.] to have a last look at it!' 'Where is it?' said I. 'Oh, in the next room on the reading-desk.' 'Well,' said I, 'if you don't like to go in and get it, I'll fetch it for you.' And remembering well the position of my reading-table, which had been close to the door of the retiring-room, I darted in, hoping to snatch the manuscript without attracting the attention of the audience, with which the room was already nearly full. I had been used to deliver my reading seated at a very low table, but my friend Thackeray gave his lectures standing, and had a reading-desk placed on the platform, adapted to his own very tall stature, so that when I came to get his manuscript it was almost above my head. Though rather disconcerted, I was determined not to go back without it, and so made a half-jump and a clutch at the book, when every leaf of it (they were not fastened together) came fluttering separately down about me. I hardly know what I did, but I think I must have gone nearly on all fours, in my agony to gather up the scattered leaves, and, retreating with them, held them out in dismay to poor Thackeray, crying, 'Oh, look, look, what a dreadful thing I have done!' 'My dear soul,' he said, 'you couldn't have done better for me. I have just a quarter of an hour to wait here, and it will take me about that to page this again, and it's the best thing in the world that could have happened.' With which infinite kindness he comforted me, for I was all but crying, at having, as I thought, increased his distress and troubles. So I left him to give the first of that brilliant course of literary historical essays with which he enchanted and instructed countless audiences in England and America.''

Mrs. Ritchie was there with her grandmother and her younger sister, and she has recorded her impressions: how the room was crowded, and how she did not recognise her father's voice when he began, ''In treating of the English Humourists of the Eighteenth Century, it is of the men rather than of their works,'' etc., though soon it softened and deepened, until it sounded again like the familiar tones. She remembers, when it was all over, the applause of the audience crowding up to shake hands with the lecturer, the proud and happy look of her grandmother, and the drive home, when her father, in high spirits, made jokes, and they all laughed and were very jolly.

It is necessary to pause here a moment to speak of the style in which the lectures were delivered. I can only offer an impression based upon the study of the letters and reports of various distinguished critical members of the audience that Thackeray appeared on the platform simply as a well-bred gentleman reading, to a large circle of acquaintances, certain essays with which he was well acquainted.

Mr. Marzials says "the secret [charm] lay in an admirable quiet delivery, that without due emphasis or pause for effect, gave the hearer the full value of every sentence." Charlotte Brontë wrote that the lecture she heard was "delivered with a finished taste and ease which is felt but cannot be described," and that she "admired the gentlemanlike ease, the quiet humour, the taste, the talent, the simplicity, and the originality of the lecture"; while another lady—Caroline Fox—thought he read in "a definite, dry manner, but makes you understand what he is about."

Longfellow recorded that the lectures were "pleasant to hear from that soft, deep, sonorous voice," and Motley, who, some years later, heard a lecture on *The Four Georges*, wrote: "I was much impressed with the quiet, graceful ease with which he [Thackeray] read—just a few notes above the conversational level,—but never rising into the declamatory. This light in hand manner suits well the delicate hovering rather than superficial style of the composition. He skims lightly over the surface of the long epoch, throwing out a sketch here, exhibiting a characteristic trait there, and sprinkling about a few anecdotes, portraits, and historical allusions, running about from grave to gay, from lively to severe, moving and mocking the sensibilities in a breath, in a way which I should say was the perfection of lecturing to high-bred audiences." Finally, when he went to America, the representative of the *New York Evening*

Post expressed himself as follows: "His [Thackeray's] voice is a superb tenor, and possesses that pathetic tremble which is so effective in what is called emotive eloquence, while his delivery was as well suited to the communication he had to make as could well have been imagined. His enunciation is perfect. Every word he uttered might have been heard in the remotest quarters of the room, yet he scarcely lifted his voice above a colloquial tone. The most striking feature in his whole manner was the utter absence of affectation of any kind. He did not permit himself to appear conscious that he was an object of peculiar interest in the audience, neither was he guilty of the greater error of not appearing to care whether they were interested in him or not."

As all the opinions I have seen are of this tenor, and as there are no dissentient voices, it is needless for me to add anything more. When, however, the different styles of the lectures by Thackeray and Dickens are compared, it should be remembered that Thackeray's audience, especially in London, consisted entirely of the most highly cultured class, for a discourse on literary men of the eighteenth century would naturally not appeal to the comparatively unintellectual in the same way as a dramatic reading from *Nicholas Nickleby* or *Dombey and Son*. The two performances must, of very necessity, have borne to each other the same relationship as nowadays do the pieces performed at the Lyceum and the Adelphi or Drury Lane theatres; each is admirable of its kind—and there the comparison ends.

As soon as the course was delivered Thackeray, with his daughters, went abroad. "Traveling as Paterfamilias, with a daughter in each hand, I don't like to speak to our country-folks; but give myself airs, rather, and keep off from them," he wrote to Mrs. Brookfield. "If I were alone I should make up to everybody. You don't see things so well *à trois* as you do alone: you are an English gentleman; you are shy of queer-looking or queer-speaking people; you are in the *coupé;* you are an earl;—confound your impudence, if you had £5,000 a year and were Tompam, Esq., you could not behave yourself more high and mightily. Ah! I recollect ten years back a poor devil, looking wistfully at the few napoleons in his *gousset,* and giving himself no airs at all. He was a better fellow than the one you know perhaps; not that our characters alter, only they develop and our minds grow grey and bald, etc. I was a boy ten years ago, breathing out my simple cries in *The Great Hoggarty Diamond.*"

It was during this Continental ramble that he revisited Weimar, and he saw again both Madame Goethe and Herr Weissenborne, who had taught him German, and who had never lost sight of him, and knew of his fame, and had read his books. He enjoyed his holiday: it was not very gay, perhaps, but his children were pleased, and that more than contented him. "As for my dear young ones," he said in a letter, "I am as happy with them as possible: Annie is a fat lump of pure gold, the kindest, dearest creature, as well as a wag of the first water. It is an immense blessing that Heaven has given me such an artless, affectionate companion. . . . Oh! may she never fall in love absurdly, and marry an ass! If she will but make her father her confidant, I think the donkey won't long keep his ground in her heart."

But soon he was compelled to return to London. He had indeed written to Mr. Hayward on May 23: "The truth is that the lectures won't do. They were all

friends, and a packed house, though, to be sure, it goes
to a man's heart to find among his friends, such men as
you and Kinglake and Venables, Higgins, Rawlinson,
Carlyle, Ashburton, Hallam, Milman, Macaulay, Wilber-
force, looking on.''   But the lectures did do.   They
were an undoubted success—''there is quite a *furore* for
them,'' Charlotte Brontë wrote—and he had been invited
to repeat them by Young Men's Associations and Literary Clubs in all parts of the country.   America, too,
made offers that were too tempting to be summarily
refused, and which later on were conditionally accepted,
though Thackeray could not be induced to sign anything
until he was actually in New York.   Friends, especially
Sir Edward Hamley, remonstrated with him, and argued
that a man of such talents should not spend his time in
such a manner; and I think Thackeray agreed with them.
He told Lady Cullom that no one could conceive how it
mortified him to have to make money by lecturing, and
once, when speaking of Carlyle, he exclaimed: ''*He*
would not go round making a show of himself, as I am
doing.   But he has lectured!   He did it once and was
done with it.''

Still, money had to be made, an hour's reading was
often as profitable as a fortnight's work—and so eventually arrangements were made for him to deliver the
Humourists at Oxford and Cambridge, at Edinburgh,
Manchester, Liverpool, and many other places.*

As soon as it was announced that he would visit Edinburgh Dr. John Brown (who one day astonished the
world by dedicating the second series of *Horæ Subsecivæ*

*''Thackeray says he is getting tired of being witty and of the
great world,'' Fitzgerald wrote in 1851; ''he is now gone to deliver
his Lectures at Edinburgh, having already given them at Oxford and
Cambridge.''

to Gladstone *and* Andrew Dick *and* Thackeray *and* Ruskin—a strange quartet) hastened to invite the lecturer to stay with him while fulfilling his engagements in the city. Thackeray's reply (which I take from Mr. Peddie's *Recollections of Dr. John Brown*) gives an idea of his system of work, when he has a system at all.

"KENSINGTON, *October* 9, 1851.

MY DEAR DR. BROWN,—I find your letters on my return home from the country, and thank you for them and your kindnesses all. I don't know yet whether it will be December or January when I shall behold Rutland Street and my friends there. I want to go to Cambridge in November if the scheme is feasible, but can't move in the matter until the vacation is over, and my friends in Cambridge are returned thither. The Gates of Liverpool and Manchester are also open to me, and I shall take these places either before or after Edinburgh, as seems best to my advisers. Until the men are back in Cambridge in about a week, I can't therefore say when the Titmarsh-Van will begin its career. But as I don't intend to touch the proceeds of the lectures myself (beyond actual travelling charges) and resolutely invest all the winnings for my two girls and their poor mother, I'm bolder than I should be otherwise in the business, and determined to carry it through with brazen resolution. In order to this end you see I must work as if nothing had happened, and am under stringent engagements to write a novel which will come out as I sail for America. Now to do this, I must have my own way, my own lodgings, factotum, liberty, cigar after breakfast, etc., without all of which I can't work; and the forenoon being spent in study, the afternoon in healthful exercise, *then* comes the evening when we will trouble Dr. Brown to go down for that, etc., etc. You have brought me into very good company in print. I daresay there are good fish still in the sea.

"With my best thanks and regards to Mrs. Brown,
"Believe me, yours very faithfully,
"W. M. THACKERAY."

The novel at which he was working with such assiduity was *The History of Henry Esmond, Esquire: a Colonel in the service of Queen Anne, written by himself.* The half title runs: *Esmond, a Story of Queen Anne's Reign. By W. M. Thackeray.*

It was to enable him to devote himself to this great work that he ceased to contribute to the periodicals, for *Esmond*, unlike *Vanity Fair* and *Pendennis*, was to be published, not in monthly parts, but as a whole, in three volumes.* It also required much collateral reading, and Mr. Eyre Crowe, who from April, 1851, was Thackeray's secretary and amanuensis, has related how the author, with him in attendance, spent much time in the Library at the British Museum, where, after much preliminary reading and research, in a room allowed him for the purpose by Sir Anthony Panizzi, he dictated the General Webb and Marlborough and Cadogan incident. More of the book was written at the Athenæum Club, where the Secretary of Committee placed at his disposal the use of one of the side rooms of the large library; and much was done at the Bedford Hotel while his children were with his mother, and Major Smyth in Paris, and his own house was in the painters' hands.

*"I have given up, and only had for a day or two, the notion for the book in numbers; it is much too grave and sad for that," Thackeray wrote in a letter quoted by Mrs. Ritchie in the Biographical Introduction to *Esmond*.

While *Esmond* was in course of composition, Mr. Vizetelly, on the part of Messrs. Smith & Elder, offered Thackeray £1,000 to write a novel for them. Subsequently Mr. George Smith himself called and repeated the offer. "There's a young fellow just come," Thackeray said, as he burst into the room where his daughters were sitting. "He has brought a thousand pounds in his pocket; he has made me an offer for my book: it's the most spirited, handsome offer. I scarcely like to take him at his word: he's hardly more than a boy; his name is George Smith; he is waiting there now, and I must go back." The offer was ultimately accepted, and henceforth Messrs. Smith & Elder became his publishers-in-chief.

Once before Mr. Vizetelly had made Thackeray an offer on behalf of a publishing firm. Mr. Bougie, in 1846 or the following year, had commenced to issue a series of brochures called *Social Zoölogies*, the first number of which, *The Gent*, by Albert Smith, had been phenomenally successful. It was determined to have the best writers obtainable for future volumes, and at Mr. Bougie's request Mr. Vizetelly applied to Thackeray, with whom he was then in close intercourse, to write as many volumes as he chose to undertake at the price of a hundred guineas each—this, it will be remembered, was double the amount he was receiving for a monthly part of *Vanity Fair*, including the etching of a couple of plates. "He frankly admitted that the offer was a tempting one," Mr. Vizetelly has recorded, "but he eventually declined it, by reason, it was said, of his strong disinclination to ally himself with anything that Albert Smith was connected with. . . . Thackeray, who had an abhorrence of things vulgar, found Smith's *mau-*

vais gout more than he could stand. When brought into contact with him he treated him with contemptuous toleration, showing him outward civility; but the occasional observations which he permitted to escape him disclosed his true sentiments respecting Albert's mountebank ways." This statement is, however, somewhat discounted by Albert Smith himself, who, writing to George Hodder, mentions that he had spent an evening with Thackeray at the Cyder Cellars, staying until three in the morning, and that "he is a jolly fellow, and no 'High Art' about him."

But to revert to *Esmond.*

"Thackeray I saw for ten minutes," Fitzgerald wrote on June 8, 1852. "He was just in the agony of finishing a novel: which has arisen out of the reading necessary for the Lectures, and relates to those times—of Queen Anne, I mean. He will get £1,000 for his novel. He was wanting to finish it, and rush off to the Continent, I think, to shake off the fumes of it."

The book was actually finished on Saturday, May 28, when Thackeray gave an informal and friendly dinner-party to celebrate the occasion. It has been said by Mr. Vizetelly that the publishers had expected the work would relate to modern times, and were in the first instance disappointed with *Esmond;* but that the sale (Mr. Smith Williams, the firm's literary adviser, told him) was so much greater than had been expected, that they sent the author a cheque, in addition to the payment agreed upon, for two hundred and fifty pounds. Trollope, on the other hand, said that Thackeray complained to him that the public did not read the book; and this is perhaps borne out by the following extract from a letter acknowledging the receipt of a presentation

Hotel Bristol. Place Vendome,

December 27. 1858.

My dear Captain Atkinson

I received your beautiful book whilst I was in London, but was in
such a state of bewilderment and botheration with my own little volume that
I hadn't heart time to perform the proper duties of gratitude and society and thank
you for your present and dedication. It was very interesting to me to see what
my native country is like now - I have far off visions of great saloons and
people dancing in them enormous idols & fireworks. rides on elephants or in
gigs, and fogs clearing away and pagodes appearing over the trees. yellow rivers
and budgerows &c - I'm always interested about the place, and your sketches
came to me as very welcome, besides being exceedingly pretty cheerful & lively.
I hope this book will succeed: It must have been an awful bile to pay.

As for that little hint about Printing House Square, I have so know the
Editors and most of the writers; and, knowing, never think of asking a favor
for myself or any mortal man. I wish your volume every success, and thank
you for putting my name on its first page. Ever yours   W M Thackeray.

copy of *Curry and Rice*, sent by the author, Captain Atkinson, in December, 1858: "As for the little hint about Printing House Square," he wrote, "I know the editor and most of the writers, and, knowing, never think of asking a favour for myself or any mortal man. They are awful and inscrutable, and a request for a notice might bring down a slasher upon you, just as I once had in the *Times* for one of my own books [*Esmond*], of which the sale was absolutely stopped by a *Times* article."

But even a thunderbolt from the "awful and inscrutable" Jupiter could only check the sale of the book for the moment. *Esmond* was bound to take its place, not only as Thackeray's masterpiece, but as a book to be ranked among the greatest works of historical fiction of any age or country.

"It is a dull, tiresome, well-written book. You'll find it dull, but it is founded on family papers"; "Esmond is as stately as Sir Charles Grandison"; "The hero is a prig";—were some remarks passed by the author upon his greatest work;* and writing from America to Mrs. Procter, he declared that the success of the book had quite surprised him, for he had only looked for a few to like it. I think, however, his real opinion

---

*He had a habit of passing criticisms upon his books—for all the world as if he had not written them—and many remarks like the following dropped from his mouth, and are to be found scattered about his correspondence. "I have just read such a stupid part of *Pendennis*; but how well written it is." "I can't say I think much of *Pendennis*—at least, of the execution," he said to Mr. J. E. Cooke; "it certainly drags about the middle; but I had an attack of illness at the time I reached that part of the book, and could not make it any better than I did." "I bought the *Kickleburys, Rebecca and Rowena*, and the *Rhine Story*, and read them through with immense pleasure. Do you know I think all three capital, and *R. & R.* not only made me laugh, but the other thing." "I have been reading *The Hoggarty Diamond* this morning; upon my word and honour if it doesn't make you cry, I shall have a mean opinion of you."

was expressed to Mr. Fields, when the publisher, in 1852, met him in Beacon Street, Boston, with the three volumes of *Esmond* tucked under his arm. "Here is the very best I can do," he said; "and I am carrying it to Prescott as a reward of merit for having given me my first dinner in America. I stand by this book, and am willing to leave it, where I go, as my card."

Meanwhile the lectures were being delivered in the provinces, and they were, as a general rule, as much appreciated in the country as in the capital. At Oxford (where he stayed with his old friend Stoddart) the readings were worth thirty pounds apiece;* and Cambridge showed itself nearly as appreciative as the sister university. At Edinburgh, too, they were a great success—a hundred subscribers and two hundred other people for the first lecture. The following, from the *Edinburgh Review*, is noteworthy: "The best of his lectures is, we think, that on Fielding; and we are delighted to read Mr. Thackeray's bold and cordial and discriminating praise of this great, but, we fear, somewhat neglected, artist—a novelist from whom the generation that is now

---

*At Oxford it was necessary to obtain the license of the 'Varsity authorities before lecturing within the precincts to the undergraduates; and Thackeray, on his arrival in the city, applied for the necessary permission to the Vice-Chancellor, who, however, was no student of contemporary literature, and was utterly ignorant of both Thackeray and his writings. This is an account that has been handed down of the interview. I cannot vouch for its authenticity: it is almost too good to be true. "Pray sir, what can I do for you?" "My name is Thackeray." "So I see by this card." "I seek permission to lecture within your precincts." "Ah! you are a lecturer; what subjects do you undertake, religious or political?" "Neither; I am a literary man." "Have you written anything?" "Yes; I am the author of *Vanity Fair*." "I presume a dissenter—has that anything to do with John Bunyan's book?" "Not exactly. I have also written *Pendennis*." "Never heard of these works; but no doubt they are proper books." "I have also contributed to *Punch*." "*Punch!* I have heard of that; is it not a ribald publication?" The account ends abruptly here—probably at this point Thackeray showed symptoms of suffocation.

passing away imbibed a heartier contempt for meanness and duplicity, and a heartier sympathy with courage, frankness, and manliness, than, we fear, is to be acquired from the more decorous narratives which form the mental food of their successors.''

Indeed, the audiences in Edinburgh were so large and so appreciative that the visit to America, that by this time he had arranged should take place about May, hung in the balance. "Why, if so much money is to be made in this empire, not go through with the business, and get what is to be had?" he asked Mrs. Brookfield. But the journey was not abandoned. "I must replace my patrimony," he told his daughters, "and make some provision for your mother and for you; and you must go to my mother's and spend the winter with her; you must work as hard as you can, and consider yourself at college in a fashion, and learn French, and a little music, to play me to sleep of an evening when I come home." Then he took them abroad to his mother and Major Smyth, in whose charge they were to be left during his absence. At the railway station at Otten, in Belgium, they parted: they going to Switzerland, he returning to England. He had to deliver some more lectures, to revise *Vanity Fair* for a cheap edition, and to correct the proofs of *Esmond*, before he could sail for America.

At the end of September he went, with Mr. Eyre Crowe, to Liverpool, where he read in the Athenæum on the Tuesdays and Thursdays (September 28, 30; October 5, 7, 12, 14); and to Manchester, in the Philharmonic Hall, on the Wednesdays and Fridays (September 29; October 1, 6, 8, 13, 15). The latter part of October was spent in London; and on October 29 they again went to Liverpool, where, on that evening, the last night in England, they dined at the house of Mr. Ratcliffe. The *pièce de resistance* at the banquet was a roasted sucking-pig—a surprise for the great man, who loved only beans and bacon better.

He was in a very despondent frame of mind, and his good-byes partook more of the nature of *Adieu* than *Au revoir*. "My dearest old friend," he wrote to Edward Fitzgerald just before he sailed, "I mustn't go away without shaking your hand and saying Farewell and God bless you. If anything happens to me, you by these presents must get ready the Book of Ballads which you like, and which I had not time to prepare before embarking on this voyage. And I should like my daughters to remember that you are the best and oldest friend their father ever had, and that you would act as such: as my literary executor and so forth. My books would yield a something as copyrights; and should anything occur, I have commissioned friends, in good places, to get a pension for my poor little wife. . . . Does not this sound gloomily? Well, who knows what fate is in store; and I feel not at all downcast, but very grave and solemn, just at the brink of the great voyage. The greatest comfort I have in thinking about my dear old boy is that recollection of our youth when we loved each other as I do now, when I write Farewell!"

On the next morning (October 30, 1852) Thackeray and Eyre Crowe, with their fellow-travellers, Lowell, just returning from Italy, and Arthur Hugh Clough, the poet, embarked on the R.M.S. *Canada* (Captain Lang). The proofs of *Esmond* had taken much longer to correct than had been expected, for the original edition was printed in the almost obsolete type of the reign of Queen Anne, and only a very small quantity of it could be obtained. Some time, too, the manuscript of the third volume was mislaid at the publishers', and it seemed as if the novelist would have to postpone his journey for at least six weeks while he rewrote it. As a matter of fact, he only received his bound copies of the book while he was on the pier, waiting for the tender to convey him to the *Canada*.*

While lecturing in Liverpool, Thackeray had seen, in a New York paper, an article containing a bitter attack on him. It was, indeed, very doubtful what reception he would meet with from the Americans, for they were still smarting under the castigation inflicted by Boz in the *American Notes;* and not unnaturally they said of Thackeray, as they thought of the Dickens Ball at the Park Theatre and the "Boz" Tableaux given in honour of his great contemporary: "He'll come and humbug us, eat our dinners, pocket our money, and go home, and abuse us like Dickens." However, it was decided to give him fair-play, and within a few days of his arrival he had changed fair-play into enthusiasm. "The popular Thackeray-theory before his arrival was of a severe satirist who concealed scalpels in his sleeves and carried probes in his waistcoat pocket; a wearer of masks; a scoffer and sneerer and general infidel of all high aim and

---

* "Thackeray's *Esmond* had recently appeared and taken the world by storm, when, one evening in November, 1852, a red-faced, mulberry-nosed, pot-bellied person clad in a shabby clerical suit, his coat fastened with pins in lieu of buttons, entered the shop, and, after introducing himself, ... drew from his tail-pocket a copy of Mr. Ralph Cudworth's sermon preached before the House of Commons on March 31, 1847, and mentioned in chapter vi. of *Esmond*. Our visitor, so he told us, had unearthed the sermon in Trinity College Library, and had called the novelist's attention to it. The venture was a failure, scarcely any copies of the reprint being sold. . . . The book was printed by Bradbury & Evans for J. Talboys Wheeler, Bookseller, over against Trinity College gateway, Cambridge, and has a dedication to Thackeray signed by James Broden."—*Some Reminiscences of Books and Men, Publishers' Circular*, June 12, 1897.

noble character," said a writer in *Putnam's Monthly
Magazine* for June, 1853. "Certainly we are justified
in saying that his presence among us quite corrected this
idea. We welcomed a friendly, genial man; not at all
convinced that speech is heaven's first law, but willing
to be silent when there was nothing to say—who decid-
edly refused to be lionised, not by sulking, but by stepping off the pedestal and challenging the common
sympathies of all he met. . . . We conceive . . .
the chief merit of Thackeray's visit to be that he convinced us of his intellectual integrity, he showed us how
impossible it is for him to see the world and describe it
other than he does. He does not profess cynicism, nor
satirise society with malice. There is no man more
humble, none more simple, and his interests are human
and concrete, not abstract."

If the Americans were delighted with Thackeray, he
in his turn was agreeably astonished at what he saw in
the New World, and his letters are full of expressions of
pleasure. "I didn't expect to like the people as I do,
but am agreeably disappointed, and find many most
pleasant companions, natural and good; natural and
well-read: and well-bred too." "Now I have seen three
great cities, Boston, New York and Philadelphia, I
think I like them all mighty well." "At Boston there
is a very good literary company indeed." "Now what
most impresses me here is that I find homes as pure as
ours, firesides like ours, domestic virtues as gentle; the
English language, though the accent be a little different,
with its home-like melody; and the Common Prayer
Book in your families. I am more struck by pleasant
resemblances than by anything else," etc., etc.

"The passage is nothing now it is over," Thackeray

declared on his arrival, when he was met by Mr. Fields.
He remained in New York for a week. Here one evening he heard Bancroft, the historian, lecture before the
New York Historical Society, and on another was initiated into the mysteries of spirit-rapping and table-turn-
ing. He met Horace Greeley, the proprietor of the
New York Daily Tribune, and in the columns of that
paper was welcomed to the States by Henry James, the
father of the distinguished novelist, who, among his
English-speaking contemporaries, ranks only after George
Meredith and the author of *Lorna Doone*. Everywhere
and by every one he was *fêted* and made much of; and
lunches, dinners, and suppers in his honour were so
numerous that he afterwards laughingly spoke of his visit
as "one unbroken round of indigestion." All the business arrangements for his lecturing had been made as far
as possible without troubling him with any of the
details. He went to Boston, where the campaign was
to be opened. "He arrived on a frosty November evening," Mr. Fields has recorded, "and I remember . . .
the enthusiasm with which he hailed the announcement
that dinner would soon be ready . . . In London
he had been very curious in his inquiries about American
oysters, as marvellous stories, which he did not believe,
had been told him of their great size. We apologised—
although we had taken care that the largest specimen to
be procured should startle his unwonted vision when he
came up to the table—for what we called the extreme
smallness of the oysters, promising that we would do
better next time. Six bloated Falstaffian bivalves lay
before him in their shells. I noticed he gazed at them
anxiously with fork upraised; then he whispered to me,
with a look of anguish, 'How shall I do it?' I described

to him the simple process by which the free-born citizens
of America were accustomed to accomplish such a task.
He seemed satisfied that the thing was feasible, selected the smallest one in the half-dozen (rejecting a large
one, 'because,' he said, 'it resembled the High Priest's
servant's ear that Peter cut off'), and then bowed his
head as if he were saying grace.   All eyes were upon
him to watch the effect of a new sensation in the person
of a great British Author.   Opening his mouth very
wide, he struggled for a minute, and then all was over.
I shall never forget the comic look of despair he cast
upon the other five over-occupied shells.   I broke the
perfect stillness by asking him how he felt.   'Profoundly
grateful,' he gasped, 'and as if I had swallowed a little
baby.' ''

The first lecture took place at eight o'clock in the
evening of November 19, before an audience of twelve
hundred people, amongst whom was George Ticknor,
the historian of Spanish literature; the others following
on November 22, 26, 29, and December 3, 6.   These
were so well attended—indeed, all the tickets were sold
before his arrival—that another course was delivered on
December 1, 7, 10, 13, 15, and 17, which also met with
great success.   One of his Boston auditors gave a good
pen-and-ink sketch of the lecturer.   "He is a stout,
healthful, broad-shouldered specimen of a man, with
cropped greyish hair and bluish-grey eyes, peering very
strongly through a pair of spectacles that have a very
satiric focus.   He seems to stand strongly on his own
feet, as if he would not be very easily blown about or
upset either by praise or pugilists—a man who scents all
shams or rumours, straightening them between his
thumb and finger as he would a pinch of snuff.''

From Boston he returned to New York—on the cars "a rosy-cheeked little peripatetic book-merchant," ignorant of his customer's identity, sold him a copy of *A Shabby Genteel Story*—where Mr. Millard Felt, representing The Mercantile Library Association, took him over the Rev. Mr. Chapin's Unitarian Chapel, from which the Rev. Henry Bellows had just retired. He was to read from the pulpit, and expressed some anxiety until he was assured that the organ would *not* play him in.

"The building was crowded to its utmost capacity with the celebrities of literature and fashion in this metropolis, all of whom, we believe, left perfectly united in the opinion that they never remembered to have spent an hour more delightfully in their lives, and that the room in which they had been receiving so much enjoyment was very badly lighted. We fear, also, that it is the impression of the many who were disappointed in getting tickets, that the room was not spacious enough for the purpose to which it has been appropriated. Every one who saw Mr. Thackeray last evening for the first time seemed to have their impressions of his appearance and manner of speech corrected. Few expected to see so large a man: he is gigantic, six feet four at least; few expected to see so old a person: his hair appears to have kept silvery record over fifty years; and then there was a notion in the minds of many that there must be something dashing and 'fast' in his appearance; whereas his costume was perfectly plain; the expression of his face grave and earnest; his address perfectly unaffected, and such as we might expect to meet with in a well-bred man somewhat advanced in years. . . . In other words, he inspired his audience with a respect for him as a man proportioned to the admiration which his books have inspired for him as an author.

"Of the lecture itself as a work of art, it would be difficult to speak too strongly. Though written with the utmost simplicity and apparent inattention to effects, it overflowed with every characteristic of the author's happiest vein." So ran a report of the "Swift" Lecture in the *New York Evening Post*, which paper Thackeray himself sent to friends in England.

He was tasting the fruits of his great popularity, and he thoroughly enjoyed himself. "I remember," Mr. Fields has recorded of the first reading at Boston, "his uproarious shouting and dancing when he was told that the tickets to his first course of lectures were all sold; and when we rode together from his hotel to the lecture-hall, he insisted on thrusting both his long legs out of the carriage window, in deference, as he said, to his magnanimous ticket-holders."

"By Jove, how kind you all were to me," he said to Mr. Reed. "I suppose I am none the worse pleased," he wrote from New York, "because everybody has read all my books and praises my lectures. . . . There are two thousand people nearly who come, and the lectures are so well liked that it is probable I shall do them over again. So really there is a chance of making a pretty sum of money for old age, imbecility, and those young ladies afterwards."*

He repeated the lectures in New York, and read them

---

*By the New York lectures he made no less than a thousand pounds, which Barings invested for the young ladies. Of the profits of the whole visit I cannot speak with any certainty. He himself in one of his letters suggested that his possible gains might amount to £2,500, but I think this is a very low estimate.

in Brooklyn. There he saw a Beatrix Esmond, to whom he lost his heart, he declared, and met the great Barnum, who wanted him to write something in the first number of an illustrated paper in imitation of the *London News*, which was just about to make its appearance under his wing. It must have been a curious interview, that one between the Prince of Anti-Humbugs, and the Prince of Humbugs.

From Brooklyn he went to Washington for three weeks, where he stayed with Mr. (afterwards, Sir Philip) Crampton at the British Embassy, and there he met Senator G. T. Davis, whose son, Secretary of the American Minister in London, was an old friend. Longfellow on Christmas Eve heard the "Congreve" lecture, and four days later supped with the lecturer at Lowell's house. "The time here has been very pleasant," Thackeray wrote to his mother. "I dined with the President [Mr. Fillmore] on Thursday, and yesterday he and the President Elect [General Pierce] came arm-in-arm to my lecture!" "Two Kings of Brentford smiling at one rose," Washington Irving (popularly known as "Old Knick" from an early work, *The History of New York, by Diedrich Knickerbocker*) murmured to Thackeray as they appeared; and surely lecturing before two Presidents is only one degree less pleasing in its intensity than to be seen walking arm-in-arm with a couple of Dukes down Pall Mall.

From Philadelphia he addressed a characteristic letter to Mrs. Brookfield. "The lectures are enormously *suivées*, and I read at the rate of a pound a minute nearly," he wrote. "The curious thing is that I think I improve in my reading; at certain passages a sort of emotion springs up, and I begin to understand how actors feel affected over and over again at the same passages of the play;—they are affected off the stage too: I hope I shan't be. . . . There's something simple about the way the kind folks regard a man; they read our books as if we were Fielding, and so forth. The other night some men were talking of Dickens and Bulwer, and I was pleased to find myself pleased at hearing them praised."

In this same letter we get a glimpse at his plans for the future. The second course of lectures and the ambition in public life were realised respectively in the *Four Georges* and the Oxford election, and the man, weary and "played out" as he was, yet managed to produce, besides other things, *The Newcomes*, *Philip*, the fragment of *Denis Duval*, and above all *The Roundabout Papers*.

"At present," runs this part of the letter, "I incline to come to England in June or July, and get ready a new set of lectures and bring them back with me. That second course will enable me to provide for the children and their mother finally and satisfactorily, and my mind will be easier after that, and I can sing Nunc Dimittis without faltering. There is money-making to try at, to be sure, and ambition, I mean in public life; perhaps that might interest a man, but not novels, nor lectures, nor fun any more. I don't seem to care about these any more, or for praise, or for abuse, or for reputation of that kind. That literary play is played out and the puppets going to be locked up for good and all. Does this melancholy come from the circumstance that I have been out to dinner and supper every night this week? Oh! I am tired of shaking hands with people, and acting the lion business night after night. Every one is introduced and shakes hands. I know thousands of colonels,

professors, editors, and what not, and walk the streets
guiltily, knowing that I don't know 'em, and trembling
lest the man opposite is one of my friends of the day
before.   I believe I am popular, except at Boston among
the newspaper men who fired into me, but a great
favourite with the *monde* here and elsewhere."

From Philadelphia he returned to New York, where,
to oblige some friends interested in a "Ladies' Society
for the Employment and Relief of the Poor," he especially composed, and delivered on January 31, at the
Church of the Messiah, in Broadway, before an audience
of about twelve hundred persons paying one dollar each,
the *Charity and Humour* discourse.   This serves as a
supplement to the *Humourist* series, for in it he compared
the eighteenth-century literature with the writings of his
contemporaries, taking advantage of the opportunity to
bestow his usual praise upon Dickens.

At this time all New York was talking of the article
in the January number of *Fraser's Magazine*, entitled
Mr. Thackeray and the United States (*by John Small*), a
playful and amusing satire on the American newspapers
and their habits of personal journalism, in which was
given a long extract from an imaginary paper, *The
Sachem and Broadway Delineator*, caricaturing the personal paragraphs that were being circulated about the
lecturer.   Although the article was not published over
his signature, it was immediately recognised as his work.
It was found as amusing in America as at home; and if,
while reading it, some hyper-sensitive persons felt a
touch of annoyance, it must have been removed when
the last page of the article was reached, for Thackeray
had written there the tribute conceded to America at
the last lecture of the first series on December 7.

"In England it was my custom, after the delivery of these lectures," he had said, "to point such a moral as seemed to befit the country I lived in and to protest against an outcry, which some brother authors of mine had most imprudently and unjustly raised, when they say that our profession is neglected, and its professors held in light esteem. Speaking in this country, I would say that not only could such a complaint not be advanced, but could not even be understood here, where your men of letters take a manly share in public life; whence Everett goes as Minister to Washington, and Irving and Bancroft to represent the republic in the Old Country. And if to English authors, the English public is, as I believe, kind and just in the main, will any of us say, will any who visit your country not proudly and gratefully own, with what a cordial and generous greeting you receive us? I look round on this great company, I think of my gallant young patrons of the Mercantile Literary Association, as whose servant I appear before you, and of the kind hands stretched out to welcome me by men famous in letters, and honoured in our country as in their own, and I thank you and them for a most kindly greeting and a most generous hospitality. At home, and amongst his own people, it scarce becomes an English writer to speak of himself; his public estimation must depend upon his works, his private esteem upon his character and his life. But here, among friends newly found, I ask leave to say that I am thankful; and I think with a grateful heart of those I leave behind me at home, who will be proud of the welcome you hold out to me, and will benefit, please God, when my days of work are over, by the kindness you have shown to their father."

And not content with the above manifestation of feeling, he had also seized the opportunity to declare his gratitude by declaring in the preface to Appleton's edition of his minor works that "he was glad to think his books had found favour with the American public, as he was proud to own the great and cordial welcome with which they received him."*

After Boston, New York, and Washington, he also visited, among other places, Baltimore and Richmond, Virginia; Petersburg, where very few seats were occupied; Charleston, where he arrived early in March, and read in the Hiberian Hall to large audiences, the most notable person being Professor Agassiz, whose acquaintance he made; and Savannah, in Georgia, where he was the guest of Mr. Low, the English Consul. Then he returned to the Clarendon Hotel in New York, where he heard of the failing health of some of the elder members of his family in Europe.

Long before the tour was over he was heartily sick of it, and nothing but the thoughts of his children would have strengthened him sufficiently to enable him to continue it. "Even when I am reading my lectures," he one day exclaimed to Mr. Bayard Taylor, "I often think to myself, 'What a humbug you are, and I wonder people don't find you out';" and writing home on February 7 he said, "In another hour that dreary business of 'In speaking of the English Humourists of the last,' etc., will begin—and the wonder to me is that the speaker once in the desk (to-day it is to be a right-down pulpit in a Universalist Church and no mistake), gets interested in the work, makes the points, throbs with emotion, and indignation, at the right place, and has a little sensation

*See Appendix.

while the work is coming on; but I can't go on much longer, my conscience revolts at the quackery." "I am getting so sick and ashamed of the confounded old lectures that I wonder I have the courage to go on delivering them," he wrote from Richmond a month later. "I shan't read a single review of them when they are published; anything savage said about them will serve them right. . . . I should like to give myself a week's holiday without my dem'd lecture-box."

In an interesting and characteristic letter, dated Clarendon Hotel, New York, April 5, 1853, Thackeray summed up his impressions of America in his characteristically straightforward fashion. He noted that *My Novel* and *Villette* had rapidly transplanted *Esmond* in popular favour; and added that though he had not made a fortune in four months, he had "a snug little sum of money." He was not horrified with the slavery of the South, but thought the negroes "in the good families the comfortablest race of menials." Of American scenery he was far from enamoured. "It is a dreary, unpicturesque country for the most part. I have not seen a dozen picturesque views in all my wanderings, nor even cared to use my pencil except to sketch a negro or two."

He longed to shut up his reading desk and get back to the Old Country, though he gratefully acknowledged the kindness of the Americans, and spoke of the many true friends he had made. The luxury of New York and the gorgeous dresses of the ladies seem to have somewhat appalled him. "Solomon in all his glory, or the Queen of Sheba when she came to visit him in state, was not arrayed so magnificently as these New York damsels."

When Mr. Crowe entered Thackeray's room, very

early in the morning of April 20, 1853, the latter, who had been consulting a newspaper, jumped up, and, in spite of his earlier intention to visit several cities in the middle and western states, said: "I see there's a Cunarder going this morning. I'll go down to Wall Street to see whether I can secure berths in her." His quest was successful. He scribbled on a card: "Good-bye, Fields; good-bye, Mrs. Fields; God bless everybody, says W. M. T."—there was no time for personal farewells—hurried down Broadway, got into a boat on the East River, reached the *Europa* to be greeted with the cry, "Hurry up—she's starting!" and landed with Mr. Crowe at Liverpool almost exactly six months after their departure.

The story of his arrival at his house has been charmingly told by his eldest daughter in the following words: "When the long summer and winter were over, and the still longer spring, suddenly one day we heard he was coming back much sooner than he had expected. I believe he saw a steamer starting for home and could stand it no longer, and then and there came off. I can still remember sitting with my grandparents, expecting his return. My sister and I sat on the red sofa in the little study, and shortly before the time we had calculated he might arrive came a little ring at the front door-bell. My grandmother broke down; my sister and I rushed to the front door, only we were so afraid that it might not be he that we did not dare to open it, and there we stood until a second and much louder ring brought us to our senses. 'Why didn't you open the door?' said my father, stepping in, looking well, broad, and upright, laughing. In a moment he had never been away at all."*

Chapters from Some Unwritten Memoirs.

END OF VOLUME ONE

PRINTED BY R. R. DONNELLEY
AND SONS COMPANY AT THE
LAKESIDE PRESS, CHICAGO, ILL.